Praise for *Australian Gospel*

"Lech Blaine is a national treasure ... His words have a way of burrowing into your heart and setting up camp there." —Jill Stark

"*Australian Gospel* is a big-hearted epic, where the pangs of terror are never far from the next belly laugh." —*The Guardian*

"This is one of the best books you will ever read. It will make you laugh. It will make you cry. But it will ultimately renew your faith in humankind and show the difference that loving parents can make to the lives of children." —Niki Savva

"Utterly unputdownable." —Sally Hepworth

"What an extraordinary family story Lech Blaine tells." —*The Age*

"A propulsive, compelling tale ... full of hope, humanity and the everyday joys and struggles of family life."—*The Saturday Paper*

"The astonishing tale of a foster family held together by ferocious love and courage. What makes a real family? Whose rights should triumph in battles over a child? Which inheritances can we escape, and which will haunt us forever? All this is explored in an irreverently joyful family saga you'll never forget."
—Charlotte Wood

"Fact is stranger than fiction but it never arrives fully formed. We need writers like Blaine to do that for us. Here he delivers a rollicking, insightful and moving account of the everyday heavens and hells we make for ourselves, and each other."
—Sarah Krasnostein

"This is the new benchmark for the quintessential Australian epic. I lost count of how many times I laughed and cried. If I was a believer, I'd say that Lech Blaine's writing is godlike. Then again, it's something better than that: enchantingly human." —**Grace Tame**

"Wild applause. Brave, funny and true." —**David Marr**

"An extraordinary true story, beautifully told." —**Tim Minchin**

"Buckle in, because Lech Blaine's story about his family will blow your mind ... Blaine is considered one of Australia's most talented writers and this story is a clear indication why ... a riveting and exceptional read." —**Readings**

"A narrative told with humour, compassion and an ever-present tension that haunts the reader from start to finish." —**ArtsHub**

"At the heart of this book lies, well, a whole lotta heart ... a bloody good yarn." —*The Conversation*

"Captivating ... at once a tremendously moving story of family life, and a profound meditation on family-making and the legacies of love, grief and trauma that get passed from one generation to the next."—**Catriona Menzies-Pike**, *The Guardian*

"This emotionally charged book reads partly as a thriller and partly as a literary memoir, creating a strange yet compelling combination ... More than anything, *Australian Gospel* is for the hopeful souls who believe love and acceptance have the power to change lives."
—*Books+Publishing*

Lech Blaine

A FAMILY SAGA

Australian Gospel

Published by Black Inc.,
an imprint of Schwartz Books Pty Ltd
Wurundjeri Country
22–24 Northumberland Street
Collingwood VIC 3066, Australia
enquiries@blackincbooks.com
www.blackincbooks.com

Copyright © Lech Blaine 2024
First published in 2024; reprinted in 2024, 2025
Lech Blaine asserts his right to be known as the author of this work.

ALL RIGHTS RESERVED.
No part of this publication may be reproduced, stored in a retrieval system, or transmitted in any form by any means electronic, mechanical, photocopying, recording or otherwise without the prior consent of the publishers.

9781760643973 (paperback)
9781743823866 (ebook)

 A catalogue record for this book is available from the National Library of Australia

Cover design by Sandy Cull
Text design and typesetting by Aira Pimping
Cover image by Cavan Images / Alamy Stock Photo

Printed in Australia by McPherson's Printing Group.

This project has been assisted by the Australian Government through Creative Australia, its principal arts investment and advisory body.

For my mother, Lenore

"The mind is its own place, and in itself
Can make a heav'n of hell, and a hell of heav'n"
John Milton, *Paradise Lost*

"If I cannot inspire love, I will cause fear"
Mary Shelley, *Frankenstein*

PROLOGUE
1

✝

Act One
5

Act Two
111

Act Three
257

✝

EPILOGUE
356

AUTHOR'S NOTE
359

ACKNOWLEDGEMENTS
361

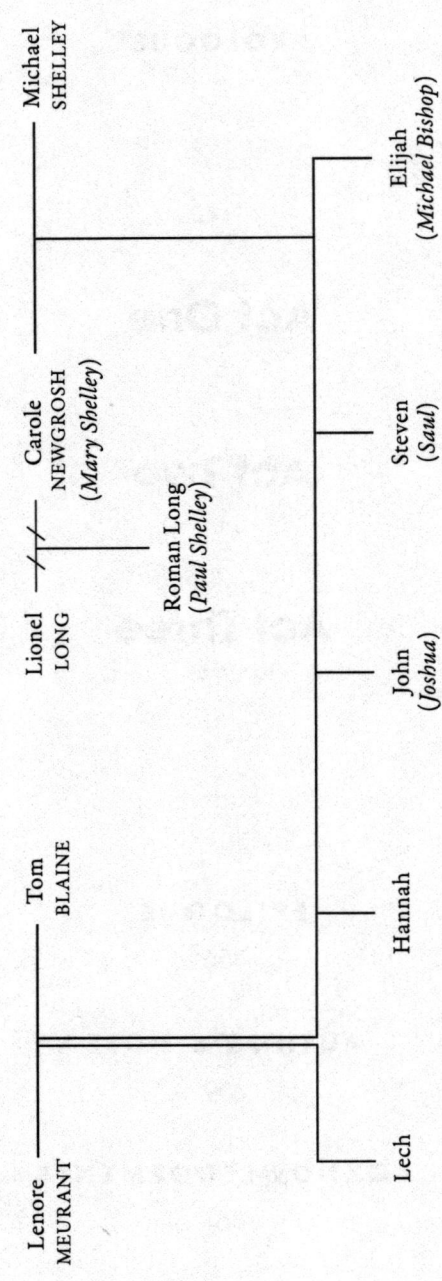

PROLOGUE

Jacki Weaver tracked me down, not the other way around. Her email was a needle in the haystack of history. The actress was seventy. I was twenty-five, a university dropout running a three-star motel in Bundaberg. Four and a half hours north of Brisbane. I was a long way from Hollywood, let alone heaven.

"I just listened to your interview with Richard Fidler," wrote Jacki. "I'm sitting in a record-breaking LA heatwave, gobsmacked and in a state of shock."

It was 2017. I pictured the sweating thespian squinting at an iPad. Saturday night in Los Angeles and Sunday morning in Bundaberg. You could get a place to sleep – or hide – for $95 at the Blaine family business. The Honeymoon Suite was occupied by Bundaberg's most decorated meth dealer.

"I mentioned to an old friend that I might seek you out," wrote Jacki. "And he said: *Sometimes it's better to let sleeping dogs lie, especially if the dog has rabies.*"

A few days earlier, on ABC Radio, I told Australia the tale of Michael and Mary Shelley. They were the biological parents of my foster siblings: Steven, John and Hannah. For thirty years, Michael and Mary travelled the world preaching the Gospel of Jesus while stalking and threatening their mortal enemies. Such as my parents,

Lenore and Tom Blaine. I was their only biological kid, conceived shortly after the arrival of my sister Hannah.

"Our children were brought up in depressing western Queensland pubs which featured the reckless indulgence of alcohol and an obsession with idiotic ball sports," wrote Michael in his manifesto. "In collusion with the Department of Child Safety, the Blaines brainwashed our children into boring Australians."

My interview was broadcast on national radio and streamable overseas. Hundreds of strangers came out of the woodwork. It was easy for them to find me. Maybe I wanted to be found. I received emails from kindred spirits: people who had also lived in fear of Michael Shelley.

"The adolescent Michael who I loved was complicated, but sweet and devoted," wrote Jacki Weaver to me. "That Michael bore no resemblance to the dictatorial young man that he became in his twenties."

I searched Jacki Weaver on Google, just to be certain. Yes: one of Australia's most famous actresses was the old flame of Michael Shelley, the Christian kidnapper whose white robe occupied my nightmares as a child. She mentioned their relationship in her memoir. I downloaded and devoured it.

"I hope that you don't think that I was referring to you with the rabies comment," wrote Jacki in a follow-up email. "Michael was genuinely very hurt when I broke up with him. There was much more to our relationship I couldn't put into my memoir. I didn't want to anger Michael and risk retribution."

In Bundaberg, grey snowflakes rained from the cane fields. I reread "To Women Everywhere", a chapter of Michael's manifesto. It was a bewildering mixture of environmentalism and Old Testament misogyny. Michael Shelley was the ex-boyfriend from hell.

"Women's liberation is better referred to as female bondage," he wrote. "Feminists dress explicitly and flaunt themselves like prostitutes. Yet these same women are outraged if men react to this obvious enticement!"

I had been trading emails with Michael. He sent me an exhaustive autobiography. It contained the who, what, where and when of his reinvention as God's prophet. The why remained a mystery. Until now, I hadn't allowed myself to imagine him as a teenager with normal dreams and desires.

"It seems strange for me to be this deeply affected so many years later," wrote Jacki. "But for many people, a first love can leave a deep impression, especially if it was intense and involved genuine love. No matter how young."

The morning shift at the motel finished at midday. I went to my other office: a windowless room with a laptop on a table. Boxes were filled with my mother's diaries, foster care files, newspaper clippings, court reports and restraining orders. There were four cork boards on the walls. The Gospel of Michael. The Gospel of Mary. The Gospel of Tom. The Gospel of Lenore.

"I'm going to write a book about the Shelley Gang one day," my mother, Lenore, used to say during the biblical shitshow of my childhood.

The book was unwritten, for a variety of reasons. It was up to me. There was one problem: I wasn't alive when much of the story happened. So, I interviewed hundreds of people for thousands of hours. I walked in the shoes of the main characters. I tried to see what they saw and feel what they felt.

Act One

‡

CHAPTER ONE

The Child Heist

Brisbane – 9 November 1983

Michael Shelley kidnapped Elijah on a sunlit Monday afternoon.

The Bruce Highway teemed with gleaming bonnets. Two thin men with ponytails sat in a gold Holden Commodore, rented back in Sydney. Michael was driving. His face was scenic as a beach. Long, sandy curls. A neatly trimmed beard. Eyes bluer than the cloudless sky.

At the age of thirty-seven, Michael was the Australian Jesus Christ or a homeless sociopath, depending on your perspective. The New South Welshman was about to declare holy war on the godforsaken state of Queensland.

"At that time Michael, the archangel who stands guard over your nation, will arise," he kept proclaiming in an educated Australian accent; Daniel 12:1.

The front-seat passenger was a nineteen-year-old hitchhiker named Glen Elliott. His eyes and hair were brown like the Brisbane River. A few days earlier, Michael had picked up Glen from a highway on the outskirts of Byron Bay. They promptly bonded over mutual mummy issues. Now Glen was a budding child abduction accomplice. Life was funny like that.

The Commodore exited onto Strathpine Road. It was half an hour north of the Brisbane CBD. Developers had bulldozed the sugar mill for a shopping centre, and timber plantations for subdivisions of snug 700 square metre blocks.

To Michael, Strathpine was just another soulless shithole on a continent stolen from Aboriginals by fat, illiterate sporting fanatics. He hated the games Australians played, the beer they drank, the food they ate, and the way they all called each other *MAAATE*. Mateship was a bonding ritual for satanists.

The Westfield Shopping Centre sign was a guiding star, red and white against a blue sky. The car park of the new shopping centre was filled with tired housewives bribing their children to stop crying with Kinder Surprises.

Michael went left. They passed a strip of video rental stores, fish-and-chip shops and used-car dealerships. Another left over the bridge above the train line. Here, the kitsch subdivision had a ridiculous classical music theme.

Chopin Street. Symphony Avenue. Beethoven Road.

It made Michael smile snidely, despite the high stakes. The brick homes were cheap enough for Australian dreamers who couldn't afford Aspley, but steep enough to keep out the fibros across the Bruce Highway in Bracken Ridge.

The Commodore reached the destination. 24 Danube Drive. A narrow one-storey home surrounded by palm trees. White bricks and brown roof tiles. A Kreepy Krauly chugged through a swimming pool in the backyard. It provided a bass line to the concerto of suburbia: clicking cicadas and chirping birds.

"Do not be anxious, Glen," said Michael to the shaking teenager.

The two men parked three doors down. They climbed out but didn't slam their doors shut. Michael left the motor running. Sweat drenched his blue jeans dark and white t-shirt see-through. The street scorched the skin of his bare feet.

Michael tied his flowing hair into a ponytail, like he was loading a rifle. He waited for the theme song of *Play School* to chime through the fly screens. *Open wide. Come inside.* Blessedly, one of Elijah's foster sisters had forgotten to lock the front door after getting home from school.

Michael opened it and stepped aside. Glen was supposed to snatch Elijah. That was the whole point of recruiting a disciple. Instead, Glen froze like a broken robot. Michael rose to the occasion. History insisted upon this.

"Despite their location being a secret," Michael wrote afterwards, "we found where Elijah lived by the grace of GOD. I did not even have to go into the house. Elijah was waiting right at the front door and rose up to meet me."

His version of events was disputed by Debbie, Elijah's nineteen-year-old foster sister. She saw a "pigtailed hippy" storm into the lounge room. Three-year-old Elijah wore a pair of budgie smugglers. He was blue-eyed and blond-haired. The son Fran and Neil Williams had always wanted. But he was also the biological son of Michael Shelley.

Elijah's foster sisters – Debbie, Linda and Cindy – were brown-eyed brunettes, like their mother Fran. Everyone in the house froze, except Michael. He snatched Elijah off the carpet. The toddler dropped a stuffed monkey.

"Mumma!" cried Elijah, reaching for Fran. She was motionless.

Michael carried Elijah through the door. Then he passed him to Glen on the front lawn. The fumbling accomplice burrowed into the backseat. Michael hit the accelerator. Glen hugged and soothed the child. Elijah was shocked and silent.

"We are going to see your *real* mumma!" said Michael.

Elijah's foster sisters chased the getaway vehicle. Debbie chanted the three letters and three digits on the yellow New South Wales number plate. It was a hymn to freeze reality. But the car slipped from the street like a dream.

The actual getaway vehicle was a white Winnebago, with a bunk above the driver's seat and Queensland number plates. It was the slowest and most conspicuous possible Trojan horse and would therefore be invisible to police.

The van sat at a campsite ten minutes west of Strathpine. In the sleeping quarters lay Mary Shelley, a forty-year-old British citizen of Jewish descent. In 1962, her face had graced the front cover of *Women's Weekly*, beautiful and euphoric. Back then, Mary was a glamourous Sydney socialite.

By 1983, Mary's brown eyes were profoundly anxious. She cradled a four-month-old baby boy named Saul. They had the same olive skin. The baby's dark hair had golden tips from Michael Shelley, his biological father. Michael was Mary's third husband. She was Michael's third wife.

The Commodore arrived, unfollowed by sirens. Glen left a letter of apology on the dashboard for failing to return the rental car, but not for the kidnapping. Michael bundled Elijah into the van. Mary presented Saul to Elijah.

"Elijah, this is your baby brother, Saul!" announced Michael.

"Hallelujah!" cried Mary.

Elijah sullenly studied his younger brother. Saul burst into tears.

Mary drove the Winnebago, as per the plan. Police were searching for a Commodore driven by a man who looked like Jesus Christ. The campervan passed unnoticed into New South Wales via the Gold Coast hinterland.

"C'mon, Aussie, c'mon, c'mon," sang Elijah, his mood improving.

It was a war cry for the Australian cricket team. Michael felt newly vindicated about the kidnapping. At school, he could never fathom why the other students worshipped the cricketers and footballers, rather than geniuses like him.

"How about a real song, Elijah?" asked Michael.

He serenaded Elijah and Saul with an acoustic cover of "Father and Son" by Cat Stevens, trying to exorcise the demon of the Australian dream from Elijah's soul. His voice was deep and sweet. But Elijah was unmoved.

"No!" cried Elijah. "C'mon, Aussie, c'mon!"

Michael seethed. Glen offered a happy medium. He drew smiling faces on two bananas and dangled them above the newly amused brothers.

"Bananas in pyjamas are coming down the stairs," sang Glen.

Safely across the border, Michael took the wheel so that Mary could breastfeed Saul. At 9 pm, they reached an unlit beach on the Mid North Coast. South West Rocks. For the first time, Elijah and Saul slept under the same roof.

Later, their names were changed by social workers to hide them from Michael and Mary. The biological brothers would be raised with different surnames in separate foster homes. Life was a lottery, especially when you were born into the bottom of society. This was how Saul Shelley became Steven Blaine, the son of Lenore and Tom.

The Book of Love

Some people create chaos. Others try to tame it. Lenore Blaine was in the latter category. In 1983, Lenore was twenty-nine. A shy bookworm, with short brown hair and hazel-green eyes. The battler had an encyclopaedic knowledge of childhood attachment theory.

"The love that organically develops between a foster child and a foster mother is priceless, because it is not payback for a biological debt," she wrote in an A4 notepad. *THE BOOK OF LOVE* was printed neatly on the cover.

The day after Elijah Shelley's kidnapping, Lenore watched *Play School* with pensive eyes. She was gripped by visions of two men bursting through the door and snatching her foster son, Trent. He was four years old. Blond-haired, blue-eyed and blissfully ignorant of Elijah's disappearance.

"Open wide!" Trent sang. "Come inside! It's *Play School!*"

Trent had been playmates with Elijah in the paediatric ward of the Mater Hospital in Brisbane. Elijah was sunburnt and underfed. Trent was pale and autistic. Elijah was assigned to Fran and Neil Williams. Trent ended up with Lenore and Tom Blaine in Ipswich, an old coalmining town half an hour southwest of Brisbane. It could've easily been the other way around.

The circumstances were different. Trent's real mother wasn't about to reclaim custody. She died shortly after giving birth to him. Yet Lenore was unsettled. The kidnapping reminded Lenore of her illegitimacy as a mother, which reminded her of some other things she was trying hard to forget.

"Mum, I have a Milo?" asked Trent, his gaze fixed on the TV.

"Sweetie, what do we say?" she asked in a warm and husky voice.

"*Please*, Mum, can I have a Milo, please?" he asked, nose crinkled.

"Of course you can," she said.

In the kitchen, Lenore poured milk into a plastic cup. She added three spoons of Milo, undissolved, Trent's preference. He triumphantly glugged it.

"What do we say?" asked Lenore.

"Yum," he said.

Lenore tugged him gently by the sleeve of his t-shirt.

"Good manners are free, Trent," she said.

"*Thanks*, Mum," he said, somewhat frustrated.

Lenore cherished these consistent little frictions just as much as the cuddles and kisses. How easy and weak to become paralysed by her foster son's vulnerability to the world. To allow Trent to piss his pants indefinitely. To let him eat ice cream for breakfast and hot chips for dinner. To treat him with pity. She loved the boy too much. So, she insisted on good manners and green vegetables. Lenore mothered him like a son, not a charity case.

✠

Tom Blaine was 130 kilos, with a dark mullet and a handlebar moustache. His existence revolved around sport. Watching it. Playing it. Coaching it. Betting on it. From the glovebox of his white Ford Falcon taxi, he ran an S.P. bookmaking operation. This was profitable and illegal on several levels.

"Ya win some, ya lose some," he told the gamblers. "But you'll always regret the winner ya didn't tip, more than the loser ya did. Believe you me."

Tom was thirty-four. For seventy hours a week, he drove a taxi, so that his family might one day live at a brick house in a lower middle-class suburb like Strathpine.

Late at night, Lenore waited for her husband on the veranda of their tin and timber Queenslander in North Ipswich. In spring, Tom wore shorts and thongs to work. A Dalmatian named Cindy licked at his cracked heels.

"G'day," he said. "How are my two favourite ladies?"

"I've been better," said Lenore, sucking on a menthol cigarette.

"Have the cops found Elijah?" asked Tom.

"No," said Lenore. "And not for lack of trying."

Lenore and Tom went inside. Lenore checked the locks. Tom moved a cricket bat to the entrance of the master bedroom. The Blaines stood at their son's door. Trent was wrapped in a blanket proudly stitched with TRENT BLAINE by Lenore. There was a tranquil expression on his face.

"Night, me little mate," whispered Tom, kissing him on the forehead.

Lenore and Tom both wore cheap false teeth. They left the dentures in mugs of water on their bedside tables. She was afraid. He was angry.

"What's the name of this snake?" asked Tom.

"Michael Shelley," said Lenore.

"And what's his religion?"

"Christian."

Tom, an atheist, preferred a candid crook to a dishonest bible-basher.

"Jesus really opened a can of worms, didn't he?" asked Tom.

"Yes, I guess so," said Lenore, an on-again, off-again Catholic.

Tom didn't know it, but he was destined to be Michael Shelley's best enemy yet. Michael would come to see that fat cabbie as the Australian Satan.

"I must admit that I actually feel quite sorry for the mother," said Lenore. "She had a child taken away from her. I'd die for Trent. And he's not even mine."

Lenore was an inexhaustible source of compassion. According to her, happiness wasn't a fait accompli, achieved chiefly through grit, as Tom insisted. There were patterns of grief and delirium happening at a deeper level. In Tom's humble opinion, some people were just bad apples. And rotten fruit needed to be crushed, not taken back to the orchard and watered more.

"Nutjobs," said Tom. "Send 'em both to the loony bin."

"Let him without sin cast the first stone, Thomas," said Lenore.

The two couples – Michael and Mary, Lenore and Tom – had more in common than met the eye. They wanted the same thing: a family to undo the damage of losing their own. Unrequited desire is life's great equaliser. It was gradually drawing the four of them together. In Australia, there was a thin line between the winners and the losers; the good Samaritans and the criminals; the saints and the sinners.

CHAPTER TWO

Original Sin: Michael

Michael Shelley's great-great-great-great-grandfather, William Shelley, was a cabinetmaker from Staffordshire. William suffered a religious epiphany. In 1797, he sailed to Australia, intending to spread the Gospel of Jesus. From Tahiti, he pilfered a record-breaking pearl deposit and 182 litres of dark rum.

In 1811, William Shelley opened a store in Sydney. The governor of New South Wales, Lachlan Macquarie, praised the Christian rum smuggler as "a moral, well-meaning man", and bestowed on him 400 hectares of land at Cabramatta. He allowed William Shelley to build a school for kidnapped Aboriginal children at Parramatta. It was called the "Native Institution".

"I am fully persuaded, that, under the blessing of God, these Natives are as capable of receiving instructions as any other untutored Savages," Shelley wrote to Macquarie on 20 August 1814, a prophecy of the Stolen Generations.

Governor Macquarie sent men in black clothes to abduct Aboriginal children for William Shelley's Native Institution. It had an observation cage for their bereaved parents. *Terra Nullius.* Translation: finders keepers, losers weepers.

Michael Shelley and Jacki Weaver met at a dance in West Pymble on Sydney's upper North Shore. It was the 1959 Christmas holidays. He was thirteen. She was twelve and a half. The Women's Christian Association hosted dances at Lofberg Oval on Yanko Road. The scout hall looked like a church built from Besser blocks, with timber windows and a corrugated iron roof.

On the dance floor, Michael locked eyes with Jacki. She was a blonde pocket rocket. 139 centimetres to be precise. Michael didn't freeze or flee. He pulled her towards him. Jacki was caught off guard by the handsome boy with shining eyes and sandy hair. He wasn't big or tough. But unlike the jocks, he wasn't tongue-tied under pressure.

Michael walked Jacki home across the oval. Cicadas clicked with an electric intensity. His intelligence was magnetic. So was hers. They were both straight-A students. Jacki hated sport, too, and pretended to have period pain during PE lessons. She had grown up listening to her father recite Shakespeare. She could perform Juliet's balcony scene off by heart. *O Romeo, Romeo! Wherefore art thou Romeo? Deny thy father and refuse thy name.*

That night, Michael kissed Jacki for the first time. It was astonishing evidence that the emotional range of Shakespeare could exist in West Pymble. He was her first true love. She was obsessed with him.

Michael attended Knox Grammar, an elite private school in Wahroonga. He unveiled Jacki as his girlfriend at a rugby union game between Knox Grammar and Barker College. The grandstands were filled with a mosaic of blazers and boaters. At last, all those upper-class sons from nuclear families understood that Michael was better than them.

His parents, John and Marie, had been prominent socialites. Their affair – which ended each of their first marriages – was plastered on the front pages of newspapers. Then, when Michael was eleven, his father moved to Mosman and married a much younger woman. Michael was raised by a single mum in a humble bungalow. The fall from grace was vertical.

But Michael had one last upper-class charm in his arsenal to impress Jacki: his father's yacht, *The White Maa*. It was docked in Kirribilli. Michael's grandfather, D'Arcy Shelley, had been the vice-commodore of the Royal Sydney Yacht Squadron.

One unforgettable afternoon, John Shelley took Michael and Jacki for a yacht ride on Sydney Harbour. Construction had begun on the Opera House. The blue body of water was lit silver. White sails swerved to capture the wind. Above the bridge, a yellow explosion: the sun! For the first time, Michael felt that he was seeing real colours.

✠

Jacki Weaver grew eleven centimetres in the space of a year. She wore Rock 'n' Rose lipstick to YWCA dances. Hornsby Girls High was up the road from Knox Grammar. After school, Michael and Jacki met in their uniforms. They caught a bus from Gordon train station to West Pymble. Someone scrawled "Jacki Weaver is the Sex Symbol of West Pymble" on the back window.

Jacki rode her bicycle to Michael's place. Her mother was under the impression they were doing homework together. On Yanko Road, gum trees shed bark onto front lawns, trunks bleeding with beehives. Fathers arrived home in shiny cars, except to Michael's driveway. His mother was scouting for a third husband at the All Nations Club in Darlinghurst.

Most afternoons, Michael and Jacki had sex in his mother's bed. Perfect and precocious, they studied the geometry of each other's textbook bodies. His was firm from childhood breathing exercises for asthma.

"I love you! I love you! I love you!" Michael chanted.

At twilight, Michael and Jacki rode their bikes back to her place. Azaleas in front gardens. Galahs laughing from gum trees. They had sex one more time next to the Lane Cove River, skin soft and slick with sweat.

Perhaps Michael's first fanaticism made him thirsty to worship perfection. Only heaven could measure up to the pleasure of those inaugural orgasms. And only hell could measure up to the damnation of getting dumped.

Jacki, fifteen, was cast to play Cinderella opposite a heartthrob named Bryan Davies. He was a number-one hit singer and a star of the TV show *Bandstand*. Jacki played hard to get, but love bloomed. It was huge news in the Sydney tabloids. Bryan picked Jacki up from Hornsby Girls High in a red Jaguar.

Michael was immaculate. Yet the people he loved kept deserting him. In his final year of high school, Michael wagged classes and stole cars. He gate-crashed parties across the North Shore with cigarettes and hip flasks of gin.

"I was running away from all of my anger and pain," he later wrote.

The enfant terrible of West Pymble still managed to get straight A's. Michael had learned some valuable lessons. Sex was the meaning of life. But in Sydney, it wasn't going to be forthcoming without fame or money.

++

Michael Shelley studied a chemical engineering degree at the University of New South Wales. The civil rights movement had hit Sydney, along with the sexual revolution. Michael's university years were a moveable feast of booze, weed, speed, Vietnam War protests and unprotected intercourse.

"As a teenager, I became very sexually promiscuous," Michael wrote later. "I slept with approximately two hundred women before the age of twenty-eight."

Michael volunteered for *Tharunka*, the UNSW student magazine. The editor was Richard Neville, another Knox old boy, who later rose to fame as hippy-in-chief of *Oz* magazine. A subeditor at *Tharunka* was a public-school graduate from Western Sydney named Beverly Fleming. She was tall and thin with black bangs and short skirts.

Beverly slept with Richard Neville. She didn't understand what all the fuss was about. Then she met Michael Shelley at the Roundhouse, a bar at UNSW.

"I've found you," said Michael.

"Who?" asked Beverly.

"The sexiest woman in Sydney."

"I'm seeing someone," she said.

Beverly was dating a curly-haired architecture major named Grahame Bond. He later starred as Aunty Jack on the ABC's *Aunty Jack Show*.

"That must be very unsatisfying for you," said Michael.

"You have a very high opinion of yourself," said Beverly.

On New Year's Eve 1964, there was a party on the North Shore with all the usual ingredients: beer, wine, amphetamines and marijuana. Eighteen-year-old Michael borrowed his mother's new VW without permission. He offered Beverly and Grahame a ride back to the eastern suburbs. A girl named Dianne rode up front with Michael. Beverly sat on Grahame's lap in the back.

Seatbelt laws hadn't been introduced yet. None of them were buckled up. Michael hit a dip in River Road. Skylarkers had removed the lanterns placed to illuminate the road works. The VW careened into excavated earth.

Michael dislocated his chiselled jaw against the thick, flat windscreen. Dianne went flying face first into the glass. Grahame suffered a cut to the lip. Beverly was unscathed. She watched bloody Dianne seemingly dying on the roadside. Michael attended to Dianne with a fractured face of his own.

Dianne survived the accident. Beverly's relationship with Grahame did not. He was the first one on a stretcher. The budding actor grew a moustache to cover up the scar. Meanwhile, Beverly had seen that Michael's brazenness at the Roundhouse wasn't a charade. He was eerily fearless.

After recovering from his injuries, Michael took Beverly on a picnic to Centennial Park. His jaw was still swollen and his expensive dentistry wrecked. Beverly assumed he wanted to apologise for the crash.

"Bev, we nearly died," he said. "I saw life flash before my eyes. You want to know what my biggest regret would have been? That we never made love."

"Are you crazy, Michael?" she asked, flushed.

Michael spoke as though he were pouring his soul into the space between them. They kissed. Beverly was light-headed with delight and desire.

"I love you, Bev," said Michael.

"I love you, too," cried Beverly.

Beverly was surrounded by people rising to fame. She slept with many of them. Michael eclipsed all of the competition in the charisma stakes. Later, Beverly realised that was because he didn't give a damn about anyone else.

At *Tharunka*, Richard Neville was succeeded by two student journalists: Richard Carleton and Allan Hogan. Later, they teamed up on *Four Corners* and *60 Minutes*. Michael became an assistant editor of *Tharunka*. Allan Hogan taught him to play the twelve-string acoustic guitar. Michael was obsessed with pre-electric Bob Dylan.

"I had a miraculous natural talent," wrote Michael.

Michael smoked marijuana heavily. At some point, he became a sperm donor, an entrepreneurial way to pay the rent. Occasionally,

Michael caught up with an old friend from Knox Grammar named Bruce Moir.

"Bruce, it's official: I have the purest semen in Sydney," said Michael.

"That's a very Hitler-esque thing of you to say, Mick," said Bruce.

The personality changes caused by recreational drugs weren't immediately obvious to Michael's new friends and lovers. But those who'd seen his sweet and sensitive side noticed a growing megalomania.

In 1966, Jacki Weaver made her breakthrough appearance in the TV series *Wandjina!* Michael ran into his first love at a party in the eastern suburbs. Jacki had just been to watch Bob Dylan live at Sydney Stadium.

"He was beautiful, Michael," said Jacki. "You would've loved it."

Michael blew up. He hadn't forgiven Dylan for going electric, or Jacki for breaking up with him. The true source of his disproportionate anger was channelled into a one-way debate about the virtues of the acoustic guitar.

"You wouldn't have a clue, Jacki," he roared. "Bob Dylan is a fraud, a fake, a sellout. He's just a talentless conman taking naïve girls like you for a ride!"

What shocked Jacki wasn't the opinion, but the way Michael expressed it. Like an all-seeing preacher. As if his was the only truth. As if any disagreement deserved damnation, especially when it came from a woman.

Love Thy Neighbour: Mary

Two long stories short: Michael and Mary Shelley were the children of cheaters. Mary's father, Sidney Newgrosh, was an Ashkenazi Jew whose family hailed from the now Ukrainian town of Brody. The Newgroshes were silversmiths to the Austrian royal family. They fled to England from the pogroms.

In 1938, Hitler invaded Austria. Sidney Newgrosh was a tall, olive-skinned jeweller in London's West End. He married a Welsh bombshell named Joan. In July 1940, the couple were walking home from dinner when the air-raid siren sounded. They rushed down some steps into a cellar. Debris from the German missiles buried the lovers in an underground bunker. They were rescued eight hours later.

Sidney was drunk with a new lust for life. According to Joan, Sidney had a fetish for hearing her describe fictionalised flings with other men. At wartime parties, he descended the stairs dressed as a woman and serenaded the guests with French and German songs. Joan claimed that Sidney would make her dance unclothed.

Their first child, Ann, was born in January 1942. In December, the couple hosted a party to celebrate the momentum of the Allied forces and the final trimester of Joan's second pregnancy. Sidney allegedly recruited an eighteen-year-old to the master bedroom for a sexual rendezvous.

Carole Sue Newgrosh – who later married Michael Shelley and changed her name to Mary – was born in January 1943. A brother, David, followed in 1945. Their mother took the bible's advice to *love thy neighbour* literally. Joan began an affair with a married man, Albert Marks. A dance-band leader, Mr Frost, found them in his flat, Joan in her lingerie.

Sidney and Joan divorced in 1950. It was a landmark case in the British legal system. The salacious details were reported alongside dapper photographs on page three of *The Daily Mirror*. Joan obtained a court order preventing Sidney from taking their children overseas. Ann, Carole and David were sent to a brutal boarding school in the Sussex countryside.

Sidney remarried a dress designer named Muriel. The marriage lasted a year. She accused him of cruelty. Sidney started seeing Molly Everitt, a model and ballet dancer who also worked as a clothes designer for the royals. She was the perfect abduction accomplice: too beautiful to raise suspicions at customs.

Sidney withdrew Ann, Carole and David from boarding school. He and Molly took them to the international airport. Carole was ten. The destination on her boarding pass: *Sydney, Australia*. She thought this was a hysterical inside joke about her father's name and ancestral homeland.

Sidney, Austria.

Sidney broke the court order. He flew his children to the obscurity of Sydney. In December, the kidnapped sisters were pictured grinning with a Christmas tree in *The Daily Telegraph*. Sidney described Australia to a local newspaper as "a mecca for carpetbaggers". At the Australia Hotel, he sold eight plates that once belonged to King William IV for £425 a pop.

Sidney and Molly got hitched. The runaway family settled in the eastern suburbs. They had thirty goldfish and an ice cream-eating dachshund named Bert. Carole attended Dover Heights Home Science High School. The Newgroshes joined a synagogue, Temple Emanuel. At Carole's Bat Mitzvah, she delivered a sermonette suggested by Rabbi Brasch.

"Smile," said the rabbi.

Carole Newgrosh had been thrust from the grey skies and anxious faces of London to a country where everyone was expected to smile all the time, even the rabbis. So she smiled, while dying on the inside. Who was she? Where was she? And when would she see her mother again?

✢

Sidney Newgrosh opened the Chelsea Restaurant on Macleay Street in Kings Cross. Visitors included Frank Sinatra, Russian ballet dancer Rudolf Nureyev and Jesus Vargas, the Secretary of Defense for the Philippines. Prime Minister Robert Menzies was a regular guest. Sidney was a chronic name-dropper. He sold ashtrays in the shape of Australia imprinted with "MR SIDNEY OF THE CHELSEA".

"Mr Sidney has children of his own and knows babies," read the menu. "He suffered during the last war and can't eat Grilled Spatchcock. Remember King Henry VIII? Remember his VII wives? How could he? We'll show you!"

Sidney sure showed them. He ditched Molly for a maître d' named Alice. They married and bought a palatial home in Bellevue Hill. Sidney threw Ann and Carole a party at the Chelsea. A fuse above the restaurant blew. Sparks flew and lit a fire. The restaurant filled with smoke. Guests evacuated, but not before the Newgrosh sisters made an impression.

"Very attractive they looked, too, in their whirling-skirted floral cottons, mingling with guests on the specially laid dancefloor," noted a newspaper.

Sidney funded a "Million Dollar Cabaret". It was the party of the year. The MC was Brian Henderson, a news anchor at Channel 9 and host of *Bandstand*. Entertainment was provided by Lionel Long, a twenty-year-old folk singer and *Bandstand* star. Carole Newgrosh wore a green dress, pinned with a single white rose. She was thin from a moderate eating disorder.

"Call me Carrie," she told Lionel.

On stage, Lionel received undivided attention. All the single young women in the room wanted to be horizontal with the TV star. Carrie sat nibbling at a Vienna schnitzel. Lionel couldn't take his eyes off the sixteen-year-old.

"You'll come a Waltzing Matilda with me," he sang.

✤

Carrie Newgrosh bobbed up and down on a brand-new yacht called *Waltzing Matilda*. Her intense eyes watched carefree Lionel negotiate a gentleman's agreement between the flapping sails and invisible wind. Beneath them glinted the godliest body of water in the world: Sydney Harbour.

It was 1962. Lionel, twenty-three, had recently released the best-selling album of all time by an Australian – also called *Waltzing Matilda*. Carrie was nineteen. If it weren't for the slit of Mosman on the horizon, she felt the yacht might glide into the sky.

Lionel wore a button-up shirt, cream chinos and boat shoes, no socks. He was so popular hosting *Sing Sing Sing* on Channel 7 that they gave him his own show. He had identified Carrie Newgrosh as the prize of notoriety. It was an odd match. Carrie was a Bellevue Hill Jew with a British accent. Irish-Catholic Lionel had been inspired to sing ballads about bushrangers and swagmen while jackerooing in the dust of the Australian outback.

At sunset, Lionel parked *Waltzing Matilda* at Rushcutters Bay. He had four more yachts docked alongside it. Lionel and Carrie walked hand in hand up the steep streets to Kings Cross. They passed the El Alamein Fountain.

Lionel and Carrie were VIP guests at the Chelsea. Sidney Newgrosh lorded over the room in a black tuxedo, a clown prince. There was a goldplated tissue box on the bar. An Italian named Salvatore Frensi played piano. Black-tied waiters delivered dinner to candlelit tables under a crystal chandelier. Lionel offered Carrie a white gold ring with a solitaire diamond.

"Yes!" said Carrie.

Their engagement was trumpeted on the front cover of *Women's Weekly*. LIONEL LONG and his BRIDE-TO-BE. The nameless brunette with red lipstick stared up gratefully at the giant face of her famous fiancé. Lionel drove Carrie to Alice Springs in a Mini Minor to celebrate.

Back in Sydney, Lionel and Carrie moved into a Bellevue Hill terrace. Lionel's pipe collection sat on a marble pedestal. There were Viennese gilt frames for the mirrors. In the garden, vines wrapped around the trellises. Carrie would sit on a timber bench with a black dog named Laddie on her lap.

"It's our own private world," she told *Women's Weekly*.

Their wedding photos were printed in *The Sydney Morning Herald*. Carrie's hair was tied into a bun with a white headdress, a curled fringe at the front. The newlyweds represented equal and opposite possibilities to each other. Lionel, that he might rise above the station of a wild colonial boy. Carrie, that she might become a happy, laid-back Australian.

Lionel's *Waltzing Matilda* was followed by bestselling albums such as *Wild Colonial Boy*, *The Bold Bushrangers* and *Songs of the Sea*. But the singer was determined to make it as an actor. The couple sailed to England on the TSS *Fairstar*. Lionel performed at dinner. In England, he made a breakout cameo as an actor in 1965's *The Amorous Adventures of Moll Flanders*, starring Kim Novak.

At sea, Carrie had fallen pregnant. She reunited with her mother, Joan, in West London for the first time since 1954. It was an emotional homecoming. Joan fetched an extensive archive of newspaper clippings, legal files and letters returned to sender. Carrie read them and wept. Lionel was the prize of her father's lies. Motherhood seemed like a chance at redemption.

A daughter named Amberwren was born in 1965. The Longs moved back to Sydney. Lionel secured his best-known acting role: as an Italian detective named Bert Costello on *Homicide*, Australia's most popular TV show.

In 1968, Carrie gave birth to a son, Roman. A few days later, in London, her mother was killed in a car crash. Carrie's grief led to postnatal depression. She slit her wrists with a knife. Doctors sent her from the maternity ward to the psych ward. They prescribed electroshock therapy.

Like Moses, Roman was left in a wicker basket at the house of Ann, Carrie's older sister. Lionel was busy filming *Homicide* in Melbourne.

Carrie was released from hospital. She was never the same after electroshock therapy. At home, tensions with Lionel escalated. Carrie couldn't handle the necessity to pretend they were a happy family for magazine profiles.

Carrie left Lionel. She moved into a rental with her two children. A heated argument over alimony led to a physical altercation. Lionel was charged with assault. The actor pleaded not guilty and received leniency.

Abattoir Blues: Tom

The worst day of Tom Blaine's life was in 1962. He was twelve going on thirteen, the only member of the working-class Blaine family to make it past primary school. In Ipswich, Tom had the sunroom of a Queenslander to himself.

"Get up, Tom," shouted his mother, Lillian.

Pikelets and peanut butter were waiting for him on the kitchen bench. He sucked the peanut butter from his thumb and banged on the bathroom door.

"Hurry up, Mum," he shouted.

Lillian was fifty-six, a squat woman of Germanic descent and temperament. Tom was the sixteenth baby to leave her fruitful womb in one piece. Now, his mother stumbled from the bathroom with her foot wrapped in a towel. Overnight, pus and blood had begun erupting from an ingrown toenail.

"What happened to you?" he asked.

"Don't ask," she said, so he didn't.

Tom prodded blood down the shower drain with his toe. In the kitchen, varicose veins erupted from Lillian's plump, bowed legs. She limped on her good foot. Tom collected a Spam and tomato sauce sandwich for his lunchbox.

"My toe is stuffed," said Lillian. "Give it a kiss before they cut it off."

Tom was nonchalant. His kin were permanently hurt. The Blaines survived daily intimations of fire and brimstone by taking the piss.

"It ain't over till the fat lady sings," said Tom, immediately regretting it. Lillian wasn't vain about being overweight, but Tom was sensitive on her behalf. She laughed with a mixture of gruffness and love. Tom felt relief.

"The fat lady is singing," she said.

"Ya not that fat," he said.

"And the Pope's protestant," she croaked.

On the way to Bremer High, Tom fetched a cigarette from his pencil case. It matched the taste of soot from the coalmines on the limestone horizon. Tom strutted through the school gates with a bewildering self-confidence. He wasn't rich or particularly big. But the Blaine brothers were gun boxers, cricketers and rugby league players. They weren't to be messed with.

Tom moved between classes while harbouring two dark secrets: he preferred arithmetic to manual arts, and he wanted to do unspeakable things to a girl named Debbie. He shared a desk with her in last period for maths.

Tom's father, John Blaine, was vice-president of the Queensland ironworkers' union. "Hoppy" was a smiley blacksmith with squinty eyes, gigantic hands and a bung leg from a mishap at the railway workshop.

If Tom – the youngest child – stayed on an A for maths, maybe his father would let him continue beyond grade eight. If he made it to grade ten, maybe he could get a cadetship at the Commonwealth Bank, rather than a trade. And if he became a banker, maybe Debbie would marry him.

Tom's daydream was spoiled by the sight of his father limping to the classroom door in a dirty boilersuit. The other students stared at the white-haired intruder. He was tailed by the able-bodied principal.

"Tom Blaine," said the principal.

"Bring your stuff," said John.

The Blaines walked through the school gates. Tom thought he was in deep shit. His father broke the silence without making eye contact.

"It's ya mum, cobber," he said. "She's crook as a dog."

John, sixty-two, looked one hundred years old. That morning, his wife had gone to the GP. A nurse attempted to numb and cut the ingrown toenail. The patient's blood pressure went through the roof. A vein in her brain burst.

"But she'll be right?" asked Tom.

"Nah, cob," said John. "She won't be right."

At hospital, Lillian had been moved from emergency to a private ward. Her white face was bright red. A doctor stitched her tongue to her bottom lip so she wouldn't choke on it. Her mouth was a fit of tubes and spit.

Tom started sobbing. Calluses covered his father's gargantuan hands, preventing the bolt-burrer from feeling much. John scratched Tom mechanically on the neck, like a pet parrot.

"You'll be right, mate," said John.

Tom's older siblings arrived at the Ipswich Hospital. A priest from the Salvation Army performed last rites. Lillian was fifty-six and unfixable.

☩

A few weeks after the death of his mother, when people stopped dropping food around, Tom found himself alone at the kitchen table with his father. Something about dusk – or maybe grief – made John Blaine seem vulnerable.

"I wanna go to the end of grade ten," said Tom. "What do ya reckon?"

"What's the point of that?" asked John.

None of the other Blaines made it past primary school, because a senior education cost money, and John was tighter than a fish's sphincter. His pockets jingled with the pennies he was stockpiling for the next Great Depression.

"I'll get a job at the … bank," said Tom, choking on the last word. "I know a bloke whose brother got a cadetship. It's a gig for life. I'll pay ya back."

John squinted at Tom sideways, grinning incredulously.

"Ya booked the operation, mate?" asked John.

"What operation?" asked Tom.

"To get ya balls chopped off!"

Tom hadn't heard John laugh so much since Lillian died. He was glad to see him smiling again. Just a shame that it came at the expense of Tom's pride.

"Ya ain't a banker's arsehole, Tommy," said John, sombrely. "You're a Blaine. I know you're a bit glum about ya mum. But no more poofter business."

Tom knew few occupations that didn't constitute "poofter business". He wasn't keen to work with his dad on the railway. And he was spooked off the coalmines by his Uncle Stanley, John's brother, who had been paralysed by a 30-kilogram shard of sandstone that fell from an underground tunnel.

Tom opted for a job at the abattoir on the Bremer River. Cow tongues washed up along the banks. On the first day, thirteen-year-old Tom got dressed in overalls and galoshes. He recognised men on the kill floor: footballers with broken noses, cauliflower ears and homicidal hands. Fifty decapitated cattle hung upside down from severed legs on s-shaped hooks.

Tom joined the meatworkers' union. He became militantly left-wing. The members went on strike at the slit of a finger. He worked from 6 am until 3 pm, Monday to Friday. A quarter of his wage went to his father for rent.

In 1966, John Blaine was forced into retirement from the railway.

It was the beginning of the end. Late one night, he burst onto the veranda.

"Wake up, me little mate!" he exclaimed.

"What's wrong?" asked Tom, sixteen now.

"Your mum's coming home," said John.

Tom's father had misplaced his marbles. But he hadn't lost that blacksmith strength. John dragged Tom to the front steps. They waited hours for Lillian to arrive. She was a no-show. The sun rose over the horizon. Tom – a wannabe bodgie – slicked back his darkening hair with a comb and Brylcreem. At half past five, he rode a pushbike past the river to the abattoir.

Tom wore a knife and sharpening steel on the belt of his apron. The beasts were killed and stripped and skinned and cleaned. Then, upon a two-metre-high steel platform, Tom split them down the middle and spread their heels apart. He gutted their kidneys, liver, heart, lungs and intestines onto a bench.

"Hurry up, ya slow fuck," yelled Tom's supervisor.

Tom stuck the next cow with everything, piercing the uterus. A calf was revealed. Tom recoiled. He slipped sideways on a burst of blood and shit. I'm dead, he thought, on the way to the concrete floor.

Tom shattered his hip. Bone broke through the skin like a hot knife. He couldn't tell which pool of blood was human and which came from a cow. Then he passed out from pain. He woke up in hospital to the sight of his father.

"Ya silly bugger," said John, grinning wistfully.

The doctors tried and failed to put Tom's hip back together. It became grossly infected. Tom nearly died. He spent months in Ipswich Hospital.

It was a bittersweet winter for the Blaine family. Tom's brother George played fullback for the Ipswich Rugby League representative team in the Bulimba Cup final. They defeated Brisbane – the favourites – 7–2. Then, Tom's sister Rita gave birth to a blond bombshell named Allan Langer. Tom wheeled himself from surgery to maternity to nurse his newborn nephew.

"He looks just like you when you were born, Tommy," said Rita.

Allan was a phoenix rising from the ashes of Tom's rugby league career. Doctors told Tom he'd be lucky to walk again, let alone play contact sport. His sisters provided an endless supply of potato bakes and meat pies.

"Redcliffe for Christmas, mate," said John. "That's just what the doctor ordered. A nice sea breeze and some ice-cold Coca-Cola. You'll be a pig in shit."

In late spring, John's kidneys capitulated. Sixty-six, he died in the same ward as his wife, a floor below his son. Tom went to the funeral on crutches, hip plastered, and twenty kilograms heavier than when he entered hospital.

"Mate, ya look like ya swallowed a sheep!" said his brother George at the wake. The charismatic football star was nicknamed "Gorgeous Georgie".

Before Christmas, Tom was freed from hospital into orphanhood. His hip was purple and filled with pins. His gammy leg was two inches shorter than the other. Tom couldn't wear a blue collar due to injury, or a white collar due to his lack of a senior certificate. He received $3.50 a week from the dole.

Tom inherited his father's second-hand bicycle collection and his mother's Salvation Army bible. Except now he was a devout atheist. On the off-chance that God existed, Tom wanted nothing to do with the prick.

Poor Bastard: Lenore

Lenore Meurant – Tom Blaine's future second wife – came from a rich bloodline of convicts. Ferdinand Meurant was a jeweller for the French royals. He shot through to Ireland during the French Revolution. In

Dublin, Ferdinand was caught forging bank notes and sent to Australia for life on the *Minerva*. He knocked up Mary Pritchard, a teenaged convict, out of wedlock.

Ferdinand's great-grandson was Kenneth Meurant, Lenore's father. After World War II, Kenneth deserted his first wife and two children. He hitchhiked through rural Australia with a swag, working as a shearers' cook.

North of Tamworth, Kenneth met Dorothy, the daughter of Catholic banana farmers. Kenneth, fifty, was short and grey-haired with black-rimmed glasses and a fading navy tattoo on his forearm. Dorothy, twenty-one, was dark-haired with hazel-green eyes. Kenneth introduced her to rum and sex.

Dorothy fell pregnant. The odd couple fled south. Just over the Victorian border, they stopped at Pyramid Hill. Fat little lambs were scattered across the land like maggots. The town – population 652 – was named after a 187-metre pile of granite, debatably shaped like a pyramid.

Kenneth got a job as a shearers' cook. He and Dorothy lived in a green canvas tent. Lenore Meurant was born on 4 January 1954, a bona fide bastard. Kenneth named his third daughter after the first one. Lenore the Second was a chubby girl with a large head and bulging hazel-green eyes.

Lenore had fond memories of Pyramid Hill, largely because she could remember so little of it. Just some flashes of placid farm animals and drunken hillbillies around a campfire, whistling through leaves and singing bush ballads.

> Once a jolly swagman camped by a billabong
> Under the shade of a coolabah tree
> And he sang as he watched and waited till his billy boiled
> You'll come a-waltzing Matilda with me!

Lenore was sure that she could recall the sense of fun, the sound of laughter. Kenneth and Dorothy hugged and kissed their bug-eyed toddler. Maybe it was the drunkenness. Or maybe the cost of their affair just hadn't sunk in yet. Once upon a time, Lenore felt like a daughter, not an afterthought.

++

Kenneth and Dorothy had four more children out of wedlock. The Meurant family outgrew the canvas tent. They relocated to a council estate in Echuca, on the Victorian border. 18 Garden Crescent. The tiny three-bedroom home had fibro slats and a brick chimney.

On Monday mornings, Dorothy cooked a massive saucepan of porridge. The five kids ate it without complaint until Friday. For dinner, Kenneth caught red fin, yellow belly, crayfish and cod from the Murray River.

On Saturday afternoons, Kenneth went to the Echuca Racecourse. He came home empty-handed, or bearing toys and fresh oysters, depending on whether or not he had backed a winner. One such afternoon, Kenneth walked through the front gate with rum on his breath and wrath on his face.

"Done my arse," he said to Lenore, before stumbling inside.

In the kitchen, Dorothy was making vanilla ice cream. You needed to half-freeze the milk and sugar, take it out and stir it, and then leave it to freeze again. That day, Dorothy had forgotten to stir. Kenneth could quickly judge his wife's sobriety by sticking his fingers into the ice cream.

"This is shithouse!" he roared. "You've been on the piss, haven't ya?"

"That makes two of us," she whispered, exiting for the pub.

"Keep your legs shut, ya mutt," grumbled Kenneth.

On weeknights, Lenore helped Dorothy collect her empty beer bottles and stash them in the shed. But the garbo, Ray, was a drinking buddy of Kenneth's. He provided a running update on Dorothy's alcohol intake.

Dorothy became more creative. She bribed Lenore with a couple of bob to hide the bottles in wheelie bins around the council estate. Soon the stubbies were accompanied by empty benzo bottles. Dorothy sourced prescriptions from a variety of local doctors. They were handing out Valium like jellybeans.

"Don't tell your dad," Dorothy told Lenore.

Dorothy wasn't the only one in the marriage running a secret scheme. Kenneth gathered five Commonwealth Bank money tins, one for each child. They were designed to be opened only once. He placed them on top of a cupboard, out of Dorothy's reach. When luck struck at the racecourse or the TAB, Kenneth divided the leftover takings equally among the piggy banks.

After a good day at the racecourse, Lenore stood at the bedroom door.

"What's that?" she asked Kenneth.

"Hey there, sailor," he said, drunk and good-humoured for once. "I'm saving you some dosh for a rainy day. Don't tell your mum, or she'll blow it."

The Meurants' sole outside entertainment came from the radio. Lenore listened to it religiously. Her favourite folk singer was Lionel Long. He glorified Lenore's lost nobility as the daughter of a shearers' cook in the bush. Lenore studied photos of Lionel. She tried to imagine being attractive to a man like him. It was impossible. Lenore was a frumpy, short-haired tomboy.

"Ugly as sin," one of the footballers at school called her.

Lenore daydreamed about Lionel Long riding into Echuca on a white horse, like the Man from Snowy River, and rescuing her from irrelevance.

✢

Lenore turned fifteen. At Echuca State High School, the shy teacher's pet topped English. She was hyperlexic. English streamed from the page into her brain. She spent hours reading novels and bush poetry at the public library.

Kenneth, sixty-seven, was suffering from Wernicke-Korsakoff syndrome, the brain disease of drinkers. Bed-ridden, he chain-smoked Tally-Hos in a white Jackie Howe singlet. Dorothy, thirty-eight, drank enough for both of them.

Kenneth's inability to go fishing, plus Dorothy's costly habits, led to a shortfall. His veteran's pension wasn't enough to put food on the table for seven. During a rare appearance at the kitchen table, he decided Lenore would quit school at the end of grade ten, so she could get a job and pay rent.

"But if I finish school, I could become an English teacher," pleaded Lenore, with tears in her eyes. "And that would mean more money for us."

"And if your mum had a dick, she'd be your dad," said Kenneth.

Lenore dropped out of school and got a full-time job at Woolworths. She paid half of her minimum wage to share a shoebox bedroom with her two younger sisters. Even after her sixteenth birthday and her promotion to shift supervisor, Kenneth still enforced a strict 9 pm curfew.

Lenore was asked on a date by a chubby mechanic named Zeek. He smelled of petrol and sweat. They went to see *Butch Cassidy and the Sundance Kid* at the drive-in cinema. Afterwards, Zeek parked alongside the Murray River.

"You gonna give me a kiss, or nah," said Zeek.

"I guess," she said.

Zeek stuck his tongue into Lenore's mouth for a few minutes. It was an interesting experience. But she felt no great sexual awakening. The mechanic slipped a rough hand underneath her b-cup bra. Lenore pushed it away.

"You think you're too good for me?" he asked. "You're not."

It was a realpolitik approach to love. Neither fumbling Zeek nor meek Lenore was flush with options. Lenore was more worried about the time.

"My dad will kill me," she said.

It was ten past nine on a Friday night. Cicadas galore. Zeek dropped Lenore back to the council estate. Kenneth was waiting on the front porch.

"Pack your shit and get out," he said.

Lenore was the spitting image of her mother. This was the eviction Kenneth wished he could inflict on his unfaithful wife. Lenore's four siblings silently watched her pack clothes into a bag. Kenneth handed his daughter a money tin as a severance package. Dorothy, benzo'd beyond emotion, couldn't make eye contact. Lenore walked to Zeek's place. He lived with his parents.

"You can crash in the shaggin' wagon," he said.

The next day, Zeek dropped Lenore at a caravan park. He had no desire to resume his courtship of the sixteen-year-old, frigid and now homeless.

"This ain't gonna work," he said.

"I know," she said, humiliated that he thought she was crying about him.

Curtis Caravan Park was surrounded by cow paddocks. There were magpies on the barbed-wire fence. Lenore walked through the front door of a petrol station that doubled as a lobby for the caravan park.

"How can I help you, love?" asked Betty, the middle-aged owner.

Betty Curtis had been the 1952 Australian Two-Mile Cycling Champion. Her legs were muscular from pedalling. Her hands were callused from dairy farming. She was a tough country woman from good stock.

"Good morning," said Lenore. "I'm looking for a place to stay."

"How long?" asked Betty.

"It might be for a while."

"So you need a place to live?"

"I hope that isn't an inconvenience to you."

Betty didn't take permanent bookings. She had no desire to attract Echuca's trailer trash. Lenore presented a dilemma. The teenager was clearly on the run from something. And yet she seemed gentle.

"I'm going to need a week up front," said Betty, softening her policy. "This isn't a charity service. We don't put up with riff-raff."

"Oh, that suits me just splendidly," said Lenore. "I was hoping to get away from the riff-raff myself. Do you have a can opener, perchance?"

Betty lifted an eyebrow, and then guffawed. Lenore handed over her long-awaited Commonwealth Bank money tin with shame and pride.

"Tough times?" asked Betty.

"I've been saving it for a rainy day," said Lenore.

Betty fetched the necessary utensil. Lenore cracked the can open, face lit with anticipation. Hope turned to dismay. The tin was filled with stainless-steel washers. Her mum had got there first and clamped the lid back on with glue. Lenore burst into tears. This was a new level of humiliation.

"I have the money!" she cried. "I work full-time. But the bank isn't open. I won't be able to pay you until Monday morning. First thing, I swear."

"First thing Monday morning," sighed Betty.

The kindness was justified. Lenore never missed rent. Betty had her first permanent tenant: a teenage girl with an addiction to literature. In the caravan, Lenore read *My Brilliant Career* by Stella Miles Franklin. She jotted her favourite sentences onto an exercise pad, and nearly rewrote the whole book.

"Provided a woman is beautiful, allowance will be made for all her shortcomings," wrote Franklin. "A plain woman will have nothing forgiven."

Betty got Lenore to babysit her two daughters. Then, during a family crisis, she got Lenore to run the servo. It was damn hard to find good help. But Lenore balanced the till to the cent. She had a magic touch with money.

"Do you want a job?" asked Betty.

"I already have a job," said Lenore.

"You're smart enough to run Woolworths," said Betty.

Lenore worked at Woolworths Monday to Friday and helped Betty on the weekend in return for free rent. She ate breakfast and dinner with the Curtises. All her spare income was deposited into a "Flee Echuca" fund.

Lenore's unofficial adoption by the Curtis family was worth more than money. For the first time, she saw how the sausage of a happy family got made. Betty was a teetotaller. She parented her children with a firm affection, a soft strength. What a wonder it was to tell someone who you loved so much "no", without angrily exploding! And then wait patiently for the tears to subside.

More than sex or drugs or money, Lenore wanted to be a mother. A mum you could learn from. A mum you could trust. A mum you could love.

CHAPTER THREE

The Decline and Fall of Western Civilisation

In 1969, Michael Shelley married Beverly, the woman he had nearly maimed in a car accident when they were teenagers. They bought an apartment in Milsons Point. Through the bedroom window, the couple glimpsed a panorama of Sydney Harbour. Michael was a corporate wunderkind for mining company Alcoa. He completed a Master of Business Administration.

"Like so many young men denied enough love by their fathers, I had ambitions to be successful, rich, famous and powerful," he later wrote.

Michael's father, John, was made an aide-de-camp to the Queen. Not long afterwards, he died of a sudden heart attack. Michael grew comatose with grief. He used speed to wake up and pot to fall asleep. Then he burst from the cocoon of his disillusionment, like a bipolar social butterfly.

Michael quit the high-flying white-collar job. He grew a bushy beard and hair down to his shoulders. The hippy entrepreneur started a wine bar in Kensington: The Decline and Fall of Western Civilisation as We Know It. The interior featured huge posters of black blues musicians. The native-title movement saw The Decline as a safe haven. So did the UNSW Gay Society. Michael's brainchild was making $3000 a week, or $150,000 a year.

Each day, Michael drank wine and chain-smoked three packets of cigarettes. Beverly watched her husband flirting with the barmaids and university students. Some of the staff and customers openly bragged to Beverly about Michael's sexual prowess, not realising that she was his wife. She was never more in thrall to him than when he treated her appallingly.

"I did not believe that I had the right to say no to a woman," he wrote.

Michael belonged to the Cruising Yacht Club of Australia in Rushcutters Bay. On Boxing Day 1972, 26-year-old "Mick Shelley" was a crew member of *Boomerang VII* in the Sydney to Hobart Yacht Race.

Michael hated the rich so much that he wanted to be richer than all of them put together. The wine bar was a start, but not enough on its own. In 1974, Michael purchased the Limerick Castle Hotel in Surry Hills.

"Look Who's Dropping Back into Millionaire's Row", read the headline in *The Daily Mirror*, beside a photograph of Michael.

> If Michael Shelley isn't a millionaire by the time he's 40, it will probably be because he's already made it by the age of 30. At 28, he already has two university degrees, two bars and a furniture company. He is planning a nightclub in Sydney and a ski-lodge at Jindabyne. In his spare time, which must be about 3 am, he likes to parachute, sail and play the guitar. With shoulder-length hair and a bushy blonde beard, Michael isn't everyone's idea of a young executive – particularly as he doesn't own a suit.
>
> "I didn't like what was happening to me in the corporate world," he says. "I was losing control over my own life, so I gave it away. I used to want to be a millionaire, but now I've modified that – I just want to make enough money to do all the things I want to do, then drop out and sail around the world."

Michael borrowed a motza to buy the Limerick Hotel, including $50,000 from Beverly's family. It was a disaster. The pub cannibalised the customer base of The Decline, but with much higher overheads. Michael kept them both afloat thanks to the compassion of some shadowy loan sharks.

++

On a Sunday morning, Michael sat at the dining table solving a Rubik's Cube with mathematics. Beverly watched her husband, trying to work out what the hell was going on inside his brilliant mind. It was like trying to hold a cloud.

"Michael, are you alright?" she asked.

Michael maintained eye contact for what felt like the first time in months. Then he broke up with Beverly, as if they were switching electricity providers.

"Bev, I need to go," he said. "This is the best thing for both of us."

Michael was zooming towards ruin. He took off on unexplained sailing voyages. Beverly heard whispers her husband had upgraded from doing drugs to smuggling them. Peter Cross – the best man at their wedding – was later outed as the ringleader of a syndicate importing cocaine from Bolivia. His partners included the hitman Christopher Flannery, aka Mr Rent-a-Kill.

As creditors circled Michael, his empire went up in flames, figuratively and literally. The Decline and Fall of Western Civilisation as We Know It burned down in suspicious circumstances. Everyone concerned was convinced that Michael lit up the building. Unfortunately, he had forgotten to renew the insurance.

The bank repossessed the Limerick Castle and the apartment at Milsons Point. Beverly, thirty-one, moved back to the western suburbs with her parents, who never saw a cent of the money they lent to their son-in-law.

Michael's life had descended into a series of half-baked schemes to save his dreams of wealth. And – once the disgrace of bankruptcy was inescapable – plots to soften the blow of rock-bottom. His richest mistress was a UNSW student named Rosemary. She had been a barmaid at The Decline before it was torched. Rosemary came from Double Bay old money.

Michael proposed. Rosemary was elated. Her parents were mortified. The wedding was held in the backyard of a stone mansion in Watsons Bay. The past eight years had thinned out Michael's entourage of friends. On the horizon, yachts dangled below Sydney's growing skyline. All that water and wealth. All that desire and bliss. All that disappointment and duplicity.

Michael strutted to the altar. He wore a pale blue suit with white shoes. Thick golden sideburns, like a blond Elvis. The puffy-faced playboy was running so fast from his unfaithful father that he had somehow become him.

☩

The marriage was a disaster. At the age of thirty, Michael was twice divorced and penniless. On a Sunday night, he drove to The Gap, a picturesque cliff in Watsons Bay. He lit a cigarette and chugged from a bottle of wine. A Good Samaritan ruined the scenic suicide attempt. Michael was taken to Prince Henry Hospital in Little Bay. The sleepy streets were lined with Norfolk Island pines, sweeping to the doors of a three-storey brick fortress.

Michael was placed in a room with no sharp objects. The heavy tranquillisers strangled his brain. In the morning, the horizon split the sea and the sky into different shades of blue. How was he still alive? And why?

The sedated libertine withdrew cold turkey from alcohol, nicotine and illicit drugs. He ate three square meals and swallowed his medication. In his first session of group therapy, Michael witnessed a hallucination of beauty: Carrie. She was the ex-wife of Lionel Long. Now she was thirty-three and officially bipolar. Michael could tell she was afraid to be seen, but maybe less so by someone like him.

"I fell in love with Michael the first time we met," she later wrote. "I was very lost and alone in this world without his LOVE + PROTECTION."

After surviving domestic violence at the hands of Lionel Long, Carrie had remarried an American film director named Christopher. Tender and intelligent, he treated her children like they were his own. But Carrie's migraines, crying fits and suicidal ideation came back in waves.

Carrie told Michael that she had been sexually abused between the ages of four and ten. Michael listened to the revelations without judgement. He didn't flinch or disbelieve her. Indeed, he reciprocated with confessions of his own family dysfunction and psychological malaise. Neither of them had ever met another person whose loneliness so closely resembled their own. The adulterous parents. The famous first love. The nervous breakdown.

For the first time, Michael cried about the death of his father, whose ashes were still in the boot of his car. The sad son wasn't cured, exactly, but he had discovered a way to soothe suicidal ideation: true human connection.

"Being a person who relied on logic, I put two and two together – if I got in touch with my feelings and actually expressed them, this relieved my anxiety," wrote Michael. "Seemed simple. But it still eludes the huge intellects of stupid psychiatrists, for whom I have the greatest contempt."

Michael and Carrie spent their convalescence on the hospital veranda. The beach was clean with no undertow. Headlands to the north and south. Michael serenaded Carrie with acoustic covers. He felt himself in her company like no one else's. She felt something less than numb. Salvation had been found in the most unexpected location: a psych ward.

The Virgin Lenore

In 1976, Lenore Meurant bought herself a one-way Greyhound ticket to Queensland. She got a job as a bookkeeper with Waltons, a department store in Indooroopilly. She rented a little unit and settled into the summer heat, sweaty but still frozen. Sometimes the best thing to do when you were unsure was to disappear and work out how you feel about everything later.

Waltons couldn't believe that the high-school dropout from rural Victoria didn't have a university degree. They kept promoting her. Lenore travelled across the state setting up auditing systems. Her best friend at work was a middle-aged clerk named Ivy, the wife of an Ipswich coalminer.

"It is strange to feel so irreplaceable," Lenore wrote in her diary.

Ivy invited Lenore to Ipswich for Easter 1978. There was an ulterior motive. Ivy's son Bruce was a root rat electrician. She wanted to set him up with Lenore, a calming influence. They were the same age: twenty-five.

Lenore was oblivious to the marriage plot and her potential attractiveness to men. On Good Friday, she drove to Ipswich in a hand-painted Holden FJ. White t-shirt and purple skirt. Hair permed for the rare social outing. Ivy's cottage looked like a tree house. Down a steep embankment, the Bremer River brewed gum leaves with runoff from the abattoir and coal mines. Lenore parked the car. She took three deep breaths.

Laughter came from the barbecue in the backyard. Men and women sat on deckchairs or eskies. They were in thrall to an interrupted sermon. Judging by their smiles, it had been a funny one. The storyteller was a bearded man with thick, dark curls. A big beer gut, but limbs muscly and sunkissed. Eyes shut, he waved tongs at Lenore like a magic wand.

"Abracadabra!" he said. "Bring me a good-lookin' woman!"

Tom Blaine was shameless as a snake. He was recently separated. His first wife, Janelle, had thought that his waistline would be an insurance policy against infidelity. She was wrong. He slept with dozens of other women.

"Keep your dick in your pants for once, Tom," said Ivy.

Ivy poured a cup of Fruity Lexia from a glinting goon bag. Lenore sat in a picnic chair. Her throat felt hoarse from cheap wine. Her cheeks blushed from the introduction. Was it a compliment? Before she could analyse and decide, the stranger was standing in front of her. He gripped a can of XXXX in one hand and extended the other. There was a tan line on his ring finger.

"Tom Blaine," he said. "It's a real pleasure for you to meet me."

The gathering guffawed. Ivy rued the late arrival of her son Bruce.

"Lenore Meurant," she said.

"Meurant," he said. "Where's that come from?"

"France," she said, proudly.

Lenore neglected to mention her French ancestor was a convict.

"Bonjour, baby!" said Tom.

This wasn't the landed gentleman that Lenore had fantasised would rescue her from the caravan park in Echuca. But Ivy watched a hard-won unguardedness spread across the bookworm's face. She probably wasn't Bruce's type, anyway. Nor Tom's. But that was for them to find out.

"What do you do for work?" Lenore asked Tom.

"I'm kind of like you," said Tom. "I spend my days counting money."

"He's a full-time gambler!" said Ivy.

"And a part-time taxi driver," said Tom, winking.

Lenore didn't remember the men being this large in Victoria, or such large men being at the top of the social hierarchy. Tom pierced a can of XXXX Bitter with a car key. He crushed it down his gullet. The crowd cheered. Lenore drank slowly, memorising the strange rituals to investigate later. She was appalled and also touched by the machismo. Who was this anonymous man in Ipswich, with an ego befitting the King of England?

"Well, he's colourful," said Lenore to Ivy.

"Tommy?" she asked. "He's a lot of fun. If you can keep up with him."

Ivy brought out a pack of cards. The table was covered with a green sheet. They played Pontoon for ten dollars a hand. Ivy was just as competitive as the men. Tom transformed from a drunken clown into a stone-cold assassin.

"That's all she wrote," he said, after raking up the takings.

Tom counted cards while dominating conversation. He spat out arcane sporting statistics. This was after twenty cans of heavy beer. Nobody argued with him. There was a shrewdness beneath the mask of lewd stupidity.

"Wanna come home with me?" he asked Lenore towards midnight.

Lenore was a shrinking violet. She felt a gravitational pull towards the larrikin. To hurtle through the universe with such certainty!

"That might be nice," she said.

"Might be nice," he scoffed.

Lenore and Tom wandered three blocks from the miner's cottage to his Queenslander. The railway workshop carved a reservoir into the dimly lit suburb. Lenore gave a heavily edited rendition of her pilgrimage from Victoria to Brisbane. She was less shy without a crowd. Tom was quieter.

"The French are deep thinkers, aren't they?" he asked.

"Don't hold it against me," she said.

"No way," he said. "I'm sick of listenin' to idiots with shit for brains."

A Dalmatian named Cindy waited at the front gate. Tom hugged and scratched the dog. In the kitchen, he poured Lenore a mug of tank water. Soon, she was undressed in his bed. They had sex without a condom.

"See ya in the morning," said Tom with a quick kiss.

The married man fell asleep, regretting nothing. Lenore – the single one – lay awake with premonitions of pregnancy. Later, when the morning sickness started, she recalled those anxious thoughts as a god-free prophecy.

Metamorphoses

Michael Shelley moved back in with his mother, Marie, and younger brother Tom. They lived in a house on the Lower North Shore of Sydney. Most of Michael's old friends had young families now. Whispers reached them about his vacation at the funny farm. They treated him with sympathy and suspicion.

Michael started a PhD on human behaviour at the University of New South Wales. The PhD was a whodunnit. What socioeconomic and psychological forces led to Michael nearly killing himself? The intellectual detective pinpointed a chief suspect. Capitalism. The Industrial Revolution replaced the kinship of local community with the worship of money.

Michael was spotted powerwalking across the Harbour Bridge to UNSW. He refused to accept lifts. The former mining executive warned old friends that car pollution would lead to the end of the world. Even public transport was immoral. The consensus: Michael Shelley had lost his marbles.

"Most people in developed countries maintain naive fantasies about the long-term viability of capitalism," wrote Michael. "So it is important to stress one inconvenient truth: Western civilisation is environmentally unsustainable."

More specifically, Michael blamed his near-miss with oblivion on two culprits: his mother and father. Marie loved him too much. John didn't love him enough. His racing mind illuminated a second suspect. Feminism. The Sexual Revolution threw the roles of men and women into complete confusion. This led to the plague of family breakdown across the West.

"Every dying civilisation in the history of mankind has shown a similar pattern," wrote Michael. "When women are liberated, complete anarchy results."

Carrie had officially split up with Christopher, her second husband. She packed up her children once again. They moved into the bottom floor of *Kooytong*, a two-storey Federation home on Lang Road. Centennial Park was across the street. Michael Shelley became part of the furniture at Lang Road.

With him, Carrie didn't feel that her amazing pain was a liability or something that she needed to cover up. Their ecstasy at finding each other was spliced with periods of deep seriousness and prolonged weeping. Insanity was an avalanche. It began with the tiniest tremor. On the veranda, Michael and Carrie recited their favourite bible passages to each other. Giddily, they opened up to random pages, like a game of religious roulette.

"At that time Michael, the archangel who stands guard over your nation, will arise," read Michael, feeling a jolt of adrenaline. "Every one of your people whose names are written in the bible will be rescued!"

The couple believed that the bible was speaking to them. A new-age curiosity about the scriptures snowballed into a folie à deux, French for "madness of two". Michael was *that* Michael, the messenger, God's right-hand man. He told Carrie that she didn't need more lithium or electroshock therapy. They were cured of future suicide attempts. The alleviation of all that pent-up dread was better than the purest drug or deepest orgasm. Needless to say, there was a flood of the latter in those doting days and nights.

"Every time I let go + become more of a woman, Michael loves me even more," wrote Carrie. "God certainly knows what He is talking about."

Michael and Carrie began acting like characters from the bible. They adopted a Nazarene dress code and hairstyles. The couple reimagined themselves as God's bodyguards for the children of Australia. Michael had a particular fixation with promiscuous single mothers.

"The only way a woman can show real love for her family is to be soft, gentle, fragile, vulnerable, quiet and serving," he wrote. "Single mothers without the guidance of a strong man have no idea how to care for children properly."

Without warning, Michael reappeared in the life of his ex-wife Beverly. She had a daughter named Katie born out of wedlock. Michael tracked down Beverly in the White Pages. He walked from Lang Road to her home in Hunters Hill. Katie was eighteen months old. The born-again Christian insisted on holding the toddler's hand during the creepy visit.

Beverly moved house and got a silent number. Michael was seen wandering the western suburbs searching for her. He wasn't hostile enough to get arrested. There were no threats. Just an unsettling obsessiveness. He left letters in the mailbox of his former in-laws. Each night, Beverly's father called to ascertain Katie's safety and ensure that Beverly had locked all the windows and doors. Beverly sent a cease-and-desist letter to her ex-husband.

"It appears on the numerous previous occasions I have discouraged you to contact me, you haven't taken me seriously," she wrote. "Therefore, I'll reiterate: please don't contact me. It would only be awkward and embarrassing."

Michael took this as an opportunity to cancel his unpaid debts.

"I spent a long time blaming myself without realising all relationships have a shared responsibility," Michael wrote to Beverly. "Consequently, I will not be sending you any more money. May your life be happy and close to God."

According to family folklore, Michael was distantly related to the poet Percy Bysshe Shelley. Percy left his first wife for a sixteen-year-old girl named Mary. Mary Shelley later became famous as the author of *Frankenstein*. In 1822, Percy Shelley went sailing on a boat called *Don Juan* off the coast of Italy. The ship sank in a storm. Percy drowned. He was twenty-nine.

"I was never the Eve of any Paradise, but a human creature blessed by an elemental spirit's company and love," wrote Mary Shelley.

In December 1979, Carrie fell pregnant to Michael Shelley. The sperm donor was going to be a real father for the first time. They married in an informal ceremony at Lang Road. This was to be consecrated at a later date, following Carrie's divorce from Christopher. Under strict instructions from Michael, Carrie changed her name by deed poll to "Mary Shelley".

"God has asked me to LOVE + CARE for the most precious man," she wrote. "His name is MICHAEL. God has called him to be a PROPHET. Michael has a ministry to children. The child abuse in Australia is appalling."

Michael had created a beautiful Frankenstein's monster. At Lang Road, Mary's family staged an intervention. Michael attacked her stepmother, Alice. At 3 am, Michael phoned Bruce Moir, his old friend from Knox Grammar. Bruce arranged to visit him the next day. Upon arrival, a handcuffed Michael was being jammed into the back of a paddy wagon.

The guitar-wielding dictator was charged with assault and sent to Long Bay Prison. He received a broken nose for preaching Jesus to the wrong prisoner. In five years, Michael had progressed five kilometres along Anzac Parade: from the wine bar, to Prince Henry Hospital, and lastly to Long Bay. What was he doing wrong? He pored over a Gideon's bible for guidance.

The Gospel of Matthew was written for this particular pickle. Michael felt just like Jesus in the Judean Desert. Satan came in the form of rapist inmates armed with cigarettes and heroin. On a higher level, society was trying to crush him into cowardice by painting a saviour as somehow insane.

"You will be hated by everyone because of me," said Jesus Christ in the Gospel of Matthew. "When you are persecuted in one place, flee to another."

Michael was thirsty for persecution, the truest proof of perfection. It was obvious that he needed to split from Sin City, for biblical and logistical reasons. Mary was expecting his child. But she would never be strictly under his dominion while sharing custody of two children with her ex-husband, Lionel Long.

"Do not go among the Gentiles or enter any town of the Samaritans," Jesus told Michael across the millennia. "Go rather to the lost sheep of Israel."

Where was Australia's equivalent of Israel? Michael looked north. And he saw a place urgently deserving of God's wrath: Queensland.

Thou Shalt Not Kill

Lenore thought that the abortion was a bad idea. Tom politely disagreed. Ipswich was a big country town. Everyone knew everyone's business. He was technically still married. The divorce would take time to process. A baby with an unwed woman would bring great shame upon the Blaine family name.

"And an abortion wouldn't?" asked Lenore, not mentioning the other sins – such as drinking and gambling – that Tom seemed proud to publicise.

They were at the kitchen table in Ipswich, dinnertime on a Monday. Lenore had moved in a month after they first met.

"You don't carry an abortion down the main street," said Tom.

"*You* don't carry an abortion down the main street," said Lenore.

There were no ultimatums. That was unnecessary. Lenore was

madly in love with Tom. She had waited her entire life for the safety net of Tom's embrace. She didn't want to risk it with a significant disagreement. The bookkeeper kept her complaints for the diary that remained at the office.

"Men never take responsibility for anything," she wrote. "Without sex, our usefulness would dry up like flowers in a drought."

Tom knew of "a place" in Brisbane. It made Lenore wonder whether he'd been there before. On a Thursday afternoon in winter, Tom dropped her to the Greenslopes Fertility Control Clinic. It was a two-storey Queenslander.

The abortionist, Peter, was pleasant yet meticulous. He scraped the life from her womb. Lenore left the room with a bit of her soul missing.

"You're a brave lady," said Tom, patting her on the leg.

Lenore didn't want to be brave. She took the week off work. In bed, she bled and bled and bled and bled, craving the dead baby like a drug.

✠

Tom went straight back to work. He didn't misunderstand the tug of motherhood out of malice. But there was a fine line between stoicism and callousness. There was no one for Lenore to share the debilitating secret with. Her mother was in a psychiatric hospital in Ballarat. Her siblings were out of touch. All the people she knew in Ipswich were affiliated with Tom.

"I'm up shit creek, Cindy," she told the Dalmatian.

In spring, Lenore returned to work. The bleeding had stopped, but the guilt was just beginning. On the streets of Brisbane, protestors demanded the closure of abortion clinics. Premier Joh Bjelke-Petersen launched a crackdown, while turning a blind eye to gambling dens and brothels.

"The bigoted hypocrite!" said Ivy at morning tea.

"What do you think about abortion?" asked Lenore, cautiously.

"I think it's nobody's business but the people with vaginas," said Ivy.

In the lunchroom, Lenore burst into tears. Ivy hugged her protégé. Lenore offered no confessions. Ivy didn't ask any questions. But she'd wondered about Lenore's recent absence from work and her accompanying glumness.

"No god of mine would judge someone for such a thing," said Ivy.

The problem wasn't God, thought Lenore, but his army of bible bashers. She would rather swelter in hell than spend eternity with any of them.

++

Lenore didn't anticipate agreeing to spend the rest of her life with Tom in a nightgown and slippers over a plate of pork sausages and mashed potato.

"Let's get married," he said. "We'll have a shitload of kids."

Tom was smitten. He just had a reticent way of expressing it. Lenore was frugal, but not greedy. She was smart, but not smug. She was calm, but not cool. She was kind, but not foolish. She offered the outgoing lone wolf something he didn't know it was possible to feel: acceptance.

"Is this a wedding proposal?" asked Lenore.

"I couldn't imagine anyone I'd rather mother my kids. Course I wanna marry ya, darlin'! Soon as the divorce comes through, it's done."

For Lenore, love was about safety, not lust. She still hadn't figured out the mysteries of female pleasure. It didn't stop her from respecting Tom, from needing him, from bleeding to protect his reputation. He was a ticket to kinship.

"Yes," she said. "Lenore Blaine. That has a nice ring to it."

They were surprising soulmates. Tom drank tea. Lenore drank coffee. He ate red meat twice a day, sometimes thrice. She preferred seafood. He had a loud clap, a loud click, a loud whistle, a loud laugh. His natural habitat was the pub. Hers was quietly reading a book on the couch.

These differences were eclipsed by philosophical similarities. Tom and Lenore were both members of the Labor Party. Their priorities? Higher wages. Better hospitals and schools. They believed that a society was judged by its treatment of the downtrodden. This was their God: egalitarianism.

Gone Walkabout

In the winter of 1980, Michael and Mary Shelley ditched all their belongings in a fit of minimalism. Mary left her two children on Lionel Long's doorstep.

"Do not get any gold or silver to take with you in your belts – no bag for the journey or extra shirt or sandals," said Jesus in the Gospel of Matthew.

Without a dollar in their pockets, the barefoot missionaries hitchhiked towards the equator. The Northern Rivers, then Brisbane, and then Central Queensland. On road signs, there were bullet holes through silhouettes of kangaroos. Real kangaroos lay mangled on the highways. It was the start of a long drought.

The skinny prophet and his pregnant prophetess stuck their thumbs into the dusty wind. Nothing but two toothbrushes, a tablecloth and Holy Bible to their name. They won sympathy from unsuspecting drivers, who received sermons about their loveless childhoods and marriages.

"Underneath the pretence of being 'laidback' and 'easy-going', most Queenslanders are brainless, bigoted, gluttonous morons," wrote Michael.

Come what may, God had a way of sheltering them. He kept a tally of the kindnesses and slights. Each day was a test for the strangers they met. Cattle ranches gave way to cane fields. Michael and Mary stayed at a motel in Mackay. He massaged her blistered feet. She trimmed his beard with blunt scissors. They washed their clothes in the bathtub and left without fixing the bill.

On and on they went, hitching lifts and never paying a cent for anything. The son of God ballooned inside Mary's womb, unhungry. They suffered hostility in Townsville. Michael admonished a public bar full of shit-faced soldiers. One of them called the preacher a "shirt-lifter", to howls of laughter.

"The most irritating aspect of Australian culture is the way drunken men laugh like braying jackasses at things that are not at all funny!" wrote Michael.

The Shelleys travelled through blazing fields of sugarcane to steep green rainforests. Mary was bursting at the seams. Michael didn't want his child to be born in the city. They caught a steam train from Cairns to Kuranda, a hippy commune high in the Atherton Tablelands.

On the Barron River, the Shelleys rented a timber cottage. It was lifted towards the sky by twenty sawn-down tree trunks. The Shelleys went skinny dipping at Barron Falls. Mary baptised Michael. Michael baptised Mary.

"My body is a temple of the Holy Ghost," she wrote.

On 8 September 1980, at 2 am, Mary went into labour. A pale, wailing baby with light hair emerged between the mother's legs. He was two weeks overdue and weighed 9.5 pounds. The father spied a penis. Michael cut and lovingly studied the umbilical cord. What to call him? Michael believed he was the reincarnation of Elijah, the prophet anticipated in Malachi 4:5–6.

"See, I will send the prophet Elijah to you before that great and dreadful day of the Lord comes," warned God in the Old Testament. "He will turn the hearts of the parents to their children, and the hearts of the children to their parents; or else I will come and strike the land with total destruction."

Pre-apocalypse, the family of three took a sabbatical in tropical paradise. Kookaburras laughed gleefully in the branches of the trees. Elijah's eyes were saturated with wrath. He cried and cried and cried and cried. Michael and Mary had never loved someone so much, except each other.

"Elijah + I have Michael 24/7," wrote Mary. "I am the weaker vessel. Baby Elijah has a stronger heart than me. We are trying to be God's children."

☩

Michael and Mary took Elijah hitchhiking. On the highways, Mary covered her baby with a cotton shawl, while Michael negotiated rides. During the day, they lay down for a nap on the nearest available stretch of grass or sand.

Mary didn't believe in detergents, washing machines or dryers. She washed her son's nappies by hand with soap and hung them in the wind.

"We never needed prams, cots, toys, bottles, dummies or books, except the bible," wrote Mary. "They are used to replace the care of a loving father."

At night, the Shelleys sought free lodging at churches. In Townsville, they located an Anglican parish. Michael rang the doorbell of the vicarage. The jolly vicar, Peter Hill, was grey-haired and double-chinned. He had just sat down to watch *Ripping Yarns* with a coffee and a plate of sliced meats.

Peter apologised to his wife, Patti, and answered the door. He discovered a barefoot couple with a blond baby. The man reminded him of a better-groomed John the Baptist. The woman was wearing a white ankle-length dress. She carried a bouquet of flowers. He estimated that they were in their twenties.

"Michael, Mary and Elijah," said Michael. "And you are?"

"Peter," he said.

"Peter, we live by faith as the Lord directs us," said Michael. "Tonight, he has led us to you. Mary, Elijah and I require shelter for the night."

"Oh," said Peter.

"The Lord has always provided," said Michael. "He never lets us down."

The vicar hesitated. Even he was wary of people who publicised their Christianity so piously. Nonetheless, Peter recalled the innkeeper from the stable. He decided to offer Michael and Mary the meeting room in the hall. The innkeeper organised mattresses and blankets. Michael recounted their travels.

"Sounds like a good gig if you can get it," said Peter.

Michael shot the vicar a withering glance.

"We would like showers now," said Michael. "Have you got towels?"

Peter missed *Ripping Yarns*. Patti scolded him for taking three complete strangers in off the street. The Shelleys concluded their ablutions.

"You shouldn't allow yourself to be pushed around by that horrible woman," said Michael, who'd been eavesdropping on the hushed conversation.

Peter was gobsmacked. He caved in to Michael's demands more out of exhaustion than agreement. The Shelleys insisted on eating before sleep. Michael and Mary were aghast at the lack of dates. Peter offered them fresh fruit and eggs. Michael seized a tin of pineapple juice from the fridge.

"Ah, yoghurt!" said Mary, taking out the container.

Michael had a list of non-dietary requirements. First, he needed a shirt so he could wash his own. Secondly, he needed ointment for Elijah's sunburn. Thirdly, he needed a guitar so he could sing the dehydrated baby to sleep. Peter obliged. In return, Michael and Mary would have to leave before 8 am. The vicar had a part-time gig as a chaplain at the Townsville RAAF base.

"Did you really lead them to us, Lord?" prayed Peter before sleep. "Next time, please don't send Christians. Heathens are easier to deal with."

The next morning, Peter and Patti got up at 6.45 am. They made a clatter in the kitchen. Mary rose at 7.45 am to check on Michael's shirt. It was still wet. She refused Patti's offer to use the dryer in the laundry. Five minutes before their scheduled check-out time, Michael demanded a fresh round of showers.

"Sorry," said Peter. "We need to leave. And so do you."

Michael was apoplectic. He accused Peter of abusing his body with junk food and encouraging soldiers to kill by being a chaplain for the RAAF. He berated Patti for touching his laundry without permission, for not looking after her husband properly, and for working a full-time job.

"I've had just about enough," shouted Peter, cracking up. "Maybe you should get a bloody job! And stop sponging off everyone. You're a bludger."

Michael was delighted by the outpouring of profanity.

"You bludge off Jesus Christ!" shouted Michael at the top of his lungs. "You do nothing of substance, and yet you make a living from His name!"

Holy Matrimony

At the altar, Tom Blaine touched himself on the crotch, a nervous tic, as if to reassure himself that his dick still existed. It was late spring in 1980. A balmy Saturday afternoon. Tom was getting married to Lenore in a North Ipswich backyard three houses down from where they first met two years earlier.

"When's your third wedding, mate?" asked Tom's brother George.

"Shut up, dickhead," said Tom.

After his first wedding, Tom wasn't going to be seen dead in another tuxedo. The groom resembled a West Indian one-day cricket player. He wore a maroon Hawaiian shirt, no tie. Beard trimmed above the Adam's apple. Two undone buttons to expose a hairy chest and silver neck chain. White trousers and white shoes.

There were no Meurants present. It was a Blaine family reunion. Tom's six sisters had begrudgingly forgiven him the divorce, but a few were still puzzled by Lenore. Her history had disappeared without a trace.

Adults were sometimes sceptical of "Saint Lenore". She refused to utter an un-nice word about others. Her main vice was a pot of beer with a dash of lemonade. Tom's multitude of nieces and nephews adored Lenore for the same reason. She stayed in the background and paid attention to them.

"Here she comes!" shouted one of Tom's teenage nieces.

The bride had never looked so thin or so feminine. Hair freshly permed. White dress and burgundy brooch. Some uncharacteristic lipstick. A nephew wolf-whistled. She walked down the aisle.

Lenore was led by her bridesmaid, Brigette, a schoolteacher she'd recently befriended. Tom stood at the altar with his best man, Warren, a labourer on the Ipswich railway. He was twenty kilograms heavier than Tom. Warren wore a pale blue suit, blazer sleeves cut at the elbows.

"We wish that at the end of your lives you will be able to say that because I saw the good in you, I received faith in humanity," said the celebrant.

Tom was dusty from a night on the lash with Warren. But he felt undeniably in love with Lenore. It was a more mature type, governed by a rational respect, not a fleeting physical infatuation.

"I, Thomas, take you, Lenore, to be my wife, for better and for worse, in plenty and in want, in sickness and in health, so long as we both shall live."

Lenore was a complicated woman with aspirations for averageness.

She thought that marital unhappiness belonged to social butterflies with insatiable appetites for beauty and money. None of that crap mattered to her. She would trade a million dollars and an attractive face for five children.

"I, Lenore, take you, Thomas, to be my husband, for better and for worse, in plenty and in want, in sickness and in health, so long as we both shall live."

Lenore and Tom held hands: his large and tanned and steadfast, hers thin and pale and shaking. She was twenty-six. He was thirty-one. The bride and groom traded rings. They beamed at each other in casual rapture.

"We wish children for you," said the celebrant. "Children who will learn from your best traits and try to recreate the values you instilled in them."

The celebrant pronounced them husband and wife. Tom kissed Lenore with an enthusiastic amount of tongue. The crowd cheered. A jukebox blasted the opening riff of "You Shook Me All Night Long" by AC/DC. Beer flowed from a keg. Grease wafted from a barbecue. Lenore threw a bouquet over her shoulder.

Tom whispered a spontaneous vow into the ear of his second spouse. "I'm gonna love you as long as my bumhole points to the ground," he said.

It was kind of a dream come true. They slipped into the chute of the future, drawn towards the white-hot promise of a new tomorrow.

Gimme Shelter

Michael Shelley was shocked that he got what he set out to receive: persecution. Disagreement deepened his religious delusions. It made him feel divine. In August 1981, the Shelleys arrived in Maryborough. Over a manic long weekend, they staged a tireless crusade against eight different churches.

"Modern Christian churches are spiritually bankrupt money-laundering operations that squander the most obscene amounts of wealth," wrote Michael. "True Christians sell off their assets and give the profits to the poor."

Complaints were made. The Shelleys had no money. They were arrested for harassment and vagrancy. Mary and Elijah were placed in a cell without a mattress. There was a blanket on the concrete floor. The preachers pleaded guilty. They were sentenced to six weeks' imprisonment in Brisbane.

"We had been set up by the corrupt Queensland police to remove us as an embarrassment to the churches, and terrify us into silence," wrote Michael.

Boggo Road Gaol was a barb-wired collection of redbrick tributes to the police state. Michael was placed in solitary confinement for disobeying the guards. Mary and Elijah were assigned a family cell at the Women's Prison. The supreme leader of the Women's Prison, Warden Godrich, was hardnosed. She suspected that Elijah was malnourished. Mary's one-year-old son was taken to the nearby Mater Children's Hospital for testing.

The Department of Children's Services was alerted to Elijah's existence. Susan King was a social worker with two children and a degree in occupational therapy. Each day, she visited Elijah at the hospital. Susan took great satisfaction from the fattening skin folds of the blond, bubbly baby. An enraged Michael was relocated to the Security Patients Hospital. He wrote reams of screeds condemning the "feckless feminists" in Children's Services.

"Susan King is dismayed by Mary's dedication to Elijah," he wrote, "which make her own pathetic efforts at being a woman, wife and mother look highly incompetent by comparison. She is jealous of Mary's marriage to me!"

Susan saw Michael Shelley as human proof of narcissistic personality disorder. She believed the charismatic crackpot had brainwashed

Mary. But given the Shelleys' resistance to psychiatric attention, her hopes of proving the diagnosis – and curing their mutual psychosis – were fruitless.

"God has asked me to SERVE Michael + show him REVERENCE," wrote Mary. "Whenever there is anything important to be dealt with outside our family, I do it through Michael. He stands between me + CHRIST."

✢

In October, Michael was released from Boggo Road. He collected Elijah from the Mater Hospital and organised for the release of Mary from Wolston Park. The Shelleys hitchhiked 2000 kilometres south.

Michael's old friend Bruce Moir and his wife Sue had moved to the city of churches: Adelaide. They had two young children. Bruce ran the South Australian Film Commission. The Shelleys arrived on their doorstep.

"Mick," gasped Bruce.

"Hello, Bruce," said Michael, grimacing at the nickname. "You must call me Michael. The Mick from Knox Grammar no longer exists. This is my wife, Mary, and son, Elijah. We need a place to stay tonight."

Bruce ushered them inside. Sue was horrified. They hadn't heard from Michael since he was sent to Long Bay Prison for attacking Mary's stepmother. Michael outlined their travel itinerary. They were going to hitchhike around the Great Australian Bight and sail from Perth to the Promised Land: India.

Mary barely spoke or made eye contact. Elijah chewed on his fist like it was a chicken drumstick. To Sue, the toddler looked hungry. Michael obsessively monitored the boy's feet, ensuring they didn't come into contact with the carpet. Sue cooked the Shelleys dinner. They insisted on eating in private.

"The baby is starving!" Sue whispered to Bruce in the kitchen. "Mary is completely brainwashed. We need to save them. Michael has gone bonkers."

"I just hope that God doesn't tell him to start stabbing us," said Bruce.

Bruce and Sue performed an audit of the sharp knives in the kitchen. They sealed them in the top drawer beside their queen bed, for safe keeping and potential self-defence. After supper, Mary returned to the kitchen with empty plates and a blank expression. Sue took her into the spare room.

"We can help you, Carrie," whispered Sue. "You don't seem safe or happy. Elijah is too skinny. Stay with us. Bruce will ask Michael to leave."

Mary listened politely. Sue believed she had gotten through to her. But Mary immediately told Michael about the serpent in the master bedroom. That night, Bruce and Sue didn't sleep. They clung desperately to their two children. The next morning, Sue stayed with the children in the locked bedroom. Bruce found Michael searching for breakfast in the pantry.

"Michael, this is a very distressing situation for us," said Bruce. "I'm worried about you. But Sue and I need you to leave. As soon as possible."

Michael launched into his trademark tirade. Bruce was a castrated steer. He had allowed Sue too much space in a society ordained by God to be ruled exclusively by men. Also, she was abusing their two children.

"Bruce, you are my oldest friend," said Michael. "I take no satisfaction from telling you this. If you have any conscience at all, you must divorce Sue. Or you will follow her to hell. And it might be sooner than you both think."

Michael, Mary and Elijah disappeared down the leafy street, en route to India. Sue called the police to report a threat. Bruce checked the knife collection. After the police officers left, Bruce's first call was to Jacki Weaver.

"Jacki, have you heard from Michael?" asked Bruce on the phone.

"Not since he went off the deep end," said Jacki.

"He's more than off the deep end!" said Bruce. "Michael is Australia's answer to Charles Manson. You need to be careful."

This was an extreme but not unusual response from people who encountered the Shelleys, even briefly. Bruce and Sue moved house. They became silent voters and took their names out of the White Pages. Michael had a way of finding them. Occasionally, a letter arrived.

Cattle and the Creeping Jesus

Michael, Mary and Elijah never made it to India. The Shelleys hitchhiked back to Queensland. In the autumn of 1982, they arrived in the drought-stricken town of Clermont. It was a cattle farming hub five hours west of Rockhampton. They were arrested for vagrancy. A sergeant took Elijah to be examined by a local doctor, who judged the boy to be malnourished.

"Babies are grossly overweight," wrote Michael. "They require a diet of raw vegetables, fruit, grains and no meat. Quality NOT quantity is important!"

Michael and Mary were sentenced to a month in prison. The police applied for an emergency protection order from Children's Services for Elijah. The social worker Susan King permitted it. He was placed into a foster home in Blackwater. Michael sent his son a letter, to be recited at night while making eye contact.

"Elijah, this is your dadda. I know you will understand most of this, even though you are only twenty-one months old. There is nothing wrong with you, Elijah. What is happening to you is because Susan King cannot admit her own deficiencies. It has nothing to do with Dadda or Mumma."

In Etna Creek Prison, Michael's hair and beard were cut against his will by two guards. The Shelleys were released from incarceration. Elijah was returned. The baby had gained 40 per cent of his bodyweight in three weeks.

Michael and Mary retreated with Elijah to Yeppoon. It was a popular beachside holiday spot. The Anglican church had a chapel and campsite overlooking the sea. The Shelleys arrived at 6 pm on Good Friday. The caretaker provided food and shelter. The next morning, Michael and Mary refused to leave. They abused and accosted the caretaker. He called the cops.

The police found the Shelleys resting underneath a tree. They had no fixed address and fifteen cents. Elijah was placed back into foster care. But Michael and Mary were found not guilty of vagrancy by a sympathetic judge.

"I believe there is a place in the world for the defendants to live the way they desire and their explanation is sufficiently credible," said Magistrate Loane.

☩

Elijah returned to Michael and Mary with a wicked addition to his vocabulary: "beer". The Shelleys decided to go on a public relations offensive. They did an interview with the *Capricorn Community* newspaper. The article was accompanied by a photograph of a smiling, snowy-haired Elijah. He was held by Michael, who gazed lovingly at Mary's tanned face and straight teeth.

CHRISTIAN FAMILY HAS AN UNUSUAL LIFESTYLE

"There are few who would have the courage to live a life without money, possessions and a home to return to after a hard day's work," it read. "But for the Christian Shelley family, that is their way of life.

And, despite the scepticism of some, the Lord seems to have done a pretty good job so far."

Michael knocked on the door of a cottage in Yeppoon. Two women lived there. They didn't want to leave Elijah on the street. The Shelleys stayed for three nights and three days. On the first day, while the women were at work, Mary stripped the pantry of food. On the second day, Michael rearranged their furniture, pot plants and record collections.

On the third day, one of the women engaged with Michael's sermons. This led to a torrent of "petulant, irrational, shouted abuse". He accused the women of being lesbians, and their parents of being paedophiles.

"After numerous promises to leave, a specific request to leave was met by a further verbal tirade and on this occasion was accompanied by physical violence to my person," she wrote. "Regrettably, we called the police."

Michael and Mary Shelley were arrested. They returned for a new court date with Magistrate Loane. He was repeatedly forced to pause.

"This is a court of law, and you are not to use it as a pulpit," he said.

The prosecutor related complaints of harassment from churches, charities, solicitors, motels and unsuspecting members of the general public. For two years, Cyclone Michael had spun across Queensland. Nobody had mapped the carnage until now. Loane kept the Shelleys in custody until the hearing.

"The wrath of God will be on your head!" Michael shouted at him.

In handcuffs, Michael was frogmarched from the courtroom by the police, face flaring with contempt. Mary walked barefoot in a white dress. Arms cuffed behind her back and shoulders slumped. Gaze immaculately passive.

At the follow-up trial, Michael objected to Loane sitting on the bench. Loane lost patience. He remanded Michael in custody for another seven days. Police officers dragged him from the courtroom.

Mary pursued a new strategy. She apologised for her behaviour and begged to be reunited with Elijah.

"I need him with me, Mr Loane, I miss him terribly," she said. "I do not need to see Michael. I need space on my own for time with Elijah."

Mary was remanded at Boggo Road Women's Prison for eight weeks. She and Elijah were given a family cell. Susan King monitored the situation. She hoped Mary's confinement would deactivate the folie à deux. But Michael was released on bail. He hightailed it to Brisbane for a prison visit.

Warden Godrich ordered Michael to pass Elijah back to Mary. He refused. Two police officers arrived. Michael was dragged from the room. According to the warden, Mary threatened to sacrifice Elijah. Mary was placed in solitary confinement. Elijah – nearly two now – was taken to the Mater Hospital. He was placed in the custody of his social worker.

Mary wrote Elijah a letter, to be recited each night: "Dearest Elijah, I'm sorry that those scary men took you away. They locked me up + I couldn't even say goodbye. There is nothing wrong with you, Elijah. You + me + Dadda = LOVE. That ugly lesbian, Susan, is trying to destroy what we have. We will be together soon. I know because GOD says that it won't be long."

The Fruitless Womb

Lenore Blaine's first miscarriage seemed like a minor glitch. The second caused a rising tide of doom. The third confirmed Lenore's worst suspicions: that the abortion had placed an irrevocable curse upon her womb.

> If you have made yourself impure by having sexual relations with someone other than your husband, may the LORD cause your abdomen to swell, and your womb to miscarry.

The abortionist had warned that the procedure could cause permanent changes to her fertility. Now Lenore felt as if she'd lost her bodyweight in blood. Tom's station wagon had become a hearse. All those silent journeys returning from the hospital, and to visit unhelpful specialists in Brisbane.

The fourth miscarriage produced a despair beyond grief; a black-hearted acceptance of the facts. Lenore was numb in the skull and plagued by pain in the stomach. She was no one's mum. How much blood could a woman gush?

"You've caused an enormous amount of stress to your body in a short space of time," said the doctor. "At this point, it's dangerous to keep trying."

Lenore lay in bed for days and days. Her sister-in-law, Grace, brought deep-fried food from the petrol station she ran. Grace had nine children. A conga line of nieces and nephews tried and failed to cheer up Auntie Lenore.

If only the Blaines could breed as effortlessly as their pet dog. Tom moonlighted as a Dalmatian breeder. In the backyard sat a kennel fenced with chain-link. Cindy gave birth to a litter of black and white dashed puppies.

"Strewth," Tom whispered.

Lenore envied the admiration her husband showed Cindy. He also had no shortage of young men who saw him as a father-figure. Tom was a selector and committee member for the Norths Tigers rugby league club. He coached juniors on Saturdays and seniors on Sundays.

Lenore volunteered in the canteen with Tom's sister Rita. Rita's youngest son, Allan, was seventeen and five-foot-nothing. Yet he was a rugby league prodigy. The blond halfback ran rings around the grown men. Tom assumed an ad-hoc position as Allan Langer's agent.

"Allan will play for Australia one day," Tom told the disbelieving bigwigs in New South Wales. They thought Allan was too small. Tom had a love–hate relationship with Sydney. He loved the chutzpah of Sin City but hated the assumption that people like him should stay humble.

Tom had over fifty nieces and nephews. They all stood taller in his company. He made them feel like members of the royal family. Lenore's heart swelled, and then broke. She had dreamed of being a kid who felt that way. Now, she dreamed of bringing that kid into existence.

Her infertility hurt. But life had taught her to be resourceful. There was a chronic shortage of legal custodians for the surplus sons and daughters of Australia's underclass. She studied the brochures.

"We should become foster parents!" said Lenore.

Tom didn't take too much convincing. He was no bleeding heart, but he liked a challenge, and could see the unique qualities they might bring to the role. As a rugby league coach, he knew how to tame groups of ruffians.

The Blaines applied to be foster carers. They were visited for a series of interviews by Susan King from the Department of Children's Services. The social worker subjected the Blaines to extensive psychometric testing. Tom was offended that she didn't accept their generosity at face value.

"It must've been traumatic losing your parents at a young age," she said.

"*Traumatic*?" asked Tom. "Is that a vacuum cleaner brand?"

"Trauma is a stressful event that leaves a psychological scar," she said.

"Yeah, well," said Tom. "Shit happens, love."

Lenore glared at him censoriously.

"Pardon my French," he said. "Crap happens."

Lenore was friendly and erudite, yet an enigma to Susan King. There were few women who decided at the age of twenty-eight – in the prime of their womanhood – to look after other people's traumatised children.

Usually, foster carers were family members. Or middle-aged women who wanted to continue mothering after their children flew the coop. Or Christians guided by scriptures. Lenore wasn't seeking salvation or money. Her compassion came from some inner source, not from the bible.

"Why do you want to be a foster carer?" asked Susan.

"I know what it's like to be on your own in the world," said Lenore.

Lenore and Tom were rough around the edges, but this was a plus. Susan knew the best foster carers aren't house-proud people. They don't go apeshit if something breaks, or if a child doesn't know how to use a knife and fork. The Blaines weren't allergic to imperfections. They embraced them.

"Some people come in expecting a cute little miracle baby," said Susan. "Are you prepared to care for kids with physical and intellectual disabilities?"

"Yes," said Lenore. "I'm not expecting a miracle."

The only asterisk on the application was courtesy of Lenore. Foster carers needed to be affectionate, yet not grow over-attached. Susan didn't know if Lenore would be able to maintain emotional distance from needy kids.

"I must warn you," said Susan. "Foster care isn't an adoption service. The aim of the department is *always* to reunite families. Are you prepared to care for children who might leave? For a home less welcoming than your own?"

"Yes," said Lenore. "It doesn't make a difference to our decision."

Lenore's personality made the Blaines perfect for long-term foster care placements. But Susan wouldn't be bringing an unblemished baby wrapped in a white sheet. These kids had been abandoned by their biological parents, or so mistreated that there was no prospect of reunification. Those cases were rarer. And they were often ticking time bombs.

Hide and Go Seek

Susan had two complex cases at the Mater Hospital: Elijah and Trent. Elijah was bright-eyed and affectionate. He was thin, but mentally well developed. Trent presented as "deaf and mute" to the doctors. He was born six weeks premature. His mother died of leukemia after giving birth to him. Trent's father found a new partner. The couple couldn't cope with Trent's regular outbursts of hysterical terror. He wouldn't eat, or sleep, or stop crying.

The Department of Children's Services had a clique of veteran carers for extreme cases. Margaret and Brian Clarke lived in north Brisbane. Fran and Neil Williams lived in Strathpine, not far from the Osbournes. They were close friends, whose foster kids regularly played together.

Trent went to the Clarkes. They lived in an elegant Queenslander. Brian was a successful engineer of Russian origin. Margaret had a peaceful yet firm demeanour. Trent quickly grew attached to his foster mum.

Elijah was sent to the Williams. Fran Williams was a stay-at-home mum. Neil Williams was an air-conditioning engineer. They had five brunette daughters and no sons until the arrival of Elijah. Fran rewarded Elijah's growth milestones with Cheezels and Neapolitan ice cream.

"Elijah is inquisitive," Fran told Susan. "When we stop for fuel, he needs to know where the petrol came from and how it makes the car move."

The Williams sisters – twenty-three, eighteen, sixteen, eleven and six – worshipped Elijah. In the backyard, they played hide and go seek. Elijah hid in the bushes and ambushed his foster sisters, snapping like an alligator. Pretty soon, Elijah was calling Fran "Mumma" and Neil "Dadda".

Michael negotiated Mary's release from prison. The Shelleys gate-crashed the welfare department office with a crew from the ABC. This shamed the social workers into granting visitation rights for Elijah's second birthday. The birthday party was on the tenth floor of a government building. It was attended by Michael, Mary, Elijah, Fran, Susan and two uniformed police officers.

Elijah carried a stuffed monkey. His hair had been cut without the Shelleys' permission, bastardising the Nazarene style. Michael's eyes bulged. The trainee saviour was being brainwashed into a cult of suburban dullness.

"This is Mumma Mary," said Fran.

What was that supposed to mean? Elijah only had one mumma: Mary. But Elijah cried when Mary tried to touch him. He clutched tightly onto Fran, a plain-faced woman with short hair.

"Mumma," said Elijah.

"Sweetie," replied Fran.

Fran handed Elijah a packet of Cheezels. Michael wanted to vomit.

"We don't refer to our son as sweetie, bubba, darling, or any of that other gah-gah nonsense," said Michael through gritted teeth. "Elijah is a real person."

"I appreciate you might do things a little bit differently to me," said Fran with a patronising tolerance. "But Elijah needs to fit in with our world, too."

This was the business model of foster carers. How easily the love of a mother and father could be deleted from the consciousness of a toddler.

"Fran, you cannot replace me in Elijah's heart!" screamed Mary. "No amount of houses, cars, swimming pools and Cheezels will change his DNA!"

The party was cut short by twenty minutes. The candles remained unlit, the cake uneaten. The Shelleys were physically evicted from the building. Michael began relentlessly calling the office of the Queensland premier, Joh Bjelke-Petersen. The leader of the National Party was a self-proclaimed Christian. But the supposed man of God had been ignoring the prophet's letters. He refused to see the couple when they visited his office.

Michael sent another letter. He accused Bjelke-Petersen of running a protection racket for corruption while persecuting children, Aboriginals, prisoners and the mentally ill. Michael demanded the immediate return of Elijah.

"Joh Bjelke-Petersen, the Lord whom I serve wants me to give you a direct warning," wrote Michael. "WHATEVER YOU DO TO MY FAMILY, THE GOD OF ISRAEL WILL VISIT ON YOUR HEAD MANY, MANY TIMES OVER. You are jeopardising your soul, and the souls of your family."

The Shelleys refused to participate in any further supervised visits with Elijah. They travelled to Canberra to petition the Human Rights Commission and federal government. Michael was evicted from Parliament House for causing a ruckus during question time. The couple were profiled in *The Australian*.

"Last week, Mr and Mrs Shelley approached the leader of the NSW opposition, Mr John Dowd, who demanded that Elijah be transferred back to NSW," wrote the journalist. "Mr Dowd claims that the Shelleys are being persecuted due to their religious beliefs. He points out that if a parent beats a child, he or she is normally repatriated with the child within six months."

The Shelleys' appeals fell on deaf ears. They retreated to Nimbin, a commune in the Northern Rivers of New South Wales. There, they plotted the rescue of Elijah. All Michael knew about Fran and Neil Williams was that they attended a church in the vicinity of Brisbane. He called every single congregation, providing their names and Fran's physical description.

"My wife and I met Fran and Neil on a holiday," said Michael, faking a friendliness that he didn't feel. "It would mean a lot to send them a letter."

After more than a hundred attempts, Michael struck gold. A gullible minister was delighted to provide their address. 24 Danube Drive, Strathpine.

In January 1983, Michael wrote Neil Williams a letter. It was sealed in an envelope marked CONFIDENTIAL. He predicted that 1983 would be a year of "accidents, illness and terror" for the wicked Williams family.

"Neil, I am writing this to you just prior to taking Elijah back," wrote Michael. "You are a despicable coward of a man. Elijah is being physically and emotionally abused by Fran, a sickening PIG of a woman."

Mary was thirty-eight. She fell pregnant. The baby was destined to be a Virgo like Elijah. It didn't fix the grief Mary felt about her missing son. In February 1983, she sent a letter to Fran Williams, her usurper.

"You know nothing about being a woman, wife or mother, because you don't look after your own body," wrote Mary. "You are frantic and fat. GOD cannot stand to see His precious children suffer because of ugly sadists like you."

Meanwhile, Jacki Weaver married Derryn Hinch, a famous media figure. She was his third wife. He was her third husband. Rich and promiscuous, the couple were vivid symbols of Michael's grievances with Australia. Derryn was host of the TV talk-show *Beauty and the Beast*. He publicly probed glamorous women about their carnal activities.

The newlyweds began receiving diatribes from Michael Shelley. Derryn told Jacki to forget Michael forever. He was a dangerous madman. Jacki lived in fear of Michael, but she also felt a strange affection for him. He was the boy who had taught her how to feel life's great joy: love.

The Miracle of the Mute Boy

Susan King called Lenore Blaine with some potentially good news. They needed permanent foster carers for a motherless little boy with autism.

"I need to be honest with you," said Susan. "This will take a lot of hard work. Trent is one of the most traumatised foster kids in the system."

Lenore had been waiting impatiently for such a call. She wasn't superstitious. But it was a strange coincidence. Trent had the same birthday as Tom. If he was fostered by the Blaines, they would have the same initials, too.

"I'm ready," she said.

Lenore was eager to impress Trent with her femininity. She wore a rare skirt for the first visit to the Clarkes'. Her hair was freshly permed. She forced Tom to shave and don a button-up shirt, trousers and leather shoes. Beforehand, he washed their rust-coloured Ford Falcon station wagon.

"I didn't even wear a flash shirt for our first date," he said on the drive.

"Yes," said Lenore. "I noticed that."

The Clarkes' house was much nicer than the Blaines'. Tom carried an armful of trucks and cars. Lenore was stocked up with lollies and lamingtons. The couple sat in the lounge room with Margaret and Brian. The Clarkes gave the novice foster carers a crash course in Trent's learning difficulties. He played in the sandpit out the back, staring aimlessly into space.

"Trent," called Margaret. "There are some people who want to meet you."

Margaret carried the screaming boy into the room. He was three but looked at least a year younger. Lenore grinned at Trent. She offered him a handful of strawberry-and-cream lollies. He winced at the sugar hit.

"G'day, digger," said Tom.

Trent clicked his tongue disapprovingly at the strange behemoth. He hid behind Margaret and Brian. Lenore was dying inside. Eventually, she stopped trying. Trent went back to the sandpit. Tom ate three of the lamingtons.

"Tough crowd," said Tom, coconut covering his naked cheeks.

"He must be so afraid of big people," said Lenore.

Afterwards, Trent began suffering from acute separation anxiety. He refused food. He woke up in the middle of the night, screaming. Doctors prescribed him twenty milligrams of Melleril, an anti-psychotic.

"Trent was very much back to the old psychotic Trent, who behaved like someone who was both deaf and mute," wrote the doctor. "The basis of Trent's upset is his fear of losing the Clarkes, who have been his stabling anchor."

Margaret spent hours on the phone with Lenore, reassuring her that it wasn't personal. They became foster care comrades. Still, Margaret couldn't believe that her new friend kept coming back regularly for months on end, to no avail. The lamingtons were doused with escalating amounts of jam.

"You are such a lovely little boy," cooed Lenore.

Trent's limbs were bent at odd angles. He screwed his face in silence at her kind words and cried violently if she attempted to touch him. After another failed afternoon at the Clarkes', Lenore broke down. The universe didn't want her to be a mother. And why would it? Trent could sniff her insufficiency from a mile away.

Tom pulled over to the side of the road and hugged his crying wife.

"You're gonna be the best bloody mum under the sun," he said.

Between trips to the Clarkes', Lenore pored over photocopied journal articles about child attachment theory sent by Susan. Once trust in the safety of the world has been lost, they claimed, it takes a long time to regain.

"It is risky to expect love," wrote Lenore in her diary. "Better to make the goal mutual respect and tenderness. We should not need a child's love to show them kindness, consideration, accommodation and consistency."

The Blaines paid a last-ditch visit. Lenore wore tracksuits and a t-shirt. Her perm was going flat. Tom wore footy shorts and pluggers. His beard was bushy again. He presented a Parramatta Eels jersey to Trent.

"Here ya go, dig," said Tom to Trent, who was unimpressed.

Lenore knew what it was like to be shy, to be afraid. Life had taught her to be alert to potential sources of attention, and how to prevent them.

"One day we would love you to come to our place," said Lenore in a voice perfectly hers: husky and unpretentious. "We have a Dalmatian named Cindy. And a swimming pool. Tom does the biggest bomb dives in the world!"

Trent showed no sign of budging. Lenore smiled at him in silence. She wooed the mute boy with a wild kindness. Then an anti-ultimatum.

"I'm sorry we scared you, sweetie," said Lenore. "You don't have to live with us. But I still want to stay friends. I think that you're just awesome."

At the end of the visit, Lenore and Tom walked to the door. Something stirred within Trent. The little boy gave chase. He clung to Lenore's leg. This was the first time he'd ever touched her. She would never forget it.

"Would you like a hug?" asked Lenore.

"Yep," said Trent.

Lenore lifted up his pale, bony body. Trent embraced her tightly. He started crying. She recognised them as tears of need, not tears of fear.

"Oh, sweetie," she said.

Within this elusive affinity was permission to take Trent back to Ipswich. Maybe not today, but soon enough. He would be her son. And she would be his mum. That day, love filled the space where pain had been.

CHAPTER FOUR

Mother's Milk

With the social security benefits saved from his prison stint in Queensland, Michael Shelley bought a Kombi van to shelter his forthcoming child. The Shelleys set forth for Kuranda, the same birthplace as Elijah in 1980.

The drought was over. Queensland was green again. The Kombi reached Home Hill, an hour and a half south of Townsville. Prime beef and sugarcane country. The Shelleys camped along the Burdekin River.

On 30 June 1983, Mary's waters broke, two months prematurely. Even Michael could see that the situation exceeded his paediatric expertise. An ambulance rushed Mary and her endangered baby to the Townsville Hospital. Michael trailed the high-speed rescue mission in the Kombi.

The nurses expected a dead premmie. It stunned them that such a small, weak thing could thrash with so much wrath. Michael and Mary recognised that perseverance. They named him Saul. He was the first King of Israel, reincarnated as a thin, olive-skinned baby in North Queensland.

The nurses explicitly forbade Mary from breastfeeding him.

"Mary's breast milk is of superb quality!" Michael argued.

Saul swallowed Mary's milk. His heartbeat slowed. There wasn't enough oxygen in the bloodstream. His skin turned blue.

"Some babies will die if God needs them to!" insisted Mary.

Security guards apprehended Michael. Doctors saved Saul. They provided oxygen until a light airplane to the capital became available. At midday on 7 July, Mary and Saul were urgently shepherded 1330 kilometres south. The plane glided onto the roof of the Royal Brisbane and Women's Hospital.

Mary stayed with a friend of a friend. She arrived at 8.30 am each day and left at 9.45 pm. A three-dollar cab fare each way. There were no spare beds for mothers to stay with their suffering sons and daughters. Mary launched a crusade against Dr Johnson, the medical superintendent. She was furious at the nurses' preference for S-26 formula over her personal milk supply.

"You are concerned about Saul's heart because your own heart is deeply distressed," Mary wrote to Dr Johnson. "Saul's heart would murmur only because he is separate from his chief source of LOVE + PROTECTION, MICHAEL."

Mary accused the hospital of secretly owning a stake in S-26. She berated the student nurses for referring to Saul as *darlin'*, *sweetheart*, *sweetie* and *bubba*. She accused Dr Johnson of binge eating to repress her own loneliness and of projecting that hunger onto the allegedly underfed infants.

"Dr Johnson, you are lost + alone in this world without the love of a caring man like MICHAEL," wrote Mary at 7 am on 25 July, Saul's day of release. "You will die of a heart attack if you don't express how you really feel. ♡ Mary."

Mary walked free from the hospital with baby Saul. They hitch-hiked to Rockhampton. Michael was locked up in Etna Creek Prison. En route to Brisbane, he'd been arrested for a breach of bail. The prophet represented himself in court. He called Mary as the key witness. She read from the Gospel of Matthew.

"We live our lives according to the bible," said Mary.

The prosecutor tendered a threatening letter sent to him by Michael. The magistrate warned Michael that he might be held in contempt of court.

"It is not *me* who is in contempt of court!" roared Michael. "I do not threaten people. I warn them of their fate, as part of my ministry."

Michael was released on bail. The Kombi travelled south. On Elijah's third birthday, the Shelleys idled outside his foster home. Mary wanted Saul to be near his older brother. Michael delivered Mary and Saul back to Sydney. Solo, he went on a second reconnaissance mission to Queensland. He staged surveillance on Elijah's foster home. Then he sent a final warning to Susan King, Elijah's social worker.

"We found Elijah's abusive foster home without any trouble," wrote Michael. "If you leave Elijah with Fran and Neil, I can promise you that we will do EVERYTHING to harass them and take him back. GOD is on our side."

✣

Glen Elliott grew up in Melbourne with a single mother who was addicted to Valium. At the age of nineteen, he hitchhiked to Western Australia and then clockwise to Byron Bay. The drifter was searching for nothing less than the meaning of life. The night before meeting Michael, he leaned against a tree.

"I need you to send someone to save me," Glen prayed to God.

The next day, on the highway south of Byron Bay, Glen stuck his thumb into the wind. God sent a Kombi driven by a doppelganger for Jesus. Michael Shelley pulled over and offered him a lift to Sydney. He was handsome, charismatic, telepathic.

"Glen, I can see in your eyes that you have been terribly hurt by your mother," said Michael. "But you need to stop running away from that pain. I can help you. You need to open your broken heart to the gospel of Jesus Christ."

The preacher was intense but empathetic. Glen had never felt so seen, so accepted, so prized. In fifteen minutes flat, Glen trusted Michael with his fate. Which is why he felt so outraged when Michael told him the story of Elijah.

"How can they just take someone's child like that?" asked Glen.

"The world is a wicked and vicious place, Glen," said Michael. "Very few people have as much kindness as a beautiful young man like you."

Michael love-bombed gullible Glen with the same persuasiveness that he had love-bombed hundreds of women in his previous existence as a playboy. He recruited the hitchhiker to the kidnapping so delicately that it seemed like the teenager's idea. Glen found the meaning of life: to save Elijah.

"Many are called, Glen," said Michael. "Few – like you – are chosen."

Michael and Glen drove back to Sydney. They picked up Mary and Saul from a convent. Glen rented a car with NSW number plates. Then they all raced back to Queensland. Michael was planning to trade the Kombi for a campervan.

Glen would invade the foster home to liberate Elijah. This would secure him a plus-one to eternity and spare Michael a more serious criminal indictment. Mary would be waiting nearby in the campervan with Saul.

You Win Son, You Lose Son

The kidnapping of Elijah Shelley provoked a national manhunt and media storm. "TWO PIGTAILED MEN KIDNAP BOY, 3," read the front page of *The Courier-Mail*. "BABY GRAB MANHUNT!" read the front page of *The Daily Sun*. *The Telegraph* featured a photo of nineteen-year-old Debbie holding Elijah's stuffed monkey. "BRING BACK OUR BROTHER," read the headline.

"The kidnappers should be skinned alive," said Neil Williams, Elijah's foster father. "Even if we got Elijah back, the emotional damage he suffered could be irreparable."

On Tuesday morning at sunrise, Michael and Mary Shelley took Elijah and Saul for a peaceful stroll along the empty beach at South West Rocks. It was high tide in the horseshoe-shaped bay. A lighthouse at Smoky Cape marked the spot where Captain James Cook had detected a fire in 1770.

The Shelleys were Australia's most-wanted apostles. They drove away from the ocean to the wine and coalmining hubs of the Hunter Valley, until hitting the dry, quiet country highways of western New South Wales.

The Winnebago made a pitstop at the Dubbo swimming pool, five hours northwest of Sydney. It soothed Glen's nerves to be submerged. Michael waded Elijah through the water. Mary and baby Saul were watching on. So was a horrified lifeguard. He recognised Michael's face from the news.

"Time to go, Elijah," said Michael, scooping up his son.

The Winnebago kept heading south. They spent the night in Wagga Wagga. On Wednesday, the Shelleys reached legal Jerusalem: Canberra. The Australian Capital Territory provided asylum from extradition to Queensland. The van pottered along the straight, wide boulevards, passing Parliament House and the Lodge.

Michael drove west. The Winnebago spent the night outside the city, camped at Cotter Dam. The next day, Michael and Mary had to risk their liberty. They were running out of money. The social welfare office was in Queanbeyan, just over the border, back in the snake pit of New South Wales.

On Thursday morning, Michael and Mary arrived at the office. The supervisor secretly alerted police. He asked to see the couple in a private suite.

"We don't have much time," said Michael. "Our sons are hungry."

"It will take just a moment," said the bureaucrat.

Two cops arrived on foot. They ambushed the Shelleys. The plan was to stall them until reinforcements from the Australian Federal Police arrived.

"The AFP have a warrant for your arrest," said one of the cops.

"Do *you* have a warrant for my arrest?" asked Michael.

"You really need to deal directly with the AFP."

"New South Wales police have no right to detain me in a federal office, or to prevent me from leaving without a warrant," said Michael. "Goodbye!"

Michael and Mary raced out of the building. He took the wheel of the Winnebago. She nursed Saul. Glen tended to Elijah. The shocked police officers chased them, but they had no car. They hailed a yellow taxi.

"Follow that Winnebago!" shouted one of the cops, flashing his badge.

The taxi pursued the Shelleys. The police officers wound down their windows and implored Michael to stop. He theatrically ignored them. The taxi was soon joined by two AFP sedans with flashing sirens. The cavalcade converged onto Yass Road. The campervan limped towards the ACT. It was like watching a turtle get stalked by a skulk of frustrated foxes.

"Michael, maybe you should stop," begged Glen.

Michael's sole priority was getting derailed in the ACT rather than New South Wales. He would have already deserted his right-hand man, had the teenager not been so obviously at risk of spilling his guts to the authorities.

"If we get arrested, don't you dare say boo," Michael told Glen. "For all the police know, Mary and Saul have been in Canberra the entire time."

The Winnebago nudged across the border. Michael roared victoriously. He flicked the indicator to the left and pulled up on the shoulder of the highway. Michael thrashed violently against arrest by the six police officers. He tripped and smashed his head against the rear-vision mirror of the taxi.

"Take me to Canberra!" he yelled.

The police acquiesced. Two of them took Michael to a Canberra police station. Two of them took Elijah to ACT social workers, who called Fran Williams. Elijah was delighted to hear his foster mother's voice.

"Hello, Mumma," he said. "Can we get pizza for dinner?"

Fran Williams and Susan King flew from Brisbane to Canberra. Elijah was gifted a toy helicopter festooned with tiny Australian flags. On the flight home to Queensland, he wouldn't stop singing "C'mon, Aussie, C'mon".

"Do you want to take it again?" Elijah asked the photographers waiting at Brisbane Airport. "I'm going to get my camera to take a picture of you!"

The photogenic foster boy became a front-page sensation.

KIDNAP BOY FOUND IN RAID
ELIJAH FLYING HOME FOR HAPPY ENDING
KIDNAP BOY KISSES HIS DRAMAS AWAY
OVERJOYED FAMILY REUNITED WITH ELIJAH

"Now we just want to get back to a normal life," said Neil Williams. "This little fellow has had quite enough excitement to last him a lifetime."

⋅⋅⋅

The bliss was short-lived. Fran and Neil were traumatised, their five daughters more so, Elijah the most. All suffered flashbacks and premonitions of a second abduction. Life didn't return to normal at all. Fran and

Neil desperately wanted to adopt Elijah, but Susan King was forthright.

"The Shelleys will never agree to you adopting Elijah," she told them. "Not in a million years. And one day, Michael will come hunting for him again."

Elijah needed a new home, unless the Williams were willing to move cities and change their names. But Fran and Neil couldn't just disappear. They'd be leaving behind two adult daughters, whose identities were known to Michael.

"I'm going to regret this for the rest of my life," Fran told Susan.

The overrun local social workers found a placement for Elijah near the Sunshine Coast: the Bishops, an evangelical Christian family. They lived on a farm in the Glasshouse Mountains. Susan visited the prospective carers. They seemed too rigid for such a larger-than-life little boy, but Susan didn't have the power to veto the decision without a legitimate gripe.

"Bye, Elijah," said Fran, tearfully. "We love you."

The Department of Children's Safety legally renamed Elijah Shelley *Michael Bishop*. In choosing his new first name, perhaps they were using reverse psychology. The clue to Elijah's identity was right under Michael Shelley's nose.

Michael had gotten half of his wish-list: for Elijah to be removed from Fran and Neil Williams. Why did he hate them so much? Because of how blatantly his son loved them. The idea Elijah might thrive and find happiness was more threatening to Michael's fragile psyche than the disturbing alternative.

Don't Be Discouraged

Michael Shelley was charged with kidnapping and refused bail. He was sent to the Belconnen Remand Centre. The brick and corrugated iron compound – notorious for overcrowding – was known as "the Black Hole of Belconnen".

Mary, Saul and Glen Elliott retreated to Cotter Dam in the van. The AFP had no warrant for Mary's arrest or legal grounds for Saul's removal. They interrogated Mary and Glen separately under the shadow of the dam walls.

"You're facing fifteen years in a Queensland jail," a detective told Glen.

Michael's worst fears were confirmed. Glen confessed in granular detail to the kidnapping plot, implicating Mary, too. She was charged. She and baby Saul scored a private family cell at the Belconnen Remand Centre.

The next day, Glen was arrested. He remembered a wise piece of advice from Michael: if he refused to wear the prison uniform, the guards would be forced to place him in solitary confinement. It would be much safer.

Glen spent the first seventy-two hours in solitary. He embarked on a fast. It was another suggestion from Michael, spiritual rather than legal in nature. Then he was transferred to the men's section. Glen won back Michael's trust by penning abusive letters to his mother, father and siblings.

Queensland tried to extradite Michael, Mary and Glen to Brisbane, where they would face charges for the kidnapping of Elijah. Susan King applied to make Saul a ward of the state. In Canberra, at the committal hearing, Michael demanded an open courtroom to maximise media attention.

"The essence of the matter is that my son, Elijah, was brutally abducted from his mother and father," he said. "We were rightfully taking him back."

Michael organised a QC for Glen, while electing to represent himself. At Michael's request, court proceedings were overseen by the Human Rights Commission. He appealed to the Supreme Court to disqualify a series of "biased" magistrates. The appeal was successful. The case was readjourned.

"This is the most important child custody case in the history of Australia," said Michael. "Queensland is a police state. Bjelke-Petersen wants me dead, by hook or by crook. Blind Freddy can see we won't receive a fair trial."

The Human Rights Commissioner testified that a child – in this case Saul – should never be separated from its mother, regardless of her eccentric beliefs. Michael made a public plea to the United Nations. He alleged a conspiracy between church, state, police and the media, claiming that his family were the victims of religious persecution. During an exhaustive appearance, the preacher listed his educational and parenting credentials.

"I am the only *real* Christian minister in the country," he said.

Michael was filibustering the prosecution and judge into surrender. The fatigued Queenslanders temporarily gave up on their extradition attempt. Michael, Mary, Saul and Glen had spent six weeks in the Black Hole of Belconnen. They were allowed to walk free. This was on the strict proviso that they presented themselves to a Queensland court the following year.

Michael's maniacal brain had gotten Glen arrested, but then saved him from a fifteen-year prison sentence. They embraced outside the court.

"We won't be going back to Queensland," Michael told him. "And I suggest that you don't, either. You should go away on a long, long holiday."

Glen hitchhiked west to Perth and north to Darwin, fearing arrest at any moment. He called a solicitor from a phone box in the Northern Territory. The solicitor told him that Queensland was chasing the Shelleys, not him.

"Stay off the radar and you'll be okay," said the solicitor.

Glen was twenty. He legally changed his name to Matthew. He went back to live with his father in Frankston. But his family walked on eggshells around him. They never forgave him for the kidnapping, or for the hateful screeds he had sent them from prison. Now, the only people who didn't flinch from him were Michael and Mary. He felt a magnetic attraction towards them.

++

The Shelleys retreated from Canberra to a sanctuary for religious cults: the Blue Mountains, west of Sydney. It rose a thousand metres above sea level. Sweeping valleys filled with trees slanted up to vertical cliff faces. In Katoomba, Michael lifted Saul towards the Three Sisters, sandstone triplets.

In a Kombi, Michael drove further and further into the mountains. The Shelleys arrived at a tiny village called Mount Irvine. The road narrowed to a spectacular dead end. They were surrounded by thick trees. You needed a sunroof to see a sliver of the sky.

The Shelleys stumbled upon a sixty-hectare farm called Kookootonga. There were walnut and chestnut orchards, along with lambs to shepherd. Michael knocked on the front door of a one-storey timber house. He offered his services as a jack of all trades. The owners accepted. Michael, Mary and Saul moved into a two-room hut. It had running water but no electricity.

Michael and Mary sang Saul to sleep. Then they went about the business of giving him a younger sibling. At the age of forty, Mary fell pregnant. Mary rested and nurtured Saul. He was small for a six-month-old. It was a gift to breastfeed a child while another one bloomed inside you.

Michael worked eight hours a day: planting seeds and squeezing cows' udders. He brought home fresh oranges, walnuts and honey.

On 30 October 1984, Mary went into labour on schedule. Michael personally delivered another bloody, olive-skinned son. But he perceived a difference in temperament between Saul and his brother. Where Saul had been small, the newborn was stout and roaring with rage. What to name him?

"Joshua!" said Michael.

"Oh, what a beautiful name!" said Mary.

The baby was the reincarnation of Moses' personal spy, who led Israel's conquest of Canaan, making him a hero to Muslims the world over.

"Do not be afraid; do not be discouraged," Michael told Joshua. "I will never leave nor forsake you. Be strong and courageous. You will lead these people to inherit the land that I swore to their ancestors."

Michael and Mary officially got married at Kookootonga Cottage. The only thing missing was Elijah. Michael intended to reunite the brothers soon.

The Land of Rum and Money

Lenore had been married to Tom for five years, and still frequently it seemed like she was waking up beside a stranger. By 1985, the taxi was paid off and profitable. Trent had been nurtured into a healthy, happy child, with only mild learning difficulties. He repeated preschool. But he was blooming into a little athlete. Tom dressed him in a Parramatta Eels jersey, shorts and socks.

Trent worshipped his foster father like he was Clark Kent. And yet it wasn't enough. Tom Blaine was beset by a perpetual restlessness.

"What's wrong?" Lenore asked him at dinner.

"Nothin'," said Tom, although there was a lot wrong.

Ipswich was going to the dogs. The mines had stopped digging coal. The woollen mills were killed off by tariff cuts. The railway workshop offered redundancies. Tom's coalminer and tradie mates left for greener pastures.

"It doesn't seem like nothing," she said.

"I'm just sick of the same old shit."

Naturally, Lenore had been performing a stocktake of her defects: average looks, social awkwardness, unadventurous dinners, barren womb.

"Is it me?" she asked.

"It's not you," he said.

There were no fights to provide catharsis or psychological insight. Away from the taxi customers and the rugby league players at the clubhouse, the happy-go-lucky larrikin slumped into bouts of monosyllabic grumpiness.

And then, like a veil, months of irritation lifted from Tom's face. It was Saturday morning. He was reading the classifieds in *The Courier-Mail*.

"Eureka!" he said.

After a mysterious series of phone calls, Tom announced that they were going on a last-minute holiday. Trent was beside himself with excitement. Lenore, puzzled, packed the Falcon for an unanticipated visit to the beach.

"Let's get crackalacking," said Tom.

Tom drove up the Bruce Highway. They missed the turn-offs for Redcliffe, and then Caloundra, and then Noosa, and then Hervey Bay.

"Are we there yet?" asked Trent.

"Not yet, dig," said Tom. "But it's coming."

Five hours after they left Ipswich, Tom took the turn-off for Bundaberg. It was the spiritual home of dark rum in the land down under. He drove over the Burnett River without slowing down or going into town. At sunset, the Falcon sped through endless fields of shivering sugarcane.

Forty-five minutes north of Bundaberg, Tom flicked the indicator to the left. They drove over a railway line. *ROSEDALE: POPULATION 356*, announced a rusted sign. The bush around Rosedale was a place where people were born and never left, or where they went to vanish from the face of the planet.

"We're here, dig," said Tom.

There was nothing but a church, a general store, a small school and a smattering of unhomely abodes. One more thing: a pub. Tom pulled up to the Rosedale Hotel, exultantly. It looked more like a large, rundown boarding house than a pub. White walls and a rusted maroon roof. Behind it was a campsite.

"Is there a pool?" asked Trent.

"No, dig," said Tom. "But there's a pool table. And steaks the size of a plate. And more packets of chips than you can poke a cricket bat at."

"Aw yeah!" said Trent.

At the bar sat a row of men with glazed eyes and bright red cheeks. The Blaines checked into a cobwebbed room with a double bed and a single bed. Lenore and Trent had showers in a detached communal bathroom. Back in the bar, they found Tom regaling the drunks with stories. Lenore had heard them all before. The publican refused to take Tom's money for drinks or food.

"Have you been here before?" asked Lenore.

"In my dreams," said Tom.

The Blaines ate dinner in the dining room. A T-bone for Tom, crumbed fish for Lenore, chicken nuggets and tomato sauce for Trent.

"I thought we were going on a holiday," said Lenore.

"Change is better than a holiday," said Tom.

Lenore had never been more convinced that she had married a gigantic mannequin who delivered a pithy idiom when you dropped a coin in the slot.

"What do you think?" asked Tom.

"It's a pub," she said.

"It's *our* pub," he said. "If we want it."

Lenore took a sip of her tequila sunrise.

"You're pulling my leg," she said.

"I'm fair dinkum," he said.

Tom scribbled figures on a serviette. The purchase price was underlined. He subtracted the sale price of the taxi and the house, leaving a slight surplus. Tom had been brooding over an escape plan that he was incapable of communicating. Until now, with shameless persuasiveness.

"You'd need to go over all the books and make sure they aren't diddling us," he whispered, an olive branch to indicate that she had a say in the decision.

"Why didn't you tell me you wanted to leave Ipswich?" she asked.

"I didn't want to flap my gums about it," he said.

That night, Tom showed restraint. After a game of pool, he retired from the bar at a reasonable hour to go to bed with Lenore and Trent.

"This'll be good for us," he whispered into her ear.

Tom and Trent fell asleep. Lenore was excited and slightly frightened. Tom bottled everything up, while bubbling away with latent frustrations and pipedreams. He was physically unmissable and emotionally unknowable.

++

That first Friday night at the Rosedale Hotel was mayhem. The Blaines got a babysitter for Trent. The dining room was filled with impatient families. Lenore took orders for the cook. Tom put a pig on the spit in the beer garden and paid an acoustic guitarist $100 to play pub rock covers in the front bar. Thirsty locals converged to test the mettle of the first-time publican.

"You're a long way from home," said a revved-up heckler.

"And you're a long way from a hospital, dickhead," said Tom.

Patrons included small-time farmers, large-scale marijuana growers and miscellaneous drifters. The bushies and bikies bonded over a mutual dislike of the backpackers. One of the Brits kept singing Depeche Mode over the pub-rock covers. He ignored repeated warnings not to pour himself a beer.

Tom stormed to the other side of the bar. He grabbed the backpacker by the collar and rag-dolled him across the floor. Then he dumped him on the front lawn. The Brits left. The bushies and bikies rejoiced. Numbers swelled the following night. Locals wanted to lay eyes on the pugilistic publican.

"You're a celebrity," said Lenore.

"You need to keep people on their toes," he said.

After school, Trent followed Tom around like an apprentice. A big red truck arrived from Bundaberg brimming with fresh kegs and cartons of hard liquor. Tom carried two empty kegs in each hand to swap with a full one. Trent pretended to help him carry it inside. He was rewarded with a pot of pub squash.

"You're gonna have bigger guns than me," said Tom.

Tom kept a notebook and a wad of fifties in his top pocket for anyone who wanted to have a cheeky flutter with the publican. One such punter was the local copper. He turned a blind eye to Tom's gambling syndicate and to the roaring supply of backdoor liquor on Good Friday and Christmas Day.

Lenore organised Rosedale Hotel merchandise: shirts, bottle openers and stubbie coolers. They sold like hotcakes. The pub was a money tree.

"This is ridiculous," said Lenore, after another Thursday morning of bookkeeping. "You are making double the income of the old owner."

"*We*," said Tom, kissing his wife.

Lenore bought Trent two blue budgerigars for the beer garden. Tom ran a raffle to decide the naming rights. The winner called the budgies Adam and Eve. Lenore neatly wrote THE BEER GARDEN OF EDEN with chalk on a blackboard. Tom placed a rubber snake at the bottom of the birdcage.

The only thing missing from Rosedale was a younger sibling for Trent. Lenore kept lobbying Susan King for another foster care placement.

"I might have some good news soon," said Susan.

Hungry Little Children

Michael and Mary ghosted their new court date. Queensland issued a warrant for their arrest. NSW detectives heard whispers that the missionaries had disappeared into the Blue Mountains. Cops staged a raid on the farm at Mount Irvine. Michael and Mary were taken to the police station in Lithgow. The Shelleys knew that social workers were circling Saul and Joshua.

"How many children in the world suffer no sickness?" asked Michael. "How many gain weight in perfect proportion? How many spontaneously express all of their pain and joy? The answer is none, except for my sons!"

Michael and Mary were ordered to appear at the Castlereagh Petty Sessions Court, in the sprawl of northwest Sydney. The Department of Youth and Community Services – YACS – was alerted to the existence of Saul and Joshua. A social worker named Margaret ambushed the Shelleys.

"Margaret is an excellent example of what happens when little women are set no limits," wrote Michael. "She dresses more appropriate to being a hostess at a gambling den, sporting a see-through dress that clearly displayed her breasts (OR, MORE ACCURATELY, THE ABSENCE OF THEM)."

Margaret ordered paediatric examinations of the two brothers. At night, the Shelleys paid a visit to the children's hospital in Camperdown. Saul and Joshua were examined for two and a half hours. The paediatrician judged that Joshua was slightly underfed. He suggested more regular feeding.

Saul and Joshua were returned to their parents. The Shelleys drove to South Australia in a car and caravan. They contemplated escape to New Zealand. But they couldn't bring themselves to leave Elijah behind.

The Shelleys went back to northern New South Wales. It was the end of summer. At night, a police officer spotted the nomads on the main street of Grafton. Michael was arrested for a breach of bail. He spent five weeks in Grafton Prison. Mary stayed at a women's refuge with Saul and Joshua. The stewardess reported Mary's parenting to the Murwillumbah YACS office.

The local YACS boss ordered fresh assessments of Saul and Joshua. The brothers were taken to see a paediatrician. The doctor described Joshua Shelley as "suntanned and scrawny". His rate of weight gain was too low for a baby that age. He was officially diagnosed with a failure to thrive.

Michael was released from Grafton Prison. This was the ideal time for the Shelleys to cut their losses. But Elijah was so close, somewhere beyond the Queensland border. Michael and Mary, armed with Saul and Joshua, returned to Brisbane. They were planning to attempt another rescue of Elijah.

Elijah was impossible to find this time. From public phone boxes with orange tops, Michael called Susan King's private home number. He left notes in her letterbox insinuating that her children were under threat. For years, Susan lived in fear of hearing Michael's voice when the phone rang; of seeing his enraged face when she took her children into public places.

Michael was located and arrested. He went back to Boggo Road Gaol. Mary drove from Brisbane to Melbourne with Saul and Joshua. They caught a ferry to Tasmania. The Seventh Day Adventist church paid for three plane tickets to New Zealand. There, Mary spent six weeks crusading for asylum.

✠

Mary ignored Michael's directions to stay away from Queensland. She purchased plane tickets back to Brisbane. On the eve of Joshua's first birthday, Mary took Saul and Joshua to Boggo Road Gaol. Susan King was alerted to their arrival. The social worker went to the prison, accompanied by the special branch of the Queensland police.

Saul and Joshua sat on the floor crying, while their parents yelled threats and insults. Michael accused Susan of being worse than the Nazis. Mary threatened to blow up Joh Bjelke-Petersen's office building.

Guards dragged Michael to solitary confinement. The special branch delivered Mary to a psych ward at the Prince Charles Hospital. Susan King took Saul and Joshua for a fresh round of testing. It was déjà vu. Joshua was judged to be even more malnourished than Elijah had been three years earlier.

"Because he was so superbly cared for, Joshua knew what was coming," wrote Michael. "He refused to eat properly in the month before his abduction."

Saul was only just below average weight, but he displayed a lack of language and motor skills. Susan King received a protection order from the courts. Michael and Mary were irrevocably forbidden from seeing their sons until at least the age of eighteen. Saul and Joshua were renamed Steven and John. They were placed into temporary foster care with Margaret and Brian Clarke. Susan King wrote them a storybook, illustrated with stick figures.

"Mummy Mary and Daddy Michael did not have a house," it read. "They liked to sleep outside. But Saul and Joshua weren't getting enough food to eat. They were so thin. They needed some meat in their tummies."

Undercover Publicans

Susan King required a permanent foster care placement for Steven and John, aka Saul and Joshua Shelley. Lenore and Tom Blaine came to mind. The publicans were perhaps the least suitable foster carers in Queensland – nay, Australia – to satisfy the maniacal dieting standards of Michael Shelley.

"The sum total of Australian culture is football, cricket, meat pies and beer," wrote Michael. "What a rigid, provincial way of life! The so-called Australian larrikin is just a cowardly, foul-mouthed lout. You can find them at pubs, smoking cigarettes and drinking alcohol like unweaned infants."

Lenore was a pack a day smoker. Tom was a three pack a day smoker. He had a strict daily intake of red meat. A steak sandwich and hot chips for lunch. A 300-gram rump, potato bake and three veg for dinner. Tom had been diagnosed with type 2 diabetes. This didn't lead to the introduction of new food.

"Fish is for Christians," he said. Tom's solitary nod to the health concerns of his doctor was swapping beer for scotch and Diet Coke.

Otherwise, the Blaines were perfect. Susan King needed to find a foster mother who could provide unlimited love, and a foster father who wouldn't be intimidated by the potential arrival of two unhinged missionaries.

"How would Trent like a couple of younger brothers to play with?" Susan asked Lenore over the telephone, with trademark understatement.

"Oh, Susan," said Lenore. "We thought that you would never ask!"

The Blaines were vaguely familiar with Michael and Mary Shelley, thanks to their kidnapping of Elijah. Susan was upfront about the risks. Lenore received a dossier of newspaper articles about the notorious couple and the threats they had sent to Fran and Neil Williams.

In the private quarters at the Rosedale Hotel, Tom studied the photographs of Michael Shelley.

"What is the go with this bloke?" he asked.

"He's a narcissist," said Lenore.

"An arsonist?" asked Tom, alarmed.

"No, Thomas. A narcissist. He loves himself."

Tom was relieved. He nodded, knowingly.

"So, he sniffs his own farts?" he asked.

"Something like that," she said.

The Shelleys would get no direct contact with Steven and John until they turned eighteen. Susan warned Lenore that Michael and Mary would inevitably attempt to find them. The Blaines would need to be silent voters and remain unlisted in the White Pages. All sorts of safety precautions would have to be taken on a daily basis. But Tom's arm didn't need to be twisted.

"I'm in," he said. "I'd love to meet the skinny prick."

Lenore and Tom Blaine went to visit the Clarkes in Brisbane. Susan King glimpsed history in the making. Steven and John didn't rise up and hail the Blaines as their saviours. But they eagerly accepted tenderness from the prospective foster carers. And they lit up around Trent.

"My brothers!" yelled Trent, cutting through the courtship phase.

Lenore left behind her own storybook, laminated with stickers of the Smurfs. It was a bedtime fairy-tale to be read by Margaret Clarke to Steven and John.

"Mummy Lenore, Daddy Tom and Trent would love Steven and John to come live with us," wrote Lenore. "We have always wanted three little boys."

⁜

A few weeks later, the Blaines returned in the Ford Falcon station wagon to collect Steven and John. Lenore packed the fattening toddlers into baby seats alongside Trent. Tom lifted his finger from the steering wheel at every passing motorist, a sacred ritual. Trent occasionally nodded into the rear-view mirror. Tom winked at him. He sped past the cane fields to the dense bush.

The spinifex grew higher than the car. The gum trees leaned sideways, ant mounds in their thin trunks. Steven and John were two curious little boys on their way home from the Big Smoke to the middle of nowhere. Lenore recited endless nursery rhymes to them.

"Tell 'em the yarn about the egg who topped 'imself," said Tom.

"Humpty Dumpty sat on a wall," said Lenore. "Humpty Dumpty had a great fall. All the king's horses and all the king's men couldn't put Humpty together again."

Lenore spoke with a subtle stiffness. The Blaines weren't themselves yet. Tom let rip a trademark fart, as if someone was playing the trumpet from his arse.

"Thomas!" said Lenore, winding the window down.

"Ya drop ya guts, ya grub?" Tom asked Trent.

"Pong, Dad," said Trent. "That was you!"

It was a breakthrough moment. Steven started giggling, and then John, too. The Blaines bonded over the universal humour of flatulence.

"Dad rips the biggest farts," Trent promised Steven and John.

That day, the Blaines became a family of five. Steven and John were mesmerised by Cindy the Dalmatian and Adam and Eve, the blue budgies. The three brothers shared a room in the private quarters. Lenore had knitted the names STEVEN BLAINE and JOHN BLAINE into two new blankets.

"Night, me little mates," whispered Tom, kissing them on the foreheads.

The next morning, Trent checked the chook pen for eggs. Steven followed. The petals from a poinsettia tree turned the concrete footpath into a red carpet. Lenore carried John, who couldn't walk yet. Then they took Trent to school. Lenore and Tom pushed Steven and John in separate prams.

Lenore spent her days showering Steven and John with affection. At first, Steven seemed more aware than John that something catastrophic had happened. He needed a nebuliser for his dodgy lungs. Watching his foster son have constant coughing fits made Tom reassess his lifestyle choices. He gave up smoking cold turkey, and never touched another cigarette.

John clung to Lenore as if she were his natural mother. His heart was a blank slate for love. Pretty soon, it felt as if the Blaines had always been a family of five. But Lenore was too honest to take advantage of their amnesia.

"Mummy and Daddy love Stevie and Johnnie very much," she said in their bedroom. "But Steve and John come from a different mummy's tummy."

"No!" cried Steven, rubbing her stomach. "I come from here!"

"The mummy who gave birth to Stevie and Johnnie loves you very, very, very much," said Lenore. "But she got sick. So you came to live with us."

Each night, Lenore spent half an hour at a timber desk in the master bedroom. She compiled one-page diary entries on an old typewriter. She hole-punched the paper and added it to a folder. There was a folder for each year. Tom bristled at the *click click click* of the keys as his wife hit them.

"Why do you need to write so much?" he asked.

"How am I supposed to remember everything?" she asked.

"In ya head," he said.

"Thomas, you'd be amazed how much we forget."

"You say that like it's a bad thing," he muttered.

Lenore disagreed. She wanted to remember everything: the good, bad and indifferent. Especially the indifferent. It was easy enough to dredge up moments of happiness and tragedy. She was a saviour of the small details.

The North Star

The department only had one caveat. Due to Steven's breathing problems, the Blaines needed to live closer to a hospital. Lenore and Tom put the Rosedale Hotel up for sale. In 1987, the family arrived in Chinchilla, population 4787. It was surrounded by grain farms that turned into watermelon plantations during wet season. To the north was the Barakula Forest, an endless supply of cypress pine timber. To the west was the Australian outback.

"Chinchilla's fifty-fifty," Tom told Lenore. "Half of 'em have never set foot inside a pub. And half of 'em have never set foot inside a church."

Tom got a good deal on the lease of the Tattersalls Hotel. It was a two-storey concrete pub, painted cream. Downstairs was a large front bar, a dining room, and a sprawling beer garden for the birdcage. Upstairs were a dozen rooms for rent and a three-bedroom private quarters.

"You're a big boy now, Trent," said Lenore. "You get your own room."

"No way!" said Trent.

Trent pestered and protected Steven and John. He regaled them with farfetched falsehoods, such as his ability to kill snakes and fly helicopters.

"Don't let the truth get in the way of a good yarn, dig," said Tom.

"It's true!" he protested.

Trent got his gift for confabulation from Tom. One of Tom's favourite lies was that he had been a professional wrestler named Killer Kowalski. Each morning, the boys tackled their father awake. He emitted a stream of fake snores. Then he staged a rapid resurrection. He tickled Steven and John into surrender. Trent hung from his father's back like a monkey, three on one.

"I submit!" Steven shrieked. "I submit!"

"Break it up," called Lenore. "Time for brekky."

Trent and John resisted Lenore's offers of Weet-Bix. Steven ate them to please his mother. She fed the others Vegemite on toast. Trent enrolled in grade two. Steven went to kindergarten. Their clothes were immaculately ironed. Lenore didn't see the laundry as a betrayal of feminism. It was another way to demonstrate careful attention to children who might otherwise feel unwanted.

John, three, was greedy for Lenore's attention. His face flipped between grumpiness and glee, not unlike the foster father whom he constantly studied with awe. John would tip a rainbow Slinky down the timber stairs to the front bar. Tom winked at him before the heavy drinking started.

"John the Baptist," said Tom. "How ya goin', mate?"

"Not bad, Dad," said John. "How ya goin', mate?"

"I'm flat out like a lizard drinking," said Tom.

Steven yearned for compliments from Lenore, the same way John wanted constant cuddles. But he was apologetic about being the centre of attention. Steven was a people-pleaser. He had a permanent smile to hide mild anxiety. The four-year-old brought home finger paintings from kindergarten.

"What do you think, Mum?" he asked, sheepishly.

Lenore regarded the artworks as if they were done by Picasso.

"Another masterpiece," she said. "I'm losing space on the fridge!"

Tom's business plan was simple. The cold room needed to be near zero and the beer lines cleaned once a week. Customers should feel as if they were sitting in their own lounge room, with a never-ending supply of liquor. Tom hired a chef nicknamed Cooky, the only known homosexual in Chinchilla. Cooky turned the kitchen into the town's first à la carte restaurant.

"You're shit-hot, mate," Tom told him after another roaring shift.

"Never eat anything that wasn't cooked by a poof," said Cooky.

Steven and John no longer had to worry about empty stomachs. Their personal chef provided sandwiches for lunch and counter meals for dinner.

"Never throw a free feed in the bin," Tom told them, making sure they finished every last scrap. "Ya never know when the next one's coming."

On Sunday nights, Tom shut the pub at six o'clock sharp. The Blaines drove half an hour west to the town of Miles, where there was a Chinese restaurant. The boys cracked fortune cookies with a Chinese brother and sister. Tom consumed half a kilo of Mongolian beef.

Lenore preferred honey chicken.

"You Chinese blokes are freaking geniuses," Tom told the owner, loosening his belt a couple of notches. "I could eat this stuff for breakfast."

"Food is more important than the Queen," said the restaurateur.

"Amen, mate!" said Tom.

"Amen, mate!" said Trent.

"Amen, mate!" said Steven.

"Amen, mate!" said John.

"Give it a rest," said Lenore.

To strangers, the Blaines appeared to be the quintessential Australian family: a blokey father, a softly spoken mother and three energetic sons.

✢

Tom hired an Aboriginal bouncer nicknamed Bud. The Indigenous locals were used to redneck publicans segregating their bars. But Tom had quickly won over the local Murri men through rugby league. They all claimed kinship with Gordie Langton, who occupied the wing for the Ipswich Jets. He was supplied endless chip kicks by Allan Langer, Tom's nephew.

Tom was given a dot-painted boomerang to hang behind the front bar. He had a quiet housekeeping conversation with Bud, the new security guard.

"Just keep an eye out for suss cunts lurking around," said Tom.

Bud grinned back into the bar. "You mean like all of them?"

"Nah," said Tom. "I mean the sussest cunts you've ever seen."

Tom provided a basic outline of the foster care situation.

"What should I be looking for?" asked Bud.

"A creep who looks like Jesus," said Tom. "He's skinnier than a minute to six. His missus is a sheila in a white dress. They're bad news."

Tom would never forget the winter of 1987. He had been telling anyone who'd listen that Allan Langer – twenty years old and

165 centimetres tall – would be the halfback for the Queensland State of Origin team.

The chairman of selectors was Tom's mate Dud Beattie, an old Ipswich coalminer. Tom watched the team announcement on TV in the front bar of the pub. Number six – Wally Lewis. Seven – Allan Langer. The blond bombshell had been plucked from obscurity to debut alongside "the King".

"In like Flynn!" shouted Tom. "In like fuckin' Flynn!"

Lenore sewed maroon beanies and socks for Trent, Steven and John. Allan Langer silenced the doubters, both in the southern media and within his own side. In the decider at Lang Park, Queensland beat New South Wales 10–8. Allan Langer was man of the match. David kicked Goliath's arse on national TV. Newspapers were unanimous. A star had been born in the north.

The next morning, Tom was hungover. He tucked into a meat pie and tomato sauce for breakfast, chased down with a schooner of Diet Coke.

"Flogs from Sydney think they're better than us," he scoffed to his sons.

"I want to play for Queensland!" said Steven.

"I want to play for Queensland!" said John.

"If you eat your Weet-Bix, anything is possible," said Lenore.

Steven and John received miniature Queensland jerseys, signed by Allan Langer. He provided an undeniable sense of identity. Who were they? They were the first cousins of the Queensland halfback. Rugby league was a religion. It erased all the other legal and biological quirks of their existences.

The Watermelon Harvest

Steven and John were raised knowing they had an older brother named "Michael Bishop", aka Elijah Shelley. For reasons unclear, Michael's foster parents lied to him. They told him he was their biological child.

Then that he was adopted. Then that he was fostered.

In January 1988, when he was seven, they revealed he had two biological younger brothers. A few weeks later, Michael Bishop came to stay with the Blaines during the Chinchilla Show.

"Michael!" cried Steven and John when he arrived.

"Call me Mick," he said, grinning.

Steven was almost five. John was three-and-a-half. The brown-haired Blaines hugged their blond-haired older brother. They were too young for the reunion to be awkward. Michael's crooked teeth flashed from a cheeky grin.

"This is so cool," he said.

At bedtime, as the jukebox blared from downstairs, Michael hypnotised Steven and John with a literate rendition of *The Digging-est Dog*. Their clever older brother verified Lenore's insistence that they came from another woman's stomach, hinting at mysteries beyond their comprehension.

"Mick, do you remember our real parents?" asked Steven.

"Sort of," he whispered. "It was ages ago but."

The Chinchilla Show was run by a committee of rich farmers' wives and National Party politicians. The Bunyip Aristocracy regarded the Blaines as uncouth townies and Tom as a beer-gutted clown. They preferred to drink liquor in moderation at the RSL rather than at the Tattersalls Hotel.

"The Association of Chardonnay Farmers," Tom called them.

On Saturday morning, there was a parade of floats up and down the dusty main street of Chinchilla. The prevailing themes were agriculture and patriotism. Tom had completely forgotten that he had agreed to enter a float.

At the last minute, he wrapped the rails of his trusty red truck with XXXX Bitter bunting and maroon streamers left over from State of Origin. He filled the tray with eskies of beer and plastic chairs from the beer garden.

"Who wants to sink some free piss?" Tom asked the front bar.

There was no shortage of volunteers. The float was occupied by the Tatts' most ardent barflies and four small boys in Queensland jerseys. Tom took the wheel and wound the windows down. He blasted AC/DC at full volume.

"What's the name of the float?" asked one of the judges.

"The Underdogs," said Tom.

The Underdogs didn't make the shortlist for best float. Afterwards, Lenore took the boys to the showgrounds. They scooped up handfuls of shattered watermelon and gleefully threw it at one another's faces.

The headline event of the show was a tug-of-war. Tom recruited three watermelon pickers who drank rum at the pub. They didn't look like much. But the pickers were blessed with animal strength from summers spent plucking 15-kilogram watermelons from the dirt for eight hours straight.

The 140-kilogram publican was a natural anchor. They creamed the early rounds. The team made the grand final against a quartet of tall, broad, perfectly postured cattle farmers in Akubras and R.M. Williams boots.

"Let's stick it to these silver-spoon-fed dickheads," whispered Tom.

It was class war. The flag in the middle of the rope showed no early sign of heaving either way. Trent, Michael, Steven and John cheered them on. The Underdogs gained the upper hand. Veins throbbed in Tom's face. He pressed the rope into his guts.

The white flag appeared to pass the line marking victory. Tom and the pickers went slack with satisfaction. But the umpire ignored the evidence. The farmers pulled the rope back towards them. The Underdogs crushed into each other. This time, the umpire raised his arm in the direction of the farmers.

"Are your eyes painted on, mate?" Tom asked the umpire.

Tom's drunken customer base booed from the grandstand.

"Bullshit!" they chanted. "Bullshit! Bullshit! Bullshit!"

Tom left before the presentations. He was subsequently banned from entering a tug-of-war team into the Chinchilla Show for twelve months. Back at the pub, Tom and the watermelon pickers numbed their blisters with the consumption of liquor.

Upstairs, Lenore supervised Trent, Michael, Steven and John. They filled their mouths with Skittles and watched *Scooby-Doo Meets the Boo Brothers* on VHS. Steven and John were smitten with Michael Bishop. He was smitten with them. It was as if they had never been apart. At dinner, Steven spilled the question that had been on his lips the whole weekend.

"Can Mick live with us?" he asked Lenore.

"Yeah!" cried John. "Live with us, Mick!"

Lenore thought she saw hope cross Michael's face. She wanted nothing more than for the three brothers to be permanently reunited. But it was a decision for the Department of Child Safety. And Susan King had made clear that she had no intention of wrenching him from another placement.

"Michael has his own family," said Lenore, covertly heartbroken.

Lenore and Tom would have fostered the charming boy in a heartbeat. Michael kept coming back to visit Steven and John on school holidays. He was crystal clear to his younger brothers and a mystery to himself. The name on his birth certificate – Elijah Shelley – remained top-secret.

Act Two

CHAPTER FIVE

The Plot to Kill the Premier

There was one more Shelley brother none of the others knew about. Roman Long had dark hair and thick eyebrows. In 1980, Mary Shelley had left her twelve-year-old son on Lionel Long's doorstep.

One afternoon, Roman arrived home to find Pro Hart – the famous artist from Broken Hill – sitting on the edge of his bed. He was painting.

"G'day, Ro," said Pro Hart.

"Hey, Pro," said Roman.

Lionel was more interested in being a socialite than a father.

"Hey, Dad," said Roman. "How was your day?"

Lionel's eyes were as hostile as a wild possum's.

"I'm reading, junior," he said, concentrating on a book of poetry.

Lionel refused to teach his son to play guitar.

"Do you want to listen to me sing?" asked Roman.

Lionel picked up a glass ashtray and feigned throwing it at Roman's head. Maybe he wasn't joking, though the beatings had slowed down as Roman got older. At school, the singer's son was regularly bashed up by his Catholic classmates. They weren't impressed by Lionel's famous friends.

Roman ran away from home. He was seventeen. It was 1985. He packed three woollen jumpers and bought a one-way train ticket to Brisbane.

The humidity stunned him, as did the friendliness of the Queenslanders at a public swimming pool. Roman studied a sunbaking blonde.

What was he doing so far from home? Roman's stepfather, Michael Shelley, had sent him a letter. Roman quite liked Michael. He was intense, and he had stolen Roman's mother. But he was less emotionally repressed than Lionel Long. Roman paid Michael a visit at Boggo Road Gaol.

"I can see why you make Lionel feel so insecure," said Michael. "He is jealous of your shine. You are growing into such a handsome young man!"

Roman had forgotten this sensation: to be wanted, to be loved. Michael made him feel like a son. He updated Roman on the recent kidnapping of his younger brothers by the Queensland Department of Child Safety. Roman asked if there was anything he could do to help. Michael told Roman to go home. One day soon, the Shelleys would arrive to rescue him.

First, Roman visited his mother at the Wolston Park Mental Asylum. It was a gothic hospital in sprawling parkland, west of Brisbane. Mary was dressed in all white. She was tranquillised against her will with anti-psychotics. Roman was outraged. Queensland wasn't so friendly after all.

⁕

Lionel Long chastised Roman for running away from home. This was nice. Roman had his father's undivided attention. Meanwhile, Michael Shelley was released from jail. The Shelleys arrived at Lionel's Bondi apartment in a Kombi. Michael rang the doorbell. Roman ran outside. Lionel stayed behind the locked screen.

"Ro, you aren't seriously leaving with them?" asked Lionel.

"Fuck you, Dad!" said Roman. "Your life is boring. I want my own life!"

Michael Shelley drove the Kombi to Byron Bay. They stopped at campsites along the way. It was the middle of summer. Mary was in withdrawal from the pharmaceuticals. Her spirit was beginning to lift.

"I'll show you how to play guitar," Michael told Roman.

Roman found it hard to learn the chords. Michael encouraged him to sing. At campfires, they duetted on Cat Stevens and Simon and Garfunkel songs. Michael knew how to pitch a tent and tie a knot and change a tyre. He wanted to teach Roman everything, including the Gospel of Jesus.

In January 1986, the Kombi stopped at Kings Beach, a popular nudist colony. Michael baptised Roman in the shallows of the surf. He was saved.

The Shelleys liked to hibernate in winter. The Kombi wound south towards the ski fields. The trio settled on a farm near Cooma. Roman pumped out Michael's diatribes on a typewriter. He hand-delivered them to Australia Post. The folie à deux of Michael and Mary transformed into a folie à trois.

Roman Long started to speak, eat, look and dress like Michael Shelley. The same multi-day fasts. The same thin arms and gaunt chest. The same beard and ponytail. The same flowing robes. The same excitable voice.

Roman renounced his wealthy Jewish relatives. He referred to Lionel Long as his "first father". They made it official. By deed poll, Roman changed his name to "Paul Shelley". Paul got what he wanted: a loving father. Michael got what he needed: a disciple. Queensland hadn't seen anything yet.

✢

In December 1987, Joh Bjelke-Petersen resigned due to corruption allegations. Michael Shelley saw it as a sign of divine intervention. Joh was replaced as premier by Mike Ahern. He was preoccupied by

Expo '88. A sandstone cultural precinct was plonked along the river in South Brisbane.

The Shelleys relocated to Huonbrook in northern New South Wales. It was situated between Nimbin and Mount Jerusalem National Park. They lived in a timber loft. Paul was at the beck and call of Michael Shelley.

"I need you to write the premier a letter," Michael told Paul.

"From you?" asked Paul.

"From *you*," said Michael.

Paul was afraid of writing the letter, but more afraid of failing Michael. And he did feel aggrieved about his missing brothers. He knew better than anyone that his mother suffered from mood swings. But Mary loved her children. She didn't deserve a lifetime of bereavement for being bipolar.

Premier Ahern had ignored pleas for custody of Elijah, Saul and Joshua. Michael Shelley wanted to turn the pressure up a notch. To Paul, he dictated a letter to the premier's children. In the middle, Michael got bogged down in legal minutiae. But he was building to a dramatic ultimatum.

"We need the immediate return of Elijah, Saul and Joshua," he said. "If this doesn't happen, your father is placing his life – and your lives – at risk."

Paul was stricken. This didn't sound particularly Christian.

"I can't write that!" said Paul. "It sounds like a death threat."

Michael glared at Paul with no shine in his eyes, just black wrath.

"Write it!" roared Michael.

The letter was put in an envelope and sent. Premier Ahern provided no response or public apology. Michael Shelley ordered Paul on a pilgrimage. The disciple hitchhiked from Nimbin to the Sunshine Coast. Paul arrived at the premier's residence a few weeks before Christmas 1988. He knocked on the front door. The premier's wife, Andrea, answered.

"I'm here to see Mike," said Paul, politely.

"He's not here," said Andrea, suspicious.

"That's fine," said Paul. "Thank you!"

Paul waited on the street for Mike Ahern to return home. The premier arrived in an unmarked police car. The driver was Alan Bourke, a beefy detective who was famous for solving the rape and murder of a twelve-year-old girl in Gympie. Paul Shelley ambushed the premier and his bodyguard in the driveway. He begged for custody of his brothers: Elijah, Saul and Joshua.

"I'm not here to hurt you," said Paul. "But how long can this continue?"

Paul strained to convey that he didn't wish to assassinate the premier. Unfortunately, he bore an uncanny resemblance to Charles Manson. Mike Ahern identified him as the author of what he perceived as death threats.

Ahern vanished inside the house. Alan Bourke crash-tackled Paul Shelley. He handcuffed Paul and threw him into the back of the sedan. The detective drove the teenager to a holding cell at Caloundra police station.

According to Paul, Bourke unwound a high-pressure fire hose and blasted him with water. It reminded Paul of a scene in the movie *Rambo*. Then Paul was transferred to a high-security psychiatric hospital in Chermside. He was diagnosed with paranoid schizophrenia and tranquillised against his will.

Over the following weeks, Michael Shelley sent escalating ultimatums. If Paul, Elijah, Saul and Joshua weren't returned immediately – along with $11 million in compensation – Ahern and his family wouldn't see Christmas. The government didn't pay the money. Mike Ahern installed a high-tech security system and received 24-hour police surveillance.

It was an anxious Christmas Day, especially for Paul Shelley. He had been injected with so many needles that his buttocks had become rock hard. Luckily, Paul had memorised the premier's phone number. He rang him.

"I don't think that I deserve to be here," said Paul, pleading for the Christmas miracle of a legal pardon. "I'm a non-violent Christian!"

Mike Ahern hung up. Michael Shelley cut his losses. Mary and he travelled south, away from the mess he had made, towards a new plot.

The Bad Seed

On Easter Sunday 1989, Nicole Wilson received an unexpected knock at the door. The teacher, thirty-seven, was breastfeeding a six-week-old daughter named Rachel. They lived on an isolated farm in the Southern Highlands of New South Wales, between Berry and Kangaroo Valley.

Nicole's black kelpie scampered to the front door. Cradling Rachel, Nicole opened it. Two middle-aged strangers stood on the porch.

"Happy Easter," said Michael Shelley.

Mormons, thought Nicole.

"My name is Michael," he said. "This is my wife, Mary. We are very old friends of Astrid. She said that you might have a cabin where we could stay."

Astrid was the Norwegian naturopath in Berry. Normally, she called ahead. Normally, the lodgers she sent had luggage with them. But the Shelleys didn't seem threatening. They looked hopeless and possibly homeless.

"Oh, friends of Astrid!" said Nicole. "I'm afraid I don't have much food."

"Don't apologise," said Michael. "God blesses your kindness."

Nicole showed Michael and Mary to their accommodation. It was an early settler's cabin. A swimming hole divided the main home from the rustic cubby house. The orange and grapefruit trees were empty heading into winter. Beyond the backyard was the endless forest of the Kangaroo Valley.

The next day, Michael borrowed a spade. Directly beside the cabin, he dug a hole for pissing and shitting purposes. Nicole was familiar with earth removal. Usually, the cavity got wider the further you went down. She could scarcely believe her eyes. The chute was the width of a spade the whole way down.

Mary occupied her time washing and polishing the glasses and cutlery in the cabin. Michael inspected the seemingly clean dishes for imperfections.

"This is a rotten job, Mary," said Michael. "Do it again."

The Shelleys lived off teabags and condensed milk. Nicole drank tea with them while breastfeeding Rachel. Mary watched with adoration and anguish. She had suffered six miscarriages since the birth of Joshua in 1984.

"Do you have children?" asked Nicole.

Mary looked at Michael for permission to speak. He nodded cautiously.

"I have a daughter," said Mary. "But she doesn't talk to me."

"There is nothing more precious in the world than a little girl," said Nicole.

"Do you mind if I hold her?" asked Mary.

"Of course not," said Nicole.

Mary nursed Rachel with a maternal tenderness. At first, Nicole was flattered by her wide-eyed wonder. It was just another small kindness.

"I pray to God to bless my womb with a daughter!" said Mary.

"Fingers crossed," said Nicole.

✚

The following Sunday, Nicole and her husband David took Rachel to the Berry markets. It was the first time Michael and Mary had been left alone. Back at home, Nicole noticed that some of David's cassettes were missing. She found them in a drawer of the cabin. Michael had entered the house and taken them.

"Michael, did you take my husband's tapes?" she asked.

"Everything here belongs to GOD," he said, dismissively.

Nicole left the tapes in the cabin. But she was troubled by the intrusion. That afternoon, Mary visited the house. She was less overbearing than Michael.

"I'm sorry about the tapes," said Mary. "You look completely exhausted. How about I take Rachel for a walk in the garden while you have a nap?"

Nicole accepted the offer. But she had newfound doubts about her eccentric guests. She called Astrid, the naturopath, for a character reference.

"How well do you know Michael and Mary?" asked Nicole.

"I don't know them from a bar of soap," said Astrid.

"Michael told me you were old friends!"

"No," said Astrid. "He knocked on my door a week ago looking for somewhere to stay. They seemed nice. But I'd never met them before in my life."

Nicole's consternation turned to terror. She ran to the garden. Mary and Rachel were missing. Nicole found them a hundred metres away, on the front steps of the cabin. Mary was attempting to breastfeed her daughter.

"What are you doing?" asked Nicole, snatching Rachel back.

"Can you please calm down," said Mary.

"I don't want you to touch my daughter anymore," said Nicole.

"Mary's breast milk is a gift!" snarled Michael.

The mother ran back through the garden with her daughter. Crying hysterically, Nicole locked all the doors and windows, barricading herself from Michael and Mary. She found David in his sound-proofed music studio.

"They tried to take Rachel!" she said.

The sensitive pianist was the wrong person to undertake an eviction. When he tried, Michael transformed from a preacher into a screaming banshee. Nicole ushered David inside and locked the doors. She called the police.

"You need to leave!" she yelled at the Shelleys.

Nicole couldn't see Michael. But she could hear him through the timber walls and glass windows. She would never forget the threat that he made.

"One day, I will come back and take her when you least expect it!"

The Shelleys vanished. But Nicole didn't feel safe. She drove at high speed to the Nowra police station. The local cops tried to calm her down. She got her breath back and related the insane fable.

"They were planning to kidnap my daughter!" she said.

The constable's frown was sympathetic yet sceptical.

"It must be a stressful time, having a newborn baby," he said.

"Please, don't patronise me," said Nicole. "There is something seriously deranged about these people. I'm not leaving until I speak to a detective."

Nicole sat in the chief detective's office, while he searched for Michael and Mary Shelley in the police database. Ten minutes later, face ashen, the detective returned to the office with a stack of concertinaed printer paper. He stood on a chair and dramatically raised the stack with his right hand. Then dropped the paper. It fanned from the ceiling to the floor like an accordion.

"There are five outstanding warrants for this man's arrest," he said.

Two police cars squealed in opposite directions from the station. That night, Michael and Mary stayed at a motel in Bomaderry. They evaded the police. The Shelleys caught a train to Canberra, en route to Adelaide.

Michael left behind a series of ticking time bombs. He lodged a formal complaint with the RSPCA about the treatment of the black kelpie. And another with Children's Services about the abuse of Rachel. Nicole was visited by a social worker, who quickly dismissed the baseless accusations.

Michael Shelley's face became engraved on Nicole's brain. Whenever she spotted a skinny male with a beard and a ponytail, her body vibrated.

The final surprise: Michael Shelley had planted a seed from God-knows-where in the shithole beside the cabin. It grew into an enormous cedar tree. The branches cast a serene silhouette over the waterhole. As Rachel grew up, the cedar tree was a perpetual testament to stranger danger.

The Miracle Box

At the pub in Chinchilla, Lenore and Tom Blaine provided shelter to dozens of short-term foster care placements. Some stayed for one night only. Others stayed for months. The children had suffered various levels of physical and emotional injuries. Trent, Steven and John treated them like brothers and sisters, not fine china. But then they were gone again. It was frustrating.

"Mum, can you get us a sister?" asked Steven.

"How good would that be!" said John.

"Never say never," Lenore told him.

At the age of thirty-four, she had stopped taking the pill. The three boys were settled and convinced that their foster parents were going to love them for the long haul. Lenore had never stopped craving a baby of her own.

In the private quarters of the Tattersalls Hotel, Tom impregnated his wife with relative ease. But getting pregnant had never been Lenore's issue.

"I don't want to count my chickens before they hatch," she told Tom.

"Don't crush the eggs, either," he said. "Be a bit optimistic."

Lenore's fifth pregnancy lasted less than a month. It left her like a bad period. Trent, Steven and John were none the wiser. Lenore kept the sorrow to herself. She didn't want the boys to suspect that they weren't enough.

Lenore fell pregnant again. The first month passed smoothly. Then the second, and the third. It was the longest that her womb had harboured a human heartbeat. Lenore took Tom's advice. She counted her chickens for once.

Over a Sunday roast at the pub, Tom announced the news.

"Ya mum's got one up the duff," said Tom, chuffed.

"I might be having a baby," said Lenore, worriedly.

"A real baby?" asked Steven.

"As real as the nose on your face, mate," said Tom.

"Fair dinkum," said John, looking cross-eyed at his nostrils.

The boys were overjoyed. Lenore had never felt less pessimistic. At the four-month mark, the Blaines visited Brisbane for an ultrasound.

"Would you like to know the sex?" asked the specialist.

"What is it?" asked Tom, without consulting his wife.

"A girl," said the doctor.

Tom kissed Lenore on the lips. Her adrenaline rush was followed by dread. Don't crush the eggs, thought Lenore. Soon, everyone in Chinchilla knew that the publicans were expecting. The bar was swamped with baby clothes.

Lenore woke in the middle of the night. A tidal wave of worry flooded her guts. The dam walls around the baby broke. Blood gushed onto the sheets.

"I'll call an ambulance," muttered Tom. "She'll be right."

Lenore nodded. But she knew that there was no life to save.

++

Tom decided to sell the lease of the Tattersalls Hotel. The Blaines purchased the lease of a pub in Wondai, population 1000. Tom loaded a rusted slippery-dip and swing set onto a train bound for dust and tumbleweeds. Wondai was two hours northeast. The area was a hotbed of peanut farmers and right-wing Christians. Lenore didn't mind. She was sick of Chinchilla's sympathy.

The Wondai Hotel was a two-storey timber pub with a rusted corrugated iron roof. A massive veranda hung over the footpath out the front. Wondai had two other pubs and an RSL. The first month of business was slow.

"At this rate, we'll go broke," Lenore told Tom.

"Rome wasn't built in a month," he said.

The Blaines were invited to an afternoon barbecue. The new publican carried a complimentary keg. The backyard cheered his generosity. Tom shattered a few bags of party ice, like they were piñatas. Then he put the ice in "the Miracle Box". It was an esky with a tap attached. There was a tube running to the keg. Cold beer poured from the tap.

"Tom Blaine," yelled a stranger. "The Great Man!"

Trent, Steven and John watched their foster father with reverence. To them he was a god. That manly handshake. Those large, crossed arms. The roaring laughter. Tom wasn't the most talkative person at the barbecue, but he became the centre of gravity.

"You're a popular man, Thomas," said Lenore on the way home.

Within a month, the Wondai Hotel was booming. Tom's wallet filled with fifties again. He became president of the bowls club, the golf club and the football club – the Wondai Wolves. Steven was six. John was five. Tom signed his sons up to play rugby league. He taught them to pass, tackle and kick, so they could be like Trent, who was a full-blown champion athlete.

After football training, Lenore sat on the front veranda in a rocking chair. She churned through half-a-dozen books a week. Trent, Steven and John rode pushbikes along the footpath downstairs. They evaded green ants and spiders in the daylight and mosquitoes at night.

"Dinner time," said Lenore, trying to shout, but without the heart to be harsh.

The Blaine brothers rehydrated straight from the corrugated iron tank out the back. The brass tap was swathed by a shrub of mint. Upstairs, they kissed their mum. She smelled nature's Colgate on their breaths. No grace before dinner; just the everyday prayer of adoration on Lenore's face.

A Fortress of Thorns

In Brisbane, Paul Shelley awaited trial for threatening to kill the Queensland premier. Michael and Mary rescued him in a Commodore station wagon. Paul lay down in the back underneath a blanket. Via the Gold Coast hinterland, the Shelley Gang drove south. Their hideout was a farmhouse in the Adelaide Hills.

Michael made a straw bed in the barn for a great big billy goat. He tethered the goat to the side of the barn so it could eat the grass that hid the brown snakes. Paul helped Michael plant rose bushes, a fortress of thorns.

Irritation crept into Michael's interactions with his unmedicated stepson. Paul cramped Michael and Mary's latest procreation attempts.

At the age of forty-six, Mary fell pregnant again. Michael lost interest in waging war against the Queensland state government. Paul went cold turkey on his attention. One morning, Paul woke up unable to move or speak.

"Don't be silly, Paul," said Michael.

Paul wasn't being silly. Michael put him back in the boot of the station wagon. The streets of Adelaide rushed across the windscreen. Paul couldn't see where they were going, but he trusted that salvation was waiting for him.

Michael dumped Paul at the front door of a psychiatric ward. He had no intention of risking his liberty. Police officers found Paul in the gutter. One of them jabbed Paul in the bladder with a baton. It didn't break the strange spell. The silent disciple pissed himself. He was admitted to hospital.

The paralysis ended. The hospital called Lionel Long, Paul's estranged biological father. Paul flew back to Sydney for a bitter family reunion. He borrowed $25 from the secretary of Lionel's acting school.

"What is wrong with you, Roman?" asked Lionel.

"My name is Paul!" he roared. "Call me by my real name!"

A physical altercation erupted between father and son. Paul was arrested for assault. Lionel refused to pay the insignificant bail. This was revenge for Paul's betrayal. Paul was placed into the mental health section of Long Bay Prison. A guard slammed his face into a basin.

At the trial, the judge connected the dots between Paul Shelley and the harassment of Mike Ahern. The Queensland government was notified. Paul was flown north to face charges of threatening to kill the premier and his family. Where was Michael? Paul had sacrificed his father, his identity, his sanity for the prophet. In Paul's hour of need, Michael dropped his disciple.

✟

Mary Shelley was thirty-six weeks pregnant. In the Adelaide Hills, Michael sensed social workers and police officers circling. He purchased one-way tickets to New Zealand. Michael planned to prove his parenting chops to the Kiwis. Then, he could crusade for the extradition of Elijah, Saul and Joshua.

Belatedly, Michael Shelley came to Paul's aid. From the safety of a phone box in Wellington, he provided Paul with a crash course in criminal law. It was the autumn of 1990. Paul elected to represent himself in the Brisbane District Court. *The Courier-Mail* photographed the angry Christian for the front page. He had a thick beard, frizzy ponytail and wild eyes.

The jury selection presented a media spectacle. Paul was allowed eight peremptory challenges. He exhausted them against eight female jurors.

"I need to have a male jury, otherwise I cannot proceed, due to my religious beliefs," said Paul. "Female jurors are an abomination of God."

The prosecutor, Margaret, was a blonde barrister. She implored Judge Forno to reject the peculiar request, arguing that to allow it would set a dangerous precedent, especially for rape trials.

"I don't know how he feels about the prosecution?" she asked.

Paul Shelley directed his response to the judge, not the prosecutor.

"I wouldn't have a female prosecutor," said Paul. "But I have nothing against women. Their creation on this earth is very important."

Judge Forno granted Paul's controversial demand. He cited the open hostility the defendant had already generated from potential female jurors. The decision provoked condemnation from Australia's legal community. The Queensland attorney-general appealed. The judge held firm. Paul presented his defence to an all-male jury. The trial was peppered with discursive outbursts. He accused his famous father, Lionel Long, of abuse and assault.

Paul received an unexpected godsend. The main witness, Mike Ahern, ignored the court summons. He had no desire to see his stalker in the flesh again. Ironically, Ahern had taken off on a family holiday to New Zealand.

"Mr Ahern has shown total disregard for the people of Queensland," proclaimed Paul. "He has put his own self-indulgent whims above the law."

The judge threatened to arrest the ex-premier. Paul was released on a technicality. He purchased a one-way ticket to New Zealand.

✢

Michael and Mary Shelley hitchhiked from Wellington to Whanganui, a town on the west coast of the North Island. They checked into the Acacia Park Motel. The three-star establishment sat on the Whanganui River. Michael neglected to mention his wife's pregnancy to the motel manager.

At 5 am on 18 April, Mary's waters broke. Michael performed the duties of a midwife. For two hours, Mary squatted over clean towels on the bathroom floor. A bloody baby slipped out. It had a slit between the legs.

"It's a girl!" declared Michael.

"My prayers have been answered!" said Mary.

Mary was a mother again at the age of forty-seven. She bathed and breastfed the baby. Michael tied and cut the umbilical cord. Their daughter needed a name. Hannah was the infertile wife of Elkanah. God had shut Hannah's womb and then opened it again, birthing the prophet Samuel.

"Her name shall be Hannah!" said Michael.

"Oh, what a beautiful name!" said Mary.

Hannah fell asleep in Mary's arms. None of Michael's big words could do justice to her love for that dark-haired, olive-skinned baby girl. She was Carole Newgrosh reborn, with the lifetime guarantee of a mother's love.

Forty-five minutes later, Mary squeezed out the placenta under the piping hot water in the shower. Michael lovingly studied the pancake of blood and tissue. He dismembered the evidence and flushed it down the toilet. The Shelleys ate a continental breakfast and checked out of the Acacia Park Motel.

"We left absolutely no sign of what had happened," wrote Michael.

The Saint of Flexible Expectations

Lenore begged the Department of Child Safety for a foster daughter. At long last, they found one. Rebecca was nine months old. Her biological mother, Cassandra, had grown up in foster care due to the alcoholism of her own mother.

Cassandra drank heavily during her pregnancy with Rebecca. The baby was born with foetal alcohol syndrome. Her father was one of two brothers. Rebecca never met either of them. She was fatherless.

"This would be your toughest placement yet," warned Susan King.

Rebecca was younger than any of Lenore's previous foster children. She wept relentlessly and rarely slept, requiring constant attention.

"Trent was pretty tough," said Lenore.

"He was a walk in the park compared to Rebecca," said Susan.

Kids with foetal alcohol syndrome were the hot potatoes of the foster care system for a reason. They bounced around between placements, too testing even for the benevolent. Those rejections were a recipe for low self-esteem. Which was a recipe for a continuing cycle of addiction.

"Susan, if I was desperate for perfection, I would've become a jeweller, not a foster mum," said Lenore. "Rebecca sounds wonderful."

Lenore paid a visit to Rebecca in Brisbane. She had a small face and red cheeks. In Lenore's calm arms, the baby girl frowned and wept, spat and scratched. Lenore smiled at her tears like they were diamonds. Rebecca grinned and giggled with a glee equal to the previous grief.

"How would you like to come and live with me?" asked Lenore. "You would have Daddy Tom and three big brothers: Trent, Steven and John. Mummy Cassandra can come and see us, too. You would get two mums!"

It was fate. Rebecca needed a mother even more than Lenore needed a daughter. And she needed a mother like this one. Lenore Blaine was the Saint of Flexible Expectations. The Blaines became a family of six.

⊹

Once a month, a social worker with a psychology degree named Sharon paid a visit to the Wondai Hotel. Tom stood behind the front bar with crossed arms and a thousand-yard stare. There was one customer in the pub.

"Hi, Tom," said Sharon. "Have you got time for a chat?"

"I'm a bit busy," he said. "The missus and kids are upstairs."

Tom had a deep-seated distrust of authority figures: schoolteachers, police officers, priests, parking inspectors, the Queen, and social workers. Mainly, he hated the regular reminders that Trent, Steven, John and Rebecca came with strings attached. Lenore, on the other hand, was afraid of authority, and eager to impress those who had it. Social workers were her soulmates. She regaled them with the developmental milestones of her foster kids.

Steven and John met with the social worker separately from Trent and Rebecca. Steven was Lenore's proxy. John was Tom's. Steven politely bragged about his progress in grade two. He was the smartest in the class.

"My teacher says I'm a better reader than most of the kids in grade four," said Steven. "I was like: wow! I really do love reading. So does Mum."

John hated grade one. He wanted to be at the pub, watching Tom play darts against the barflies and listening to all their tall stories. In the meeting, John death-stared the social worker like she was a potential kidnapper.

"How are you, John?" Sharon asked.

"Not bad," muttered John.

"John doesn't like reading as much as me," said Steven.

"Shut up, ya brown-noser!" said John, forehead furrowed.

"Sorry, John," said Steven. "That was rude. You can read, too."

Steven was always inquisitive about his biological parents. He asked Sharon if he could see a recent photograph of Michael and Mary Shelley.

"How do you feel about them?" asked the social worker.

"They look like nice people," said Steven. "Mum told me that my real dad was a very smart guy and that my real mum was a very nice woman."

"How about you, John?" asked Sharon.

John studied the photograph of the Shelleys. He remained in denial that he was a foster boy. He was a Blaine, plain and simple.

"That's not my real mum and dad," said John.

"Yes, it is, John," sighed Steven, rolling his eyes.

"No, it's not!" cried John. "Mum and Dad are my real mum and dad!"

Operation Good Samaritan

The Shelleys purchased a cheap car to show Hannah the country of her birth. Over the next month, they left a heroic trail of unpaid motel bills stretching from Wellington to Auckland. Michael was arrested. He spent his forty-fourth birthday in Mt Eden Prison. The entrance evoked a medieval church.

Mary acquired a car. She packed Hannah into the baby seat. There was only one place to go: the Bay of Plenty. It was on the west coast, two and a half hours south of Auckland. In Tauranga, Mary passed through the suburb of Bethlehem, en route to Judea. She pulled up at the Boulevard Motel.

Mary climbed from the driver's seat. Unfortunately, Michael had always insisted on taking the wheel, leaving his wife inexperienced with gearsticks and handbrakes. With Hannah in the backseat, the car reversed into a rubber tree.

The next day, a wrecker offered Mary $200 for the undriveable car. Mary and Hannah caught a bus to Auckland for Michael's court date. The judge considered extending Michael's bail, so that he could pay his debts.

"God needs you to release Michael immediately!" shouted Mary.

A loyal wife hindered Michael's charade of sanity. The New Zealand Department of Social Services was alerted to the existence of an erratic mother with a newborn baby. Further investigations revealed that Michael and Mary Shelley had three children in the Queensland foster care system.

Peter was a 32-year-old social worker. The long-haired free spirit wore jeans and t-shirts to work. Susan King responded to news of a fourth Shelley child with a militant urgency. In Auckland, Peter walked briskly to the courtroom. He handed the fresh intelligence to the judge.

Michael was enraged but articulate. He accused New Zealand of being in cahoots with Queensland. Mary appeared deeply haunted and possibly psychotic. She demanded a break in proceedings to breastfeed Hannah.

"Mary has locked herself in the toilet and refuses to come out," announced the police prosecutor. "This is a ploy to disrupt the hearing."

A psychiatrist collected Hannah from Mary. Michael was placed back into custody. Mary fled the courtroom for the British consulate. She was charged with abandoning a baby. Peter received a safety warrant for Hannah Shelley. Her first foster carers were two women named Anne and Mary.

※

Without Hannah, the Shelleys went back to the Bay of Plenty. Michael discovered a Christian charity group called Operation Good Samaritan. He convinced the administrator, Raymond, to lend him a church van.

"It is the Lord's van," said Raymond. "I'm sure you will return it."

Michael stole the van. They used it to wage a PR campaign across the North Island. The Shelleys lobbied politicians for custody of Hannah. After five weeks, they were arrested again. Michael was back in the newspaper.

SO-CALLED PASTOR STEALS CHURCH VAN

Michael and Mary were sent for a month of psychiatric testing at the Carrington Hospital, formerly known as the Whau Lunatic Asylum. It was a regal building in Point Chevalier, surrounded by trees and gardens.

Hannah's social worker, Peter, paid the Shelleys a hospital visit. The front door was locked. Inside, Peter discovered a novel psychiatric experiment. The doctors and nurses wore jeans and t-shirts. They were indistinguishable from the patients, and the patients from them.

In the living room, Michael sat cross-legged on a rug. He serenaded the patients with acoustic covers. A circle of captivated women clapped and cheered the troubadour. Mary was hunted on all fronts. Her daughter had been taken. Now the other female inpatients wanted to fuck her husband.

"Michael is mine!" Mary hissed at them.

Peter brought Hannah back to the psych ward for family bonding. To Michael, she appeared pale and chubby, not slim and tanned. Into Hannah's basket, he slipped a hand-written diatribe addressed to her foster carers.

"You have no business fostering children to fill the void in your dreary existences," he wrote. "You can't fake love! If you continue to abuse Hannah, you are in for a series of unpleasant surprises, all thoroughly deserved."

Paul Shelley arrived from Australia to join the crusade for custody of Hannah. He ambushed her social worker Peter on Queen Street. Paul followed him to the Waiheke Island ferry terminal, chanting accusations of child abuse.

The social worker boarded the 5.30 pm ferry to Waiheke Island, where he lived with a wife and baby. Peter bought himself a beer to take the edge off. The Shelleys, he thought to himself, were a different kettle of fish.

Gift Horses

At the age of forty-one, Tom Blaine received the deal of a lifetime. His famous nephew, Allan Langer, was selected for the 1990 Kangaroo Tour. The Australian rugby league team would play matches for two months in England and France. At Allan's glitzy wedding in Brisbane, Tom made a speech on behalf of the Blaine family. Allan offered to shout his uncle a trip to Europe.

"That's bloody unbelievable," said Tom to Lenore afterwards.

Lenore couldn't believe it either. They had four children under the age of eleven, and her husband wanted to disappear to Europe for three weeks.

"Would you be happy if I flew to Europe for a holiday?" she asked.

"You're terrified of flying!" said Tom. "And you hate holidays."

"I think you're missing the point, and not just slightly," she said.

Tom sheepishly admitted that the flights had already been booked. It was a reminder – if Lenore needed one – that Tom's priorities extended beyond his family. Whether or not she hated flying, Lenore couldn't imagine spending even a day separated from their children.

"You can't look a gift horse in the mouth," he said.

"That depends on your definition of a gift," said Lenore.

Lenore organised for Margaret Clarke – Trent, Steven and John's first foster mother – to relieve her husband from his parenting duties.

Tom flew economy from Brisbane to Sydney, to Singapore, to Paris. He caught a taxi from Charles de Gaulle Airport to a hostel in Pigalle, the red-light district. The next day, jetlagged and hungover, he strode through the miserable Paris streets in tracksuits and a XXXX

Gold spray jacket. A Brisbane Broncos beret covered his greying hair. He arrived at the Eiffel Tower.

"Is this it?" he muttered.

Tom was preoccupied on his way back to the precinct of bars and strip clubs. Two muggers picked the passport and wallet from opposite pockets of his tracksuit. He gave chase, but it was zero use, due to his bad hip. Nobody intervened to help. That night, he wrote a succinct postcard to Lenore in Wondai.

"Paris is a shithole," he scrawled. "Some bastard stole my passport."

Tom vastly preferred the gritty industrial towns of Northern England. He could walk into any pub and play darts with the coalminers until last drinks. All the battlers of Northern England could talk about was Lech Walesa. The Berlin Wall had fallen. The Soviet Union was in its final throes. Walesa – Tom's political hero – was about to be elected president of Poland.

"England needs a Lech," said a weathered old trade unionist.

Walesa was a high-school dropout. He had worked as a sparky in the shipyards while moonlighting as a trade union official and revolutionary. And he was a dead ringer for Tom, both in appearance and populist spirit.

"Australia needs a Lech," Tom whispered.

Tom couldn't stop thinking about Lech. He saw that walrus moustache everywhere: on newspaper stands, in magazines, on TVs at the freezing pubs. It had never occurred to Tom that someone like him could run a country.

╬

Lenore spent Tom's sabbatical thinking about fertility. According to Susan King, Mary Shelley had given birth to a baby girl named Hannah at the age of forty-seven. Lenore was eleven years younger. Not all hope was lost.

Steven and John were learning about a world beyond Wondai. Their father, Tom, sent postcards from France and England. Their mother, Lenore, received phone calls about the existence of their younger sister in New Zealand. Susan wanted to reunite Hannah with her biological brothers.

"Can we go to New Zealand?" Steven asked Lenore.

"I'd miss you too much, Stevie," said Lenore.

Lenore wanted to kill two birds with one stone: a foster daughter, and a biological daughter. She read an article in *Reader's Digest* about a wonder drug called Premarin. It replaced the fading supplies of estrogen in the ovaries of ageing women. A middle-aged American woman with a history of miscarriages had begun taking Premarin for menopause, not fertility. Then, at the age of forty-three, she fell pregnant and gave birth to a baby girl.

The special ingredient of Premarin? The urine of pregnant mares. Alas, Lenore's doctor in Wondai refused to prescribe Premarin for fertility.

"I'm not a witch doctor," he said.

"Lucky I'm not a witch," said Lenore.

For the first time in her life, Lenore bent the rules and took a gamble. She got one of Tom's sisters to source a Premarin prescription for menopause. Her sister-in-law posted the box of tablets to Wondai. Lenore swallowed the big maroon pills with mugs of minty tank water. She gained weight.

Tom arrived home lugging a second travel bag filled with English rugby league jerseys for his chuffed sons. He was bursting with trivia about Polish politics. Lenore was unprecedentedly horny. The Blaines slept together every night. Tom kept scepticism about the wonder drug to himself.

On the other side of the bed, Lenore silently begged God for one good egg. A baby girl named Amy Blaine. A bookworm. She saw her, not him.

The Exodus of Hannah Shelley

Michael and Mary Shelley were released from the psychiatric hospital. They regained custody of Hannah at the Auckland Courthouse. With Paul in tow, the Shelleys relocated to Waiheke Island, the home of Hannah's social worker, Peter. It was an hour-long ferry ride from Auckland to paradise.

Michael somehow found a way to rent a house with the best views on the entire island. 1 Miro Road, Palm Beach. It was a two-bedroom timber cottage. The front veranda directly overlooked the pristine white sand of Palm Beach. You could watch dolphins swimming through the turquoise seawater from the kitchen window. Snowy seabirds skimmed the ocean for fish.

Michael and Mary had the master bedroom. Hannah shared a room with Paul. Mary attempted to return her baby daughter to the breast, but her milk supply ran dry. She felt redundant. The anxiety had a similar intensity to the type that had nearly killed her following the birth of Paul in 1968. She was admitted to hospital for three days and diagnosed with major depression.

"Mary is experiencing difficulties breastfeeding her daughter," the psychiatrist wrote. "She reports subsequent feelings of guilt and distress."

Michael looked after Mary. Paul bathed his baby sister and changed her nappies. He walked Hannah to Palm Beach. A rocky cliff and phoenix palm trees sat at the eastern tip of the shoreline. Paul dipped Hannah's tiny feet in the tide. Her laugh touched his soul. He fed her banana and yogurt.

Hannah's social worker, Peter, performed regular check-ups. Mary was bedridden. Hannah was under the ad hoc guardianship of Paul. A GP reported that Hannah had stopped growing upon return to the Shelleys.

The Department of Child Welfare ordered an examination at the Auckland Children's Hospital. The paediatrician prodded and probed the baby. He stated categorically that Hannah had insufficient fat tissue.

The Shelleys had a unique way of ingratiating themselves with the medical experts deciding their fate. They plastered fliers around the hospital accusing the paediatrician of molesting Hannah. After a month in hospital, Hannah received a diagnosis of non-organic failure to thrive (NOFTT).

"Hannah was in a state of malnourishment upon admission as a result of a deprived diet," the paediatrician wrote. "The Shelleys have a rigid and intense parenting style. Their fanatical beliefs about weight are dangerous and life-threatening."

Hannah was placed back into foster care with a divorced nurse named Wendy. Her case made its way through the courts. Michael was arrested again and held on remand at Mt Eden Prison. He invited Peter for a meeting. Mary was rapidly deteriorating. Michael knew that the prosecutor would annihilate his wife's credibility on cross-examination.

"If you ensure that Hannah will be reunited with Saul and Joshua in Queensland, Mary and I will sign the guardianship order," Michael told Peter.

Michael's calculation was two-pronged. Saul and Joshua would protect their own flesh and blood from the presumably abusive carers. And if the trio were together, it would be easier to locate and reclaim them at a later date.

☩

Peter organised Hannah's audacious extradition to Australia. He flew with her to Brisbane. For hours, the social worker played peek-a-boo with the one-year-old girl. She didn't flinch as the tyres of the plane hit the tarmac.

A Queensland social worker was waiting for them at the arrival lounge. He was more businesslike than Peter. The boot of his white

Ford Falcon contained three spare tyres. Peter struggled to fit the luggage inside.

"What are all the tyres for?" asked Peter.

"We're going to the bush," said the other social worker.

From the airport, the social worker drove evasively to prevent any of Michael's disciples following them to their secret destination. Peter watched the suburban sprawl fritter away into nothingness. Highways were lined with tall gum trees. Dusty scrub was punctuated by one-pub towns.

Outside the Wondai Hotel was a line of utes and 4WDs. The Blaines waited on the front deck. Lenore, Tom, Trent, Steven, John and Rebecca.

"Hannah! Hannah!" chanted the children. "Hannah! Hannah!"

Steven and John looked at Hannah's face and saw themselves: dark hair and olive skin. The two brothers bustled to touch the bundle of joy first.

"I'm Steven!"

"I'm John!"

Peter passed Hannah to Lenore, allowing her to adjudicate.

"Aren't you a beautiful girl?" she said.

"What a unit," said Tom. "Hannah, the Big Goanna!"

The Blaines became a family of seven. Steven and John each held one of Hannah's chubby hands. Rebecca raced around euphorically. A little sister! Hannah processed the avalanche of affection with curiosity and confusion.

"Give her a break," said Trent, the protective eldest brother.

Tom welcomed Peter with a bone-breaking handshake.

"Thanks for ya help, champ," said Tom. "Tough bloody effort."

That was the extent of Tom's dialogue with Peter about the foster care placement. He wasn't particularly interested in the backstory. Inside the pub, the heathen half of Wondai was waiting to celebrate Hannah's arrival. Someone cued "Slice of Heaven" by Dave Dobbyn – a Kiwi – on the jukebox.

"Do you want some fush and chups?" Steven and John kept asking Hannah, imitating the accent they believed would soon emerge from her mouth.

Around 7 pm, Peter and Lenore took Hannah upstairs, to the heartbreak of Steven and John. Hannah needed some sleep. Lenore showed the social worker to his room. Then Lenore, Hannah and Peter sat on the veranda overhanging the street. Lenore fed Hannah for the first time. Hannah slurped greedily from the spoon offered by her new foster mother.

"Sorry about the kids going so troppo," said Lenore. "They've been dreaming about this. I'd say they're not usually that excitable. But I'd be lying."

"Your kids are beautiful," said Peter. "They seem very happy."

From Peter, Lenore gleaned information about Hannah and her biological parents. The scruffy mum spoke about child trauma with the erudition of a psychologist. Few people got to see such an incisive side of Lenore; mainly the social workers who became her inner sanctum.

"I loved Hannah from the moment I knew she existed," said Lenore. "I felt her absence. Not in some superstitious way. She needed to be here. Not for my sake. For Steven and John's sake. And for Hannah's sake."

On Saturday, Tom organised a local farmer to take Peter for a tour of a macadamia plantation. The sunburnt Kiwi came back in the late afternoon. "Drinks are on me," said Tom, pouring a beer for Peter and a scotch for himself. The main thing they had in common was a fondness for alcohol.

The following afternoon, the flash government car arrived from Brisbane. The Blaines gave Peter a kilo of salted cashews as a thank-you present. He hugged Hannah goodbye. Rebecca wanted a hug, too. The three boys gave him a firm handshake while making direct eye contact, imitating Tom.

Peter usually had a sinking feeling in his stomach when he left a child with new parents. All too often, the placement was the least-worst option. That day, there was no guilt or dread. Hannah had won the foster care lottery.

✢

Peter saw Michael Shelley one more time. It was at the child safety offices on Queen Street in Auckland. Peter gave Michael some photographs of Saul and Joshua – aka Steven and John – courtesy of Lenore. Michael sat leafing through the pictures of his sons. In one of them, Steven wore a t-shirt that read "Ipswich Swimming Club", a hand-me-down from a cousin.

"Oh, you can tell so much from a photo, can't you?" asked Michael, with a sinister grin.

"Michael, forget it," said Peter. "They don't live in Ipswich."

Michael left the office. But he never stopped yearning for the return of his biological children, or to learn the identities of their foster parents.

CHAPTER SIX

The Good Egg

The wondrous arrival of Hannah made my mother clucky. In her diary, she was able to pinpoint the orgasm that produced my conception with precision. It was the Sunday night after the departure of Hannah's social worker. Mum put the kids to bed. Dad shut the pub. They sat on the veranda together.

"I always pictured five kids," said my father.

"Six has a nice ring to it," said my mother.

Mum was still taking the Premarin. Dad whistled his mating call. The Blaines retreated to the dark master bedroom. The deed was done.

"Good one?" asked Mum.

"That was enough cum to knock up an elephant!" he said.

Mum's bloodlessness was followed by the rising bile of morning sickness. The boys went to school. Rebecca entertained Hannah in their shared room. My mother peed onto a pregnancy test from the chemist. It was positive. So was the second. She didn't tell Dad until they went to bed that night.

"What are you so happy about, Larry?" he asked.

"I might have some good news," she said.

"We won the lotto?"

"Maybe," she said. "I'm pregnant!"

Mum passed the four-month mark – the previous record – with flying colours. Her stomach craved vanilla slices from the Wondai Bakery. My brothers attributed her growing weight to the intake of those pink and yellow pastries.

Over a Sunday roast, Dad announced the news to my siblings. There were no mixed emotions for Trent, Steven and John. They hailed my mother's womb like it contained baby Jesus himself. Rebecca and Hannah ditched their Cabbage Patch Dolls for the real McCoy. They spent days tickling Mum's stomach and whispering gibberish to me, competing for ownership.

"My baby," said Hannah.

"My baby!" said Rebecca.

At the six-month mark, in mid-spring, an ultrasound at the Kingaroy Hospital showed a nugget of humanity without any glaring deformities. This time, the expectant mother didn't want to know the sex of the baby. Due to her "geriatric pregnancy", the doctors made preparations for a caesarean.

Mum cut back from a packet of smokes a day to half-a-dozen. The Department of Child Safety chipped in for a cleaner and paid my parents a special grant to buy a minibus. Steven begged Mum to let him take a photo of her baby bump. This sounded like the definition of counting her chickens.

"I'm not sure, sweetie," she said.

"Come on, Mum!" said John.

Mum stood on the stairs at the Wondai Hotel, barefoot in a maternity dress. Hair cut short. Hands behind her back to emphasise the bun in the oven.

"Three, two, one," said Trent, Steven and John. "Say cheese!"

My mother summoned a smile to disguise her anxiety.

"Cheese," she whispered.

The Christmas of 1991 was pretty biblical. Excitement enveloped Wondai, like a rumour of a visit from the Queen. Mum received enough clothes for a hundred babies. She set up a cot in the master bedroom.

"Amy Blaine," she whispered to me. "See you soon, beautiful."

⁓

My emergence into the world had been pencilled in for 22 January 1992, a humid Wednesday afternoon. Mum and Dad made the final drive past the sawmills and peanut farms to the Kingaroy Hospital.

Twelve-year-old Trent, in his final year of primary school, had been given the honour of joining Mum and Dad on the best day of their lives. He came armed with a brand-new video camera.

"Boy or girl?" asked Dad.

"It's gotta be a boy," said Trent. "For sure."

"We'll see," said Mum.

"What should we call him?" asked Dad.

"Victor," said Trent.

"Victor?" asked Mum. "Why on earth *Victor*?"

"Like our lawnmower," said Trent, earnestly.

Mum was less obsessed with the name of the baby than with its mere existence. She had a back-up plan for the unforeseen expression of testicles.

"I like Jamie," she said.

"Amy or Jamie," said Tom. "Shit, I thought you were creative!"

After thirteen years of infertility, the miracle was matter-of-fact. My mother's body was draped in a green sheet with a slim flap. The anaesthetist injected her veins with a cocktail of painkillers. Her butt and legs felt heavy and aflame. She passed out. The obstetrician slit a straight line across her stomach. An enormous head surged through the temporary exit.

"I haven't seen a cranium quite that large," said the obstetrician.

"For all the brains, mate," said my father, tapping his temple.

I was varnished in a thin veneer of blood and crying at a polite volume, a vital sign of life. The umbilical cord was cut. The obstetrician removed the placenta from a seeping uterus. The scrub nurse placed me into a container for a bath. Dad studied the lotto ticket of my genitals for the ultimate jackpot.

"You little ripper!" he shouted, loud enough for Trent to hear, but not loud enough to penetrate his wife's drug-induced stupor.

All of a sudden, the abyss didn't frighten my father quite so much. He had done the deed. The meaning of life, as he loosely knew it. To pass the torch of blood and name. To keep the flame of his parents' love burning.

The nurses had run out of the blue sheets for boys. I was wrapped in a pink one. Trent aimed the video camera at the door of the operating theatre.

"It's a girl," he sighed with disappointment when Dad appeared.

"Nah, dig," said Dad. "They've stitched up ya poor mum."

Mum was relocated to the postnatal ward. She awoke to her husband and son grinning deliriously. Dad was nursing a pink-sheeted bundle of joy.

"It's a girl," Mum muttered groggily.

"Sorry, love," said my father, clicking his tongue. "It's a boy."

It went back and forth like this for a long time. *It's a girl! It's a boy! It's a girl! It's a boy! It's a girl! It's a boy! It's a girl! It's a boy!* Trent could barely breathe, it was so funny. My mother waved desperately at the evidence.

"Why would they give a pink sheet to a boy?" she asked.

Dad unwrapped the pink sheet to reveal the only data that mattered.

"My kid's got a dick!" he roared victoriously.

"He's perfect," she said, snatching me from his arms.

My mother couldn't rewrite history. But she could give me a childhood free of indifference and an adolescence unblemished by rejection.

None of the midwives thought it necessary to educate the 38-year-old mother with six children about the surprising complexities of breastfeeding.

"Hold that thought," she told me. "We'll figure it out."

Dad had bigger fish to fry. The registrar arrived. At the Kingaroy Hospital, my father intuited the emergence of a great political figure.

"Lech Jack Thomas Blaine," he said, sombre.

Thomas for him, of course. Jack for his dead older brother and the nickname of my dead blacksmith grandfather. Lech for Lech Walesa, the knockabout electrician who emancipated Poland from the communists.

"That's the future prime minister of Australia, mate," said Dad, winking at the perplexed registrar.

"Lech Blaine," said Mum, tasting my name, and deciding she liked it.

And that was that. The Blaines became a family of eight.

Chummy Hillbillies

My stay at the Wondai Hotel was brief. Mum and Dad borrowed $30,000 from the bank. They bought an acre of bushland known locally as "Chummy's Hill". It was nestled halfway between the pub and the golf club. Dad hired arborists to cut down the gum and wattle trees out the front, leaving a patch of red dirt and ant mounds.

Next, my parents paid a visit to Brisbane. A removable home salesman showed them a series of Queenslanders. They were far too small. My father studied a rectangular timber building at the back of the saleyard.

"What's that?" he asked.

"It's a disused maternity hospital," said the salesman.

An inspection revealed a commercial-sized kitchen, dining room and fireplace in the lounge. Plus four bedrooms that had housed women during the final moments of pregnancy, divided by two matching bathrooms.

"We'll take it," said my father, reaching for the wad of cash in his pocket.

Our removable Australian dream arrived on a semitrailer. The hospital sagged in the middle where it had been cut in half. Once in place, it was glued back together. A plumber linked the kitchen and bathroom to the town water supply. An electrician provided light. A concrete driveway was poured, leading to an open-air carport. Dad built a picket fence for the front yard.

In winter, my parents sold the lease of the Wondai Hotel. We relocated to Chummy's Hill. Dad bought a waterbed for the master bedroom from the *Trading Post*. It was cheaper than a normal bed, due to the patched-up leaks.

"Can we really afford a waterbed?" asked my mother.

"At that price, we can't afford to *not* buy one," said my father.

My father bought a corella for a birdcage at the end of the driveway. It was a white cockatoo, with orange feathers around its eyes. Dad named his spirit animal Jack. He had a huge, sharp beak and was psychotically excitable.

"G'day, maaaate!" Jack squawked at visitors.

My mother bought a spirit animal of her own: a tiny brown fox terrier. The female dog pottered around the house, shy and silent, nuzzling into whoever was presently available for a cuddle. Mum named her Sage.

The final pieces of the jigsaw puzzle were a front and back lawn for Mum to hose and Dad to mow. Dad's mate Doc was a supervisor at the Murgon meatworks. He slipped Dad a set of keys for the abattoir gates. There was a lush meadow beside the feedlot.

On a Sunday afternoon, Dad drove his one-tonne Falcon ute to Murgon. John sat in the front. Trent and Steven travelled in the tray of the ute, holding rusty shovels like child soldiers. They filled the ute to the brim. Back at Chummy's Hill, my brothers helped Dad lay the squares of stolen grass.

"One more trip," said Dad.

He was lying through his teeth. It took five more trips to cover the dirt around the house with fertilised turf. They stopped as night fell. For the next few days, the smell of manure emanated from underneath their fingernails.

"You beautiful boys," said my mother.

At sunrise, kangaroos skipped past the back fence. In the afternoon, kookaburras sat on the branches of gum trees, laughing on behalf of the koalas. Mum checked my cot like it was a safe containing a million-dollar bill.

"Good night, Bubby Little Jack," she sang as I fell asleep.

Giving birth made my mother love her foster children even more. She got to see them bond with her own flesh and blood. They didn't begrudge Mum's shifting focus. They loved me just as much as she did.

⸸

My parents were running out of money. Dad got a job as a part-time bartender at the Wondai Bowls and Golf Club. Mum received roughly fifteen dollars a day for each foster child, and extra for the regular emergency placements.

Dad wanted to acknowledge the grit that Trent, Steven and John had shown during renovations. He searched the *Trading Post* – his personal bible – for a reward. And he found the one: "FREE GIANT TRAMPOLINE". On a Sunday morning, Dad left for a secret visit to a farm near Mundubbera.

"Where are you off to, Thomas?" asked my mother.

"I'm going to see a man about a dog," he said.

His mate Doc provided a spare pair of hands. The trampoline had seen better days. It was one of those big rectangular ones, pre-safety restraints. Corroding springs. A hole at each corner that a small child could fall through.

"You sure this thing is ridgy-didge?" asked Doc.

"Can't look a gift horse in the mouth," said Dad.

"Roger," said Doc.

They arrived home in the ute. My father beeped the horn repeatedly. Everyone rushed outside. Steven and John couldn't believe their eyes. For years, they had been petitioning my parents for a trampoline. Dad and Doc moved it from the ute to the dirt paddock just beyond the back fence.

"One at a time," said Dad, a nod to Doc's safety concerns.

Steven sprinted for the trampoline. John ankle-tapped his brother into the dirt. All eyes were on him. John's first jump was tentative. The second was more ambitious, but hardly befitting of this history-making moment.

"Do a mickey flip," said Trent.

On the third jump, John soared towards heaven.

"Woah!" said Rebecca. "He's flying to the sun!"

On the fourth ascension, John attempted a gravity-defying mickey flip. To Steven's chagrin, he nailed it. Rebecca and Hannah shrieked with delight. On John's return to earth, the mat of the trampoline evaporated. The acrobat went straight through the weathered canvas. He thudded into the dirt.

"Aaaaahhhhhh!" screamed John.

"Where'd you get this piece of crap from?" asked Mum.

"They sold me a lemon!" said Dad.

"*Sold?*" snickered Doc.

Rebecca and Hannah screamed furiously at their brother.

"Game-wrecker!" chanted Trent. "Game-wrecker!"

John held his arm in a makeshift sling, humiliated. Steven was over the moon. Speechless, I was being initiated into the chaotic world of the Blaine family. We made our own fun on a tight budget and often got what we paid for.

1992 was the finest year of my father's life. I was baptised into the Blaine family faith: rugby league. My favourite toy was an Allan Langer doll. He was the captain and halfback for the Brisbane Broncos. On game day, Mum dressed me in a miniature Broncos jersey with a number seven on the back.

"This is the year of the Bronco," said Dad.

In September, the Broncos made the grand final against the St George Dragons. My father hated the Saints. He reefed out $500 of fifties – stashed away for financial emergencies – from the pocket of his wedding blazer.

"Multi, mate," he told the TAB attendant in Kingaroy. "Allan Langer first try scorer. Broncos by thirteen-plus. Allan Langer Clive Churchill Medallist."

My Auntie Lil and Uncle Viv visited Wondai for the Sunday arvo grand final. Monosyllabic Viv – a railway worker – resembled Hulk Hogan. Lil, small but loud, dispelled the myth that sport was just for men.

"Lazarus is going to smash these weak pricks!" she declared, referring to the Broncos' front-rower Glenn Lazarus, nicknamed The Brick with Eyes.

In the lounge room, everyone concentrated on the idiot box. Debbie Byrne sang "I Still Call Australia Home". Yothu Yindi performed "Treaty". Dad watched in horrified silence as the Dragons nearly scored in the corner.

"C'mon, Alfie," he muttered, pouring a double nip of Johnnie Walker.

Alfie bucked the weight of expectation. He ran on the fifth tackle and side-stepped a Saints defender, before passing to Alan Cann. Then he looped around Cann, who put the halfback untouched underneath the black dot.

"Allan Langer!" said the commentator. "The new king of rugby league!"

Chummy's Hill erupted. My brothers group-hugged Auntie Lil. She sprouted tears of joy. Dad raised me up towards the altar of the television.

"Go! You! Good! Thing!" he yelled.

In the second half, Allan Langer scooted from dummy half to score another try, leaving four defenders clutching at thin air. The Broncos won 28–8. Allan was awarded the Clive Churchill medal for player of the match.

"Nobody's calling him *too small* anymore!" shouted my father.

Dad gripped his older sister with relief. Sport was the cheapest opiate available to ordinary people. Priests had been replaced by athletes and cathedrals by stadiums. God was dead. Long live the Brisbane Broncos.

The Happiness Academy

What's a worse fate: to come from an unhappy family, or a once happy family? Chummy's Hill set our expectations too high. There were a thousand fights, to be sure. But that's because six dissimilar children were seeking delirious glee at every available opportunity and grew outraged should it be denied to us.

"This little piggy went to market," said Dad, fingers pricked. "This little piggy stayed home. This little piggy had roast beef. This little piggy had none."

Steven filmed my first birthday on the video camera. The lounge-room smelled of balloons and blown-out birthday candles. The walls were filled with portraits of tigers. My father had procured them from the *Trading Post*.

"This little piggy went: Wee! Wee! Wee!" said Dad. "All the way home!"

Dad's thick fingers were particularly ticklish. I bit my tongue and foamed from the mouth with laughter, new front teeth puncturing my gums. Trent and John took over from Dad to wring out my giggles like a wet towel. Rebecca and Hannah ran around the lounge room, squealing as if they were being tickled.

"This! Little! Piggy!" yelled Rebecca. "This! Little! Piggy!"

Rebecca – four – had recently been diagnosed with ADHD. My birth delighted and disturbed her. I stole Mum's attention. Rebecca retaliated by blowing out my birthday candles and popping the balloons. Now she used the alibi of This Little Piggy to pinch my soft skin with her sharp nails.

"Becca!" said Trent. "Gentle!"

I began shrieking with sorrow. Trent and John went outside to play backyard cricket. Steven stayed behind to document the anthropological treasure-trove. Hannah collapsed onto the carpet, wailing on my behalf, as if we were conjoined twins. She always had a visceral empathy for me.

"This happens every time you play This Little Piggy," said Mum.

It was the final Friday night before the start of the school year. In the carport, Dad provided quarterly haircuts with a set of clippers. Trent, Steven and John received identical number ones. Rebecca's hair was too long and curly for my father's shears. Mystifyingly, he blessed Hannah with a mullet: number two on the top and sides, plus a chaotic rat's tail hanging at the back.

"Oh my God," said Mum. "You can't do that."

Hannah's haircut was Michael and Mary Shelley's worst nightmare. But nobody thought much about them, except Mum. She kept a meticulous archive of newspaper clippings about their activities. The supply had recently dried up.

"What's good for the gander is good for the goose," said my unapologetic father. He gave himself a DIY mullet in the bathroom mirror.

The next morning, Mum dressed Rebecca for the first day of kindergarten. My brothers banged their spoons against the table and chanted over their bowls of Weet-Bix: "Becca! Becca! Becca! Becca!"

Mum and Rebecca left hand in hand for kindy. It was rare mother and daughter bonding time. My brothers walked to Wondai State School. Trent was starting grade eight; Steven grade five; John grade four.

Hannah and I formed a secret subcommittee of siblings. We were left with my father. He wore a white Jackie Howe singlet and boxer shorts. Hannah tucked into Vegemite on toast, cut into quarters. She cringed at the crusts.

"Eat your crusts, Goanna," said Dad. "Or your mullet will fall off."

"Noooo!" cried Hannah, stuffing the crusts into her mouth.

Dad had a shower before work. He spent the day feeding shandies and salted peanuts to retirees at the bowls club. Mum dressed Hannah and me in colour-coordinated outfits from the op-shop. Red t-shirts and black shorts. Red legionnaires caps with black flaps at the back for neck protection.

"Twins!" said Hannah, even though she was twenty-one months older than me and vastly advanced for her age, both physically and intellectually.

In the lounge room, surrounded by the tigers, my mother recited nursery rhymes. Hannah begged her for something with more teeth.

"I love a sunburnt country," said Mum. "A land of sweeping plains. Of ragged mountain ranges. Of droughts and flooding rains. I love her far horizons. I love her jewel-sea. Her beauty and her terror. The wide brown land for me!"

I had no idea what it meant, and nor really did Hannah. But we liked the rhythm of the words, and the way Mum's eyes lit up when they rhymed.

My mother mopped and vacuumed. She washed and ironed clothes for eight people. Country music warbled from her record player: Slim Dusty and John Williamson. Hannah pretended that I was her baby. Then Mum put me in a second-hand pram from the 1960s. The three of us picked Rebecca up from kindergarten. Trent, Steven and John made their own way home.

"Mum, I'm hungry!" cried Steven.

"Nice to meet you, Hungry," said my mother.

Mum sat at the dining-room table with Trent, Steven and John until their homework was done to a satisfactory level. She was a harsh taskmaster. Afterwards, they rode pushbikes around Chummy's Hill. Around 5 pm, Dad emerged like a bunyip from the bush track leading to the bowls and golf clubs.

At sunset, my father duped Rebecca and Hannah into doing a road race. This took the edge off Rebecca, so that she would fall asleep more easily.

"Becca's gonna win," said John, trailing behind her on a bike.

Mum was breastfeeding me in a rocking chair on the front patio. Steven ambled around the corner, hand in hand with three-year-old Hannah.

"Here comes Hannah," said Mum. "Slow and steady wins the race."

"Goanna!" shouted Dad, chuckling into the dusk. "Goanna!"

Dad insisted that my mother didn't need to lift a finger before or after dinner. In the kitchen, he wore a prank apron. It featured the graphic of a six-pack, along with the graphic of a massive penis underneath a fabric flap.

"Dad, what's for dinner?" asked John.

"Shitonastick, mate," said my father. "Shit. On. A. Stick."

In reality, Dad was an excellent cook – much better than Mum. His speciality was home-made rissoles. He would crack a few eggs into a kilo of mince and add breadcrumbs, garlic, herbs, diced onions and grated carrot. Plus – most importantly – a copious dash of Worcestershire Sauce.

"The secret ingredient," he said.

Dad had bought a ten-seater table from the *Trading Post*. Each night, it hosted an eating competition. The Blaines ate every scrap of food from their plates, and then wiped the grease up with triangles of white bread and butter.

Following dinner, Trent, Steven and John alternated between washing, wiping and putting the dishes away. Whoever was on wiping duties took the opportunity to whip the other two on the legs with a wet tea towel.

On the back pergola, Mum watered the lawn with one hand. In the other hand, she switched between a cigarette and a stubbie of XXXX Gold.

"This is heaven," she said, when Dad delivered her a fresh stubbie.

Upon Chummy's Hill, my mother discovered true happiness. In lieu of her estranged family, she built herself a makeshift tribe. For the first time, she wasn't in a state of longing: not for money, love or a baby.

Never Tear Us Apart

Chummy's Hill seemed like a sanctuary from Michael and Mary Shelley. Each day, my mother had an instant coffee on the front patio with our next-door neighbour Trish. She was the manager of the Wondai Swimming Pool.

"Guess what?" asked Mum.

"You're mad and I'm not?" asked Trish.

Trish was the one person in Wondai my mother told about the Shelleys. Perhaps because Trish's husband, John, was a local copper.

"Lenore, you're trying to tell me that Steven, John and Hannah are fostered?" asked Trish, incredulously. "And their real parents are in a Christian cult? And they threatened to knock off Joh Bjelke-Petersen?"

"Pretty much," said my mother. "You can't tell a soul. We're basically in witness protection. Except the witnesses can't remember anything."

Steven and John were aware that their biological parents presented a possible danger to them. Mum kept them insulated from the full extent of the Shelleys' madness. But they knew their names had been changed for a reason.

"What *actually* happened to my real parents?" Steven asked Dad.

"They lost the plot, mate," Dad told him, without going into the details about Steven's premature birth, or his lifesaving plane ride to Brisbane.

"Do you reckon they'll find the plot?" asked Steven.

"Probably not, mate," said my father.

Visits from their older brother, Mick, reminded Steven and John that they weren't real Blaines. Mick let slip little details about the kidnapping. John sensed a showdown in the future, like *Home Alone*, his favourite movie. Whenever he got too scared, John pictured my father. Then he felt safe.

++

Mick Bishop, aka Elijah Shelley, had moved back to where his foster care journey began: Central Queensland. His foster parents, the Bishops, bought a farm near Rockhampton. They enrolled Mick at a Catholic school, St Brendan's, in the coastal town of Yeppoon.

At St Brendan's, Mick was a fish out of water. He preferred basketball and rap to rugby league and country music. His two heroes were Michael Jordan and Tupac. The boarders from the bush referred to him as a wigger: a white n****r. Mick regularly rode to St Brendan's for weekend detentions.

The Bishops believed in corporal punishment. Mick neglected to mention these floggings to his social workers. The Bishops gave up on their foster son. In December 1994, Mick came to live with the Blaines until Susan King could find a new placement for him.

"He can stay here!" Mum told Susan.

"I don't think that would be a wise idea," said Susan, cryptically.

Susan delivered Mick from Rockhampton to Wondai. Steven was eleven. John was ten. Hannah was four. Underneath the roof of the carport, Mick hugged his brown-eyed, olive-skinned siblings with tenderness.

"I've missed yas," he said.

Rebecca and I joined the embrace. It didn't take much for us to love someone. A brother of Steven, John and Hannah was a brother of ours.

Not all of us felt the same way. Trent hovered on the fringes. Now fifteen, he was six foot one, with broad shoulders and not an ounce of fat on him. He was a state swimming champion.

"What's up, dude?" Mick said coolly.

"Nice earring, Mick," said Trent.

The teenage foster boys couldn't remember bonding as toddlers in the paediatric unit of the Mater Hospital. That summer holidays, they were competing to be seen as the alpha older brother by Steven, John and Hannah.

Mick came armed with a mixtape of gangster rap. Mum let him play it on the cassette player, to make him feel at home. We all waited for the music to start. The first song was "Doggy Dogg World" by Snoop Dogg. An f-bomb was promptly followed by an n-bomb. Dad hit the roof. He pulled the cord from the power point to prevent any further obscenities.

"What the hell was *that*, mate?" asked Dad.

"It's Snoop Dogg," said Mick.

"No more Snoop Dogg," he said.

In some ways, we were living in a time capsule on Chummy's Hill. Mick heralded the Americanisation of the Great Southern Land.

‡

The main event of the Blaine family Christmas Day was an annual backyard cricket match. In the middle of the paddock stood two thin gum trees roughly twenty metres apart. They were wickets. The earth between them was the pitch. Rebecca, Hannah and I watched the game while sitting on a pile of firewood.

Dad wore white zinc on his nose and strapping for an old tennis elbow. The 140-kilogram bartender bowled left-arm wrist spin off two steps.

"Howzat?" my father appealed to himself, the opening bowler and official umpire, after he trapped John plumb LBW with the first ball.

"No LBWs, Dad!" protested John. "And no golden ducks!"

"You'd be out if there was, mate," Dad reminded him.

The red nut looked like an 8-Ball in my father's huge hands. He had been a wrist-spinner since the meatworks injury in 1966. That summer, every junior cricketer in Australia wanted to be a spinner thanks to Shane Warne.

Bowlers received a minimum of six balls. After that, Dad muttered "OVER" following two dud balls in a row. It sent a shiver down the bowler's spine. Cricket brought strapping Trent down to earth. He was an erratic fast bowler. Given the height of his eldest son, Dad didn't feel bad about mercilessly pulling and hooking Trent's bouncers across the back paddock.

"Over?" asked Steven.

"No, mate," said my father. "Not just yet."

This was the benefit of being umpire. Dad edged closer to another Christmas Day century. Trent was succeeded by Steven. Dad met his match. Steven was ambidextrous. He could bowl right-arm *and* left-arm wrist spin.

Dad entered the mid-nineties. Steven swapped the ball between each hand until the final moment of delivery. It looped from his small left hand and landed outside the off stump. Then it spun and hit the gum-tree stumps.

"Bugger it," muttered my sunburnt father.

Mick was theatrically indifferent to cricket. The game petered out. Trent, Steven and John went to play basketball with Mick in the carport. Dad attended to the leg of ham in the oven. We all sat at a plastic table in the carport. Mum took immense pleasure from a plate of prawns.

Rebecca, Hannah and I paid more attention to chocolates from our Christmas stockings.

An extension cord ran to a cassette player. At the end of "True Blue" by John Williamson, Mick stood up. Without permission, he slipped in a different tape. Mum watched with apprehension. Dad stared daggers at the gangster-rap fanatic. But the smart-arse grin vanished from Mick's lips.

"This one is for Hannah," said Mick. "Merry Christmas, little sister."

A familiar synth string section blared from the speakers. It was "Never Tear Us Apart" by INXS. Hannah beamed with embarrassed elation, the centre of Mick's attention. Mum started bawling her eyes out.

"That was a cracker," said Dad. "Merry Christmas, Mick."

In the opening week of 1995, my mother waited impatiently for the Department of Child Safety to reopen. Then she called Susan King.

"We really would love Mick to stay with us for good," she said.

There was no gentle way for Susan to break the news. A placement had been found for Mick on a cattle farm west of Rockhampton.

"We don't think that it would be the right decision for Michael to live with you," said Susan. "Either for him. Or for Steven, John and Hannah."

Susan worried that Mick would undermine my parents' authority and unsettle the attachment between Steven, John, Hannah and the rest of us. She anticipated another foster care break-up for Mick and grief for his siblings.

"Have you asked Michael what he wants?" asked my mother.

"I have," said Susan. "He wants a fresh start."

This was the part my parents would never understand. Why wasn't the unwanted foster boy begging to live with them? It was complicated.

Mick couldn't love my parents the way Steven, John and Hannah did. And my mother and father would never love him the way they loved the others.

South of Eden

A bitter feud was brewing between my parents. Mum was comfortable raising her children in a humble home on the minimum wage. With an eye on the future, my father wanted to blow up the Wondai idyll and embrace the free market.

"We can't just keep living pay cheque to pay cheque," said Dad.

"Why not?" asked Mum. "It's not like we're destitute."

Dad missed the wad of fifties in his top pocket. But most of all he craved the exhaustion that followed a twelve-hour shift at the pub. Physical proof he was a provider, not a bludger. My parents had a mortgage on a cheap home, with no superannuation. If he died tomorrow, there'd be barely enough to pay for the funeral expenses, let alone to leave behind a financial legacy.

"There won't be anything left for the kids when I'm dead," said Dad.

"Money won't buy them love," said Mum.

Money wasn't everything, but it had a basic bearing on the shape and scope of human fate. Dad had watched the sweet little boys and girls who grew into teenagers in the bush. A high school certificate, if they were lucky, followed by a menial blue-collar job. Some ended up drug addicts.

"What's Trent gonna do?" asked Dad. "Get a job at the meatworks?"

My mother found it ironic that her husband – a booster of the Aussie battler – was so opposed to his own children becoming one. She prioritised togetherness over personal achievement. Dad was a collectivist in theory. In practice, he believed an individual would sink or swim on their lonesome.

"What's wrong with a job at the meatworks?" she asked.

"Lenore, my hip is still the colour of a beetroot!" he said.

My father's life had been thwarted. The lives of his children would be unthwarted – their bodies unscarred by the ball-and-chain of class.

Dad started inspecting rundown pubs across rural Australia. He drove alone to Cunnamulla, Charleville and Lightning Ridge. Finally, he discovered a cheap lease on a pub in Toowoomba. *The Country Club Hotel*. It was big enough to make some money and small enough to run basically on your own.

We were oblivious to the perilous state of their marriage. The arguments happened late at night in the master bedroom. Mum stubbornly refused to leave Chummy's Hill. Trent was in high school. Steven and John were about to start. If the decision was put to a vote, Mum would win.

"Have you asked the kids what they want?" she asked.

"This isn't a democracy," said Dad. "They need a bit of tough love."

"That's not love. You're just greedy."

"I'm greedy? Take a look in the mirror."

"How on earth am *I* greedy? Money means nothing to me!"

"Pretty simple, Mother Teresa," he said. "You'd rather the kids be losers than world-beaters on their own two feet. You need 'em to need you."

"I'd rather get a divorce than move to Toowoomba!" she said.

My father smiled at his wife with evil delight.

"You wanna divorce?" he asked. "Do me a friggin' favour! We'll split this shitbox fifty-fifty. You can go back to stacking shelves at Woolies."

A divorce was impossible. There was Buckley's chance that the Department of Child Safety would leave five foster kids with a moneyless single mother. Mum chose love: for her children, not her husband.

✢

My parents sold the house on Chummy's Hill. We packed the minibus with as much stuff as possible. The journey was two-and-a-half hours south. Mum drove the minibus, with Trent, Steven, John, Rebecca and Hannah. Dad and I drove separately in a black Ford Falcon with a trailer on the back.

The Blaines invaded Toowoomba from the north. It was a big country town toppling from the side of the Great Dividing Range. Eighty thousand people, 800 metres above sea level. The mountain had once been a volcano. Those ancient soils fertilised spectacular parks and flowerbeds.

The pub was stuck in the no-man's-land of Mort Estate, between the old money of the eastern suburbs and the sprawl of the western ones. Mort Estate was populated by a decaying railway station, factories, boarding houses and council flats. Graffiti covered the termite-infested picket fences.

The Country Club Hotel was very different from the country clubs in Hollywood movies. The green roof was rusted. The paint on the brickwork was peeling. But to me, it seemed like a cathedral: huge and beautiful. We pulled into the carpark. A mulberry tree hung above the cracked blacktop.

"Yum! Yum! Yum! Yum!" I chanted.

"They're all yours, champ," my father said to me.

At the door of the minibus, my mother bristled. She carefully avoided any insinuation that I was more important than her non-biological children.

"The tree is yours, too," she said to Rebecca and Hannah.

"Bloody hell, Lenore," grumbled Dad. "It was a figure of speech."

Trent, Steven and John helped him lumber the furniture upstairs. Rebecca, Hannah and I gobbled mulberries. I ate more than my sisters. The berries were sweet, but the ripe ones were running out.

Rebecca and I reached for the same piece of fruit. She was closer to it than me.

"That was m-m-mine, Becca!" I stuttered at high pitch, crying.

"Finders keepers, losers weepers!" squealed Rebecca.

Hannah offered me a perfect mulberry. Mum watched on. She was irritated by Hannah's kindness, and by me accepting it without true gratitude.

"That was yours, Hannah," she said. "Lech is being a greedy-guts."

"I've had enough," said Hannah with a sheepish grin.

Mum spotted a willingness to lie about what was mine. To take and not give. A stream of selfishness running between my father and me. I could sense her disapproval, and it shocked me, such a strong and foreign quality.

"I'm sorry, Mum," I cried. "I was hungry!"

"I know, sweetheart," she said. "But your sisters were hungry, too. Do you want to know the nicest feeling in the world? Seeing someone who you love even happier than you. It makes you feel like the Incredible Hulk on the inside!"

"Aw, yeah," I said. That didn't sound like the Incredible Hulk at all. I wanted to ask Dad about it, but he was too busy moving the furniture.

╬

Rebecca was seven. At night, she paced the private quarters of the pub, making a pigsty. Mum was a sponge for her frenzy. She struggled to fall asleep, even with Clonidine pills for insomnia. Then she kept wetting the bed.

"I did it again," Rebecca cried, lifting her sheets to show my parents.

"It's okay, Becca," said Mum. "I'll just chuck them in the wash."

Mum tried to prove how unashamed she was of Rebecca's incontinence. For the next week, they shared a bed together in one of the spare bedrooms.

"Let me tell you a story," whispered Mum before bedtime, brushing Rebecca's curly hair. "There once was a couple named Lenore and Tom."

"That's you?" asked Rebecca.

"That's right!" said my mother. "Lenore and Tom couldn't have babies. So they fostered three little boys named Trent, Steven and John. But Lenore always wanted a little girl. One day, they got a daughter named Rebecca."

"That's me!" said Rebecca, giggling.

"Lenore couldn't believe her luck! Rebecca had the most beautiful laugh. It made Lenore so happy to hear it. Rebecca was the bravest little girl in the world. Lenore didn't feel so brave. But she felt braver around Rebecca."

Sharing the bed made Rebecca's nervousness worse. It seemed like a test. She wet the bed for seven nights straight, waking up in the same sopping sheets as her mother. The shame was inconceivable. So was the fear of rejection. Rebecca believed that she would get sent somewhere else to live.

"Hannah doesn't wet the bed," shrieked Rebecca. "Lech doesn't even wet the bed! You don't love me. You don't want me. I'm a spastic."

Mum smiled kindly at Rebecca's tear-streaked cheeks.

"Becca," she said. "Read. My. Lips. You could wet the bed every night for the rest of your life, and I'd still love you. You're my daughter! All the things that make you feel strange make me love you even more."

Rebecca never wet the bed again.

The Lonesome Chosen One

Mick Bishop went to live with foster carers named Donna and Barry. They were down-to-earth cattle farmers with two biological daughters and a son. The family lived on a property in Alton Downs, west of Rockhampton.

Mick helped Barry round up the cows for milking. But Mick dropped the portable milking machine. It was wrecked. Mick sprinted behind a tree, flinching from the flogging he expected to receive from Barry.

"Where are you off to, mate?" asked Barry, bemused.

Mick sat fearfully at the kitchen table. It took a long time to reassure him that he wouldn't be physically punished.

"Not your fault, bud," said Donna. "Accidents happen."

Mick enrolled at North Rockhampton State High. He wore a maroon shirt and shorts with basketball shoes. At school, he showed no lack of bravado with the opposite sex. But he always dumped them before the crunch.

"Donna, can I ask you a question?" whispered Mick one afternoon.

"Shoot," said Donna.

"What's a head job?" he asked.

Donna raised her eyebrows. His previous foster carers, the Bishops, had kept him sheltered from the sins of the world. Now, he was learning on the run.

"It's when someone pleasures you – *downstairs* – with their mouth," said Donna, blushing but determined to be upfront. "Or when you pleasure them."

"Do you and Barry give each other head jobs?" he asked.

"That's none of your friggin' business, Mick!" said Donna.

Donna coached Mick's basketball team. She sent the teenage boys for ten suicide drills at a time. Mick dreamed of playing for the Chicago Bulls.

"You need a back-up plan," Donna told him.

"I'll work for Microsoft," said Mick.

At North Rocky High, Mick received As for IT, science and maths. His brain worked in a similar way to Michael Shelley's: supernaturally rational when it came to numbers, and erratic with matters of human emotion.

⁕

Mick refused to visit Toowoomba for his annual family reunification. He seethed with a resentment towards my parents that Donna couldn't understand.

"Why do I always have to visit them?" he asked Donna.

"Well, why don't you get 'em to come up here?" she said.

Mick was delighted by the idea. He floated the proposal with his social worker. The Department of Child Safety was cautious. It was much safer – and cheaper – for Mick to visit his three siblings at their well-established home.

Eventually, the department relented. With his savings from fencing, Mick bought Chicago Bulls caps for Steven and John, and a top-of-the-range Barbie doll for Hannah. He had elaborate visions of showing them how to milk a cow. Of playing basketball with his younger brothers. Of reading nursery rhymes to his little sister. Of cooking them fresh eggs for breakfast.

My father agreed to take Steven, John and Hannah to Rockhampton. The department paid for them to stay at a cheap motel.

"This is bullshit," Mick told Donna. "Why aren't they staying here?"

"Baby steps, Mick," said Donna. "Hannah's just a little girl."

There were no sleepovers. Mick's social worker had a strict itinerary for the bonding sessions. Mick met Steven, John and Hannah at designated locations. The basketball courts. McDonald's. Go-karts. He took them to see *Space Jam* at the Rockhampton cinema. He bought Hannah a choc-top ice-cream.

On the final day of the visit, Mick, Steven, John and Hannah went swimming together at Yeppoon beach. Hannah was six. She hung off Mick's shoulders like a monkey. The social worker insisted on taking a photo.

"Cheese," said the social worker.

"Cheese!" yelled Hannah.

"Cheese," whispered Mick.

Mick mucked around with his brothers and tickled his little sister under the armpits. But the holiday was missing spontaneity. Steven and John, thirteen and twelve, seemed to feel slightly sorry for their older brother.

"Thanks for having us here," said Steven. "I hope you're alright."

Mick felt like a criminal. Why was the department afraid of him? What had they told Steven and John? Just as they all started to loosen up, the playdate was over. His brothers strolled back to my father, who wasn't Mick's father.

"Catch ya later, Mick," said John.

Hannah ran towards Dad. She jumped into his arms. Mick couldn't stomach the reminder that his siblings had a centre of gravity, minus him.

"How are ya, Goanna?" asked my father.

"I'm good, Dad," said Hannah. "But I miss Mum."

"Well, let's hit the frog and toad," he said.

Steven, John and Hannah went home to Toowoomba. Mick stayed behind. It was their final reunion. Maureen reminded Mick to call his siblings on their birthdays. But he couldn't bring himself to dial the number.

The Heart of the Matter

Trent moved out of home. The Blaines became a family of seven. My parents enrolled Steven and John at St Mary's, a Catholic school with an illustrious rugby league program. Mum took them to an op shop to buy second-hand uniforms.

"Your dad's busting a gut to do this," she said.

Steven made the A-team for rugby league but struggled to mimic the machismo of his teammates. He was beloved by teachers for his high grades and good manners. Secretly, the high achiever was besieged by social anxiety.

"Don't worry, mate," my father told him. "Be happy."

John made the Bs for rugby league and struggled academically. He was determined to keep the fact that he was a foster boy a secret. This double life made him shyer than when the Blaine family lived in Wondai. At St Mary's, John soaked up his strange surroundings with dark brown eyes.

"You can sit with me," said Steven. "You'll make mates eventually."

Steven and John were best friends. They spent all their spare time together. Each afternoon, the brothers manned the bottle-o of the Country Club Hotel. There was a loophole in the liquor licensing act allowing minors to serve alcohol if they were related to the publican. Dad paid them five dollars an hour, cash in hand. They played pool between serving customers.

John was the under-twelves state champion for eight-ball. Steven's forte was rugby league. He collected representative jerseys. In the irregular updates dispatched to the sport-hating Shelleys, the social workers omitted the athletic achievements of their sons.

※

My father worked ten-hour days. Sometimes thirteen hours on Fridays and Saturdays. He was fatter, greyer and paler than when we had arrived. And much grumpier. There was less time to cuddle. He always looked like a man who had just survived a cyclone: skin damp, hair dishevelled and eyes blank.

Fatigue was the basis of his business model. And it worked. The profit allowed my parents to save a deposit for their first investment property: a fibro shack bought for $40,000, rented by a man with five cats. This was followed by a second.

"A home should be somewhere to live, not to rent out," said my mother.

"That's why you'd never be rich without me," he said.

"Who's rich?" she asked. "Not us! We can barely afford the repayments. And you're going to have a heart attack if you keep working this much."

Dad's grandiose plan was to buy a property for each of his children and have the loans paid off by the time he retired, provided he didn't die first.

"Just you wait, Lenore," he said, tapping his temple.

In a way, they were both right. The property market was about to enter an everlasting boom. Meanwhile, my father suffered a catastrophic heart attack. It was lunchtime on a Monday. He was tucking into a steak, bacon and onion sandwich. He looked profoundly tired. This was nothing too unusual.

"Are you alright, Thomas?" asked my mother.

"Never been better," he mumbled. She went back upstairs to do the bookwork. Suddenly, it felt like a giant was smashing a sledgehammer against my father's chest. His jaw was sore, like the giant had punched him, too. Dad stumbled to the phone behind the counter of the front bar. He called 000.

"My heart is buggered," he told the operator, slurring his words.

"Where are you?" asked the operator.

"The Country Club Hotel," he said.

"Have you been drinking, sir?"

"I'm not drunk," he mumbled. "I'm the fucking publican!"

Dad didn't yell for his wife. He took his glasses off. He poured himself a pot of Diet Coke and then waited. The ambulance arrived. The publican went belly up behind the bar. Cardiac arrest. At least the pain went away. He was forty-nine years old. A drunk jumped upstairs to get my mother.

"Sorry, Lenore," he said, cap in his hands. "Tom's brown bread."

Mum ran downstairs. The paramedics had shifted her husband to the ambulance. Dad died with thongs on his feet. There was no light at the end of a tunnel, or white horses, or awesome epiphanies.

Just an implacable blackness.

"Come on, Thomas," cried Mum, squeezing his hand.

The paramedics grimaced with a professional sympathy. On the way to hospital, they electrocuted his heart with a defibrillator, mostly for the widow's closure. Mum rushed from denial to anger. She slapped Dad across the face.

"I told you this would happen," she shouted. "Don't be a coward!"

The ambos fried his hairy chest a few more times. The electrical currents tricked my father's heart into beating. His grey eyes flashed open wide. He glanced at Mum suspiciously. Then he passed out, while continuing to breathe.

My father was rushed to surgery. He had a major blockage of the left pulmonary artery. AKA: the widowmaker. The others were also clogged with fat. The doctor inserted stents, restoring the flow of blood and oxygen.

"Thank God!" said Mum. That day, she was a relapsed Catholic.

Nature vs Nurture

Doctors told my father that he needed to get out of the pub business or risk another heart attack. My parents sold the lease of the Country Club Hotel. They bought a worker's cottage for $70,000. 31 Gowrie Street, Mort Estate.

It was a thin four-bedroom house. A fat camphor laurel erupted from the street over the chain-link fence. A long concrete driveway led to a timber garage. Blocks of wood were piled beside it. The kitchen was from the 1950s. A gas lantern hung over the woodfired stove. We made peace with the mice.

"A mouse is a sign of good luck," said my father.

"How do you figure that, Thomas?" asked my mother.

"No mouse in a house with no food," he said.

Dad bought us a new Dalmatian named Mazda. Steven got a job

at a sports store. John got a job as a trolley pusher. They pooled their savings to buy a ping-pong table for the back patio at home. Steven slept in the granny flat. Next to his bedroom door was a dartboard filled with a million slits.

My parents purchased the lease of a corner store at the end of our street. It was a cobwebbed shop. The brick walls were cream. The concrete floors were painted dark red. On the left side of the counter sat a hot box filled with deep-fried food. On the right was a stockpile of chocolates and lollies.

The so-called "milk bar" was obsolete. Nowadays, everyone bought their milk cheap from Coles or Woolworths. Dad paid Rebecca, Hannah and me to take turns helping him to clean the shop and restock the soft drinks. We received a dollar for morning shifts and two dollars for night shifts.

"Carpe diem," my father told Hannah after a 6.30 am wake-up call.

"What's that mean?" she yawned.

"It's Latin," he said. "*Squeeze the day*, mate."

Hannah had Michael's nose and crooked teeth, with Mary's brown hair and olive skin. But the Shelleys' biological daughter showed deep disrespect for gender norms. Tall for her age and fit like my older brothers. Hannah cut her hair short. She preferred shorts and t-shirts to skirts and dresses.

"My beautiful tomboy," Mum called her.

Dad signed Hannah up for an under-tens cricket team. She wore a big-brimmed Greg Chappell hat. All her teammates and opponents were boys. But Hannah was one of the best players in the age group. The all-rounder batted right-handed and bowled left-handed, thanks to lessons from my leftie father.

At the age of seven, I was a boisterous bookworm. Short and chubby. The build of my father. The hand–eye coordination of my mother. Mum took me to the library. Dad took Hannah to the nets for batting practice. I read the dictionary for shits and giggles, but

I couldn't hit a cricket ball to save myself.

"Your mother's son," Dad called me.

++

In the summer holidays, Rebecca went to stay with her biological mother at a motel. Hannah and I rollerbladed around the Mort Estate for hours. She was fearless. I was afraid. Mum insisted that we wear helmets, wrist guards and knee pads. Dad called for more speed as we flew down the hill past the shop.

"Give it some gas, ya bludgers!" he yelled.

Hannah held my hand tightly, so that I would stop panicking. We were a sight to see in full flight: a tall tomboy and a small bookworm. Different ages and DNA, and yet joined together at the hip.

"Lech-sta! Peck-sta! Read all about it!" yelled Hannah.

Dad handed us cans of Fanta and chocolate Paddle Pops from the door of the corner store. At home, Hannah and I dumped the rollerblades in the shed. Mum turned on the sprinkler in the front yard. We washed off the dirt and sweat. The sun was hot. The grass was wet. Our tongues were metallic from the town water. We honeyed them with the Fanta and Paddle Pops.

"This is good shit," I said, making an ice cream spider in my mouth.

I turned off the brass tap with my milky, wrinkled hands. Hannah swapped the sprinkler for a spray gun. I turned the tap back on at full blast. She aimed her weapon of choice at Mazda, the flea-ridden Dalmatian.

"Hasta la vista, baby," she said in an Austrian accent.

Hannah pulled the trigger. The sopping dog scampered to the safety of the concrete driveway. Our lungs hurt from all the laughter flooding out.

"Do the hose trick!" I said.

She aimed the spray gun at the leaves of the thick tree out the front. The mist hit the rays of light and slowed them down. A homemade rainbow. No one in their right mind would trade this much fun or love for money.

✢

On Christmas Day 1999, there was a sense of anticipation in the summer air. It was six days until the new millennium. The apocalypse might be coming.

Steven and John bought Mum a Mexican walking fish for Christmas. Overnight, they put the gift in her fish tank as a surprise.

"Where's all my fish gone?" asked Mum in the morning.

The Mexican walking fish had eaten them all. As the youngest child, it was my job to hand out the Christmas presents. Mum gave Dad a pair of Adidas massage thongs. He gave her a bottle of Joop.

"Joop is a man's cologne, Thomas," said Mum.

Dad had been hoodwinked by the pink packaging.

"Shit," he said. "Ya kiddin' me?"

"I kid you not," she said.

Dad tested the Joop on his neck and wrists and enjoyed the scent. From that moment onwards, he exclusively wore Joop.

Hannah unwrapped a Gray-Nicolls cricket bat from Steven and John. My parents gave her a New Zealand World Cup cricket jersey. It was teal with black silver ferns fanning across the chest. This was the solitary nod to the citizenship on her passport. In sporting contests, she went for the Kiwis.

Hannah put both presents to use in the annual backyard cricket match. Over the rear fence was a horse paddock without horses. Steven and John had been cultivating a grass pitch. There was no gate. We had to stand on a rusty step ladder, climb over the high fence, and jump onto the trampoline.

"Stuff that," said Dad. He entered through the neighbour's place.

I opened the batting that day. My father lobbed up underarm lollipops. I kept missing them. Steven and John didn't take it easy on me. Sledging was a family tradition. They nicknamed me "Trevor". As in Trevor Chappell, the worst cricketer in the Chappell family.

"This is unfair!" I cried to Dad. "You're a grown man!"

"Cool your jets, big fella," said my father.

Dad handed the ball to Hannah, as a way to level the playing field. Her left-hand medium pace hit my middle stump. I refused to leave the crease. She bowled a hat-trick against me. I threw the bat over the fence.

"Bullshit!" I shrieked at high pitch.

"Watch ya language, mate!" said Dad.

I sat cross-legged at fine leg. Through my tears, I pretended to read the Roald Dahl novel – *James and the Giant Peach* – that my mother had given me for Christmas. But I was spying on Hannah's approach to the crease. I prayed to God that she would get clean bowled first ball by Dad.

Hannah bit her tongue in a trance of concentration. She hit my father's left-arm wrist spin against the neighbour's back fence with a cover drive.

"Don't go easy on me, Dad," said Hannah.

"I'm not," said Dad. He was delighted by his daughter's freakish hand–eye coordination, yet slightly embarrassed at getting smashed. "There hasn't been a kid this good since Jesus opened the batting for Jerusalem!"

I was green with envy. She was the son he always wanted, not me. Dad called *OVER* on himself. Hannah dished out the same treatment to Trent.

"Goanna!" cheered my father from wicketkeeper.

Hannah knew that she was fostered. But she wasn't bothered by the circumstances of her birth. It was just a funny bit of trivia. Anyway, she talked like a Blaine. She dressed like a Blaine. She played sport like a Blaine. As far as Hannah was concerned, Michael and Mary Shelley were on another planet.

CHAPTER SEVEN

The Resurrection

Michael and Mary Shelley spent the 1990s roaming the north and south islands of New Zealand. Up north, they went between the Bay of Islands, Omapere, Bream Bay, Hahei, Onemana, Lake Tarawera and Taupo.

"We received over $200,000 in compensation, paid justly by New Zealand taxpayers," wrote Michael. "I bought a number of computers, so that I could take this GOD-given opportunity to expand the scope of my Ministry."

By boat, the Shelleys reached the feral perfection of the South Island. The sky was 95 per cent cloud. They settled on a farm in Kenepuru, a drowned valley in the Marlborough Sounds, a strip of low-lying islands.

Paul Shelley pruned a kiwi tree in the front yard. He left fresh fruit and roses on Mary's bedside table. Michael and Paul took turns cooking dinner. Paul bought an Austin Maxi, a five-door hatchback. He put an ad in the newspaper seeking parts. An elderly man offered him a free engine block and gaskets. In the barn, Paul installed the new engine with Michael's help.

The Shelleys looped through Kaiteriteri to Kaikoura and Christchurch. They wound south to Lake Manapouri. The water was formed by the melted ice from a glacier. It was surrounded by the Cathedral

Mountains. Tour guides referred to four directions: North, South, West and Hope.

Everywhere that Mary went led to emptiness. She knew nothing about her daughter, except that Hannah was living with Saul and Joshua. There were no phone calls. The Shelleys were sent occasional photographs and school report cards. They were heavily redacted. Social workers airbrushed out any information that might help Michael and Mary locate their children.

Mary got more and more depressed. Whatever the virtues of Michael's beliefs, she blamed herself for losing Hannah. The Shelleys went back to Waikato on the North Island. Mary was admitted to a psychiatric hospital in Hamilton following repeated suicide attempts.

"She was suspicious and refused to talk," read the report.

Paul, entering his mid-twenties, was getting restless. He made a run for it. The disciple moved to a boarding house in Auckland.

✢

It took the approach of the new millennium – and Michael Shelley's promise of the apocalypse – to shock Mary from her bereavement. The Shelleys travelled to Wellington. They met with New Zealand's Commissioner for Children.

"We can't intervene in the laws of another country," he said.

"But you intervened to steal my daughter!" said Mary.

Michael and Mary sent reams of desperate letters about Hannah to New Zealand social workers and bureaucrats, to no avail. Mary went straight to the top. She wrote to Jenny Shipley, New Zealand's first female prime minister. Mary demanded the government pay for her airfares to Queensland.

"You are a child abuser and deviant of the worst kind – worse than Adolf Hitler," wrote Mary. "You will pay dearly for it. ♡Mary, GOD's maidservant."

In grey-skied Christchurch, Mary was admitted to Sunnyside Hospital under the Mental Health Act. Upon her release, the Shelleys went back to Auckland. Mary caught a taxi to the TV3 studios. She refused to pay the fare. Then she gate-crashed breakfast TV, crusading for the liberation of Hannah.

Mary was charged with credit fraud and trespassing. After getting released, she visited the Rotorua child welfare office twice in one month. Her desperate requests for a five-minute phone call with Hannah were denied.

In Queensland, Hannah had a meeting with social workers about the possibility of phone contact with Mary Shelley. Mum was encouraging, but Hannah was unenthusiastic. It was decided that Mary needed to submit to a psychiatric evaluation before the request could proceed further.

Michael and Mary sought shelter at a motel. Mary missed the scheduled psychiatric assessment, due to the flu. She called the child welfare office and delivered a very specific threat to a senior social worker.

"I'm going back to Queensland to find Hannah!" yelled Mary. "And when everyone least expects it, I will take her back while she is sleeping!"

Michael and Mary barged into the Blenheim child welfare office. They were asked to leave. In the waiting room, Michael foisted a bible on a foster child. He grabbed the terrified minor and refused to let go. A male social worker interrupted the half-hearted kidnapping.

Queensland granted Mary permission for a phone call with Hannah. It would be supervised on both ends by social workers. Mary changed her mind. A phone call wasn't enough. She needed to see Hannah in the flesh.

Michael tracked down the private phone number of Anna Bligh, the Queensland minister for child safety. He left eight messages on Bligh's answering machine. They started off diplomatically enough, before descending into misogynistic diatribes. All roads led back to Australia.

✠

On 1 July 2000, Michael and Mary Shelley arrived at Anna Bligh's home in Highgate Hill, a suburb of inner-city Brisbane. It was 4.15 pm on a Saturday afternoon. The government minister was inside with her husband, Greg, and their two sons, aged twelve and seven. Greg answered the front door.

Michael handed Greg a cardboard parcel. It was addressed to SAUL SHELLEY in blue ink and covered with pictures cut from magazines.

"Anna," called Greg. "There are people here to see you."

Anna Bligh appeared. She immediately recognised the Shelleys. They chatted for fifteen minutes on the front steps of the renovated Queenslander.

"My daughter was taken from us," said Mary. "I need to see her."

The minister listened to their complaints with the amicability of a seasoned politician. She promised to deliver the parcel to the department.

"New Zealand told you I have a history of using firearms and bombs," said Michael with a disconcerting grin. "Blasphemy! We are totally non-violent people. Do you really think someone like *me* would try to blow up your house?"

Michael gave Bligh his phone number. The Shelleys left the residence on foot. The mention of explosives freaked out the politician. She called the bomb squad. They evacuated the surrounding houses before defusing the parcel. It contained a handwritten book of Michael's favourite song lyrics.

The Devil's Lettuce

Mick Bishop – aka Elijah Shelley – graduated from high school and enrolled in an IT degree at Central Queensland University. At roughly the same age as his biological father, Mick discovered the devil's lettuce: marijuana.

His foster parents suspected drug use. They sent Mick on a run to the tip in the farm ute. While he was gone, they searched his car. His foster dad located a sandwich bag of cannabis in the armrest of the back seat.

Mick cut all contact with them. He moved into a Queenslander around the corner from the uni. A bong sat on the back table. Mick was soothed by communion with the other stoners. They were lost but not lonely. Everything was warm and funny. While high, the past seemed like a walk in the park.

Next door was a student share house. Latoya was thin and pretty. Her maternal grandfather was an Aboriginal didgeridoo maker. Her maternal grandmother was a Sri Lankan émigré.

In a green Holden Commodore, Mick took Latoya lapping up the main street of Rockhampton. Tupac blared from the speakers. Mick drove Latoya to the top of Mount Archer, overlooking the ochre-tinted horizon. He lit a joint and rapped all the words to "No Diggity" by Blackstreet.

"Latoya, I can't stop thinking about you," he said.

"Oh, Mick," she said. "I think you're gorgeous."

Mick was Latoya's first true love. He was brash and passionate. Their life together became a humid haze of bodily fluids and bong smoke. Soon, university fell by the wayside. Mick became a full-time dope dealer. He shaved his skull. Latoya watched her boyfriend beat the shit out of a customer. Self-defence was high on his list of priorities. Contraception wasn't.

"Mick, I'm pregnant," said Latoya one afternoon.

"True?" asked Mick.

"True," she said.

"What are you going to do?"

Latoya had already decided to have the baby, regardless of Mick's attitude towards fatherhood. She made peace with the possibility he might not stick around.

"I'm keeping it," she said.

Mick skipped from the dim flat into the street. He raised a fist of glee to the bright blue sky. Latoya was giddy. The love of her life wanted a kid, too. They ran to the nearest phone box and called her parents to deliver the news. Mick didn't ring a single soul. His kin seemed light-years away.

The couple moved into a little unit on the Fitzroy River, in the suburb of Berserker. Latoya gave birth to a baby boy: Jason Charles, or JC for short.

"I'll see youse tomorrow," said Mick to Latoya.

Mick didn't see his partner and child tomorrow, or for a while. The women in her life claimed that some men were like this. Fatherhood freaked them out and tested their desire for the new mother. Then Mick reappeared at their flat. He was distant with Latoya but affectionate with Jason.

"He's beautiful," said Mick, cradling his baby.

✠

Michael Shelley somehow discovered that his son Elijah was in Rockhampton. The Shelleys rushed to Beef City. They gate-crashed the local child safety office. Without disclosing Mick's identity, a social worker facilitated a phone conversation between the Shelleys and their eldest child.

"WHERE ARE YOU?" roared Michael Shelley.

"I can't tell you that," said Mick Bishop.

"We need your help to find Hannah," said Mary.

"Piss off," said Mick, hanging up.

It was a blast from the past, and not a nice one. *Blood runs thicker than water*, thought Mick. If the Shelleys kidnapped him, what was stopping them from kidnapping Jason? Mick developed a suspicion that he was being followed. He believed an intruder was moving furniture around the flat at night. The police pulled over his green Holden Commodore for speeding.

"Licence," said one of the cops.

Mick's licence had been lost due to a string of hooning offences.

"I don't have one," he said.

"What's your name and date of birth, son?"

"Elijah Shelley," he said. "September 7, 1980."

The police officers couldn't find him in their database of Australian citizens. Mick was placed in the backseat of the cop car. The police officers located a serrated knife in his glovebox, and a non-commercial quantity of pot in the armrest. They also found the liar's wallet, which contained an ID card for Central Queensland University. His real name was Michael Bishop.

Mick was charged with speeding, driving unlicensed, weapon possession, drug possession and providing a false identity. He didn't have the money for a good lawyer, or any hunger to publicly clarify his identity.

"What do you plead?" asked the judge.

"Guilty, Your Honour," said Mick.

The judge gave him a year; six months with good behaviour. Mick was sent to Etna Creek Prison. His biological father had served time there in the early 1980s. It was a high-security jail half an hour north. The blue sky summoned red dust from surrounding cattle farms. They were dried out from drought. Mick entered jail a pothead and left an intravenous speed addict.

++

With three mouths to feed, Mick Bishop dealt more drugs than before he went to jail. He sat on the couch, amazingly blazed, listening to music over the cries of his one-year-old son. He kept his stash in Jason's nappy bucket. The boom box reverberated through the walls, shaking his son's cradle.

"Can you just fuck off?" asked Latoya.

"Sweet," said Mick.

Mick disappeared on a bender. Latoya suspected he was with a serious drug dealer. At 3 am, she stumbled up Glenmore Road, baby Jason asleep in her arms. On the dark street, sirens spun silently beside the mother and son.

"What are you doing out at this time of night?" asked a police officer.

"I'm just goin' for a stroll," said Latoya.

"North Rocky's a dangerous place at this time of night," said the police officer. "Lots of druggos in this town now. Hop in. We'll give you a lift home."

The cops dropped Latoya and Jason home. The sun rose, with no sight of Mick. He materialised in the afternoon, strung out and unapologetic. Mick slept for nearly as long as he was gone. Then he awoke to the cries of Jason.

"It never stops," said Mick.

"You'd rather party than be a father!" said Latoya.

"I'd rather die!" yelled Mick, burying his face in a pillow.

Latoya didn't know much about mental health, but Mick's regular threats to kill himself seemed like statements of intent, not cries for help.

"Mick, I think you need some help," she said. "This is too much."

"I'm always too much," he whispered. "Just leave me alone."

Mick saved the bouts of euphoria for his mates and the bouts of despair for Latoya and Jason. Between the gloom and glee were moods of paranoia. One afternoon, he found a syringe atop the medicine cabinet.

"What's this?" he asked Latoya, grabbing her stiffly by the wrist.

Latoya stared at the needle in his hand and at the blame on his face.

"It's not mine," she said. "You know I hate needles."

"I can't fucking trust you!" he shouted, shoving her against the wall.

"Oh, get fucked, Mick!" she screamed. "It's probably yours, ya junkie! Or one of the drug-fucked mates you keep bringing round here."

Mick hit Latoya. It wasn't the last time. She was numb for a moment. Then pain consumed her skin. Mick showed no sign of remorse. His irate face had become unrecognisable. Or maybe she had seen him clearly.

"You weak piece of shit," whispered Latoya. "Just fuck off."

"I'm going," he said, grabbing his stash from the nappy bucket.

Latoya had no exposure to domestic violence. She had never dreamed of getting hit by someone she loved. Yet she also didn't dream of telling her parents or ringing the police. Latoya was afraid of Mick Bishop. But she was more afraid that he would leave the flat and never come back.

Warmer

One lunchtime, Michael and Mary showed up at the office of the Queensland director-general. It was on the seventh floor of a skyscraper in the Brisbane CBD. Michael carried a large bag. He visited the disabled toilets three times in fifteen minutes. The receptionist alerted security to a potential bomb threat.

"God will punish you, you fat slut!" Michael shouted at her.

Michael had one clue to the location of his missing children: Saul's shirt in that old photo. Ipswich Swimming Club. The Shelleys sniffed around my father's hometown, getting warmer, but still an hour away from Toowoomba.

"Ipswich is a hell on earth!" wrote Michael. "The climate is awful, the architecture ugly, the people fat and angry. No wonder there are so many drug addicts."

Michael and Mary visited the Ipswich office of the department. Mary stood on a coffee table, demanding to know the whereabouts of her children. The Ipswich office had no access to their highly classified foster care files. Mary grabbed the glasses from the face of a social worker. She snapped them in half.

Michael and Mary paid another visit to Anna Bligh at 11.30 pm on a Sunday. The family were woken up by banging on the door. Bligh's mild-mannered husband dealt with the wild-eyed missionaries through the security screens. Dogs barked at the squabble. Dimly lit faces filled the windows of the adjacent houses. Some of the braver neighbours stood on their porches.

"I'm not leaving until I see Hannah!" said Mary.

"That's impossible," Greg said.

"Anything is possible!" said Mary. "How would you like it if we kidnapped your children? And kept them hidden in the middle of nowhere?"

Anna Bligh feared physical assault. She remained inside, comforting her sons. The walls lit up with red and blue lights. The police officers asked the Shelleys to leave. Michael complied. He vanished onto the streets of Highgate Hill. Mary refused. She was arrested and taken to the watchhouse.

Anna Bligh took out a restraining order against the couple. The Shelleys were charged with unlawful stalking and menacing a government agency. Boggo Road Gaol was out of action. Michael was remanded in Wacol Prison. Mary was sent to John Oxley Hospital, a modern alternative to the Wolston Park Asylum.

Mary was kept with murderers in the Whitlock Unit. A psychiatrist noted her mood swings, rapid speech and religious delusions. She was diagnosed with paranoid schizophrenia. Four male nurses and two female nurses held her down while doctors injected zuclopenthixol into her posterior.

"There was an obsessive reliance on drugs to manage emotional distress, and virtually no emphasis on individual and group therapy," wrote Michael.

The hospital was pervaded by the scent of sweat and cigarette smoke. Mary was bullied by the other patients. Natasha smashed Mary over the head with a plastic bag of CDs. Anthony pulled her long, grey hair. Rodney flashed his penis. Mary ate alone. Michael called three or four times a day from Wacol.

"I feel irritable, anxious and depressed," Mary told Michael. "The drugs give me nightmares. They turn all of the patients into shuffling zombies."

Between phone calls with Mary, Michael became a jailhouse lawyer for his fellow inmates. He implored them to appeal their sentences. Then, in the serenity of the early morning, Michael penned letters to his enemies.

"I need to give you an unequivocal warning," Michael wrote to Matt Foley, the Queensland attorney-general. "What you do to me or my wife, you do to HIM who sent us. Justice will prevail, but you may not be around to see it."

++

Steven Blaine was a shy academic trapped inside the body of a football jock. The St Mary's house captain had a square jawline, dimples and a six-pack. He spent Saturday nights reading science fiction and watching history documentaries.

"I think I want to study accounting," he told Mum, the bookkeeper.

"How wonderful!" she said.

Mum took credit for his intelligence. Behind her back, social workers agreed it was an inheritance from Michael Shelley. More importantly for Dad, Steven was entering his prime as a rugby league player. Both his shoulders needed reconstructions from a willingness to crunch players heavier than him.

Steven delayed the surgeries, risking incapacitation. He was selected in the Queensland Confraternity team – the best Catholic schoolboys in the state – alongside Johnathan Thurston, his teammate from St Mary's. Steven was voted St Mary's player of the tournament over the future NRL star.

The trial for the Queensland under-seventeen team was in Brisbane. On the bus to the game, Steven listened to a Pearl Jam mixtape on his Walkman. He was the best second rower on the field. But when they announced the Queensland team, Steven's name wasn't read out over the loudspeaker. He got a lift home to Toowoomba with my father and me. Dad promised to lobby various NRL clubs to offer Steven a professional contract.

"You can make the NRL, mate," said Dad. "You just need to get bigger."

Secretly, Steven was relieved. He didn't love rugby league. It was Dad's religion, not his. At the macho training camps, Steven suffered chronic imposter's syndrome. The only thing that kept him going through the social anxiety and physical pain was a crippling fear of my father's disappointment.

✠

In November 2000, Steven graduated from high school. My parents reluctantly permitted him to attend Schoolies Week on the Gold Coast. It was just before the boozy coming-of-age ritual that Steven received a letter from his biological father. Michael Shelley was still on remand in Wacol Prison. He berated "Saul" for not responding to any of his previous letters.

"Joshua and you have clearly been neglected and abused by your atrocious foster parents," wrote Michael. "I will see you both soon. I expect an apology, or at least a good explanation. Your father – your only father – *Michael*."

Steven read the letter over a bowl of Nutri-Grain. He slipped into an unfamiliar rage. This physical specimen was no longer afraid of

Michael Shelley. He handwrote a blistering response in pencil on a sheet of A4 paper.

To my supposed "father",

Not everyone on this earth has pointlessly devoted their lives to God. Me personally, I'm an atheist. It is quite obvious that your pathetic way of life was more important than keeping us. I blame your manipulative ways for the fact that my biological mother is in a mental institution. You've brainwashed her with a false reality.

How dare you criticise my real parents. It was they who saw me off on my first day of school. It was they who taught me how to ride a bike. It was they who helped me through the good times and bad times. So when you have some spare time – I imagine you have quite a bit in jail, what a role model! – think about all the things that you have missed. I've been waiting to write this letter for a long time. I'll leave you with the following statement: I will never consider you my real father.

Saul Shelley

Steven drove to Surfers Paradise for seven days and seven nights of alcohol-fuelled obliteration. A letter was waiting upon his return to Toowoomba.

"WHO DO YOU SERIOUSLY BELIEVE YOU ARE TO TALK TO ME LIKE THAT?" asked Michael. "Your meaningless existence consists of servitude to a sporting and academic obstacle course. I cannot believe that any son of mine would want to study something as trivial as accounting."

Steven was accepted into a commerce degree. He declined to pursue an NRL career. In this way, he managed to dissatisfy both Tom

Blaine and Michael Shelley, the rival gods competing to shape his fate with their desires.

My Sister's Keeper

Mum signed Rebecca and Hannah up for field hockey. Their jerseys were green and black. Dad knew nothing about hockey, but he witnessed intimations of greatness. Hannah saw the ball more clearly than those around her. And she sat older girls from fancy private schools on their backsides.

To Hannah's amazing shame, she had begun to grow boobs. All of her teammates were thin and flat-chested. They wore expensive sports bras. Hannah felt fat, slow and poor in comparison. Mum bought her some cheap, uncomfortable bras from Kmart. Both were blushing in the changeroom.

"You're becoming a woman!" said my mother, clicking her tongue.

"This sucks, Mum," said Hannah. "I'd rather be a boy."

Hannah had beaten Rebecca to the punch. Rebecca was flat-chested. She stuffed tissues in a boob tube that Mum bought her out of sympathy.

"Where are *my* tits, Mum?" asked Rebecca. "These things are bee stings!"

"Nature takes its own sweet time, Becca," said Mum.

Hannah's first period happened when she was eleven. She ignored the discharges, until my mother saw dried blood while doing the washing.

"Let's go for a wander to the shop," said Mum.

"What for?" asked Hannah, suspiciously.

"It's a surprise," said Mum.

The surprise was a discount packet of pads from my father.

"A period means you can have a baby one day!" said my mother.

"Gross, Mum," said Hannah, blushing.

Femininity was still a mystery to Mum. Her mother had never taken her to buy bras or pads. She found it much easier dealing with male puberty.

++

Rebecca, Hannah and I went to the primary school at the end of our street: Toowoomba North State School. It was a two-storey, Depression-era brick building. Thanks to ADHD, Rebecca had been marked as a problem child.

Grades six and seven had been merged. The teacher decided to sit my sisters next to each other. She thought that Hannah would be a soothing influence, rather than a source of torture for Rebecca. The younger sister was well mannered. She never spoke without putting her hand up first. And her hand kept rising, because Hannah knew the answers to everything.

"Brown-noser," whispered Rebecca.

"Idiot," whispered Hannah.

Each time that Hannah got a question right, Rebecca felt a jolt of shame. Each time that Rebecca got in trouble, Hannah felt a jolt of pleasure.

One lunchtime, the sisters played cricket with the grade seven boys. Hannah was better than all of them. Rebecca concentrated on fielding.

"Mine!" Rebecca cried.

Hannah swooped in front of Rebecca and caught the ball one-handed.

"You're such a try-hard!" yelled Rebecca.

Hannah threw the ball to the wicketkeeper. She gave the finger to Rebecca. The older sister had suffered enough. She dug the sharp nails of both hands into Hannah's forearms. Then she dragged hard enough to draw blood.

Hannah screamed. The principal came running. Mr Nelson was a tall man with grey hair and sunglasses. He wore a white button-up shirt with cargo shorts and thick white socks to the knees. Hannah showed him the gashes.

"How could you do this to your own sister?" Mr Nelson asked Rebecca.

There were a million reasons. Rebecca couldn't pick just one.

"Want to know where violence will lead you in the real world?" he asked.

"Where?" asked Rebecca.

"Prison," said the principal.

Rebecca received a suspension and a week of detentions. Hannah went home with Band-Aids on her arms. The scratches stung. But she was calm. My mother would receive proof of Rebecca's maliciousness.

"Hey, Mum," said Hannah.

Mum was hanging washing on the line. She appeared from the other side of a white sheet. No sympathy on her face, just disappointment.

"I can't believe this, Hannah," said Mum. "How many times have I asked you to protect your sister? You just wait until your dad gets home, miss."

"Mum, I've got scars on my arms!" she said.

"You can't see Rebecca's scars," said my mother.

Hannah ran laps around the back paddock. Her brain composed detailed narratives about why Mum hated her. That night, she sat with Dad on the patio.

"Never – *ever* – dob on ya sister," said my father, as if he was a mafia boss and Hannah a *caporegime*. "We keep our brouhahas in the family."

"Mr Nelson saw it!" she said.

"Hannah, life doesn't come so easily to most of us," he said. "Your sister needs a bitta love. Not sittin' in a detention room coppin' shit from Mr Long Socks."

Hannah was dizzy. She was being punished for Rebecca's sins. The next day, Hannah passed the principal's office. Mr Nelson checked on the scratches.

"I imagine that your sister got into big trouble," said the principal.

"Nup," said Hannah. "*I* got into big trouble."

The principal was flabbergasted by the depravity of Hannah's foster parents. What kind of upside-down moral world were these bogans living in?

"Well, she's in big trouble with me," said Mr Nelson.

Hannah savoured this affirmation. Steven's perfectionism was a coping mechanism for anxiety. Her perfectionism was a coping mechanism for female rage. At the end of the year, she was elected school captain.

Snakes and Ladders

At the Ipswich District Court, Michael Shelley came face-to-face with the man he threatened to kill: Mike Ahern. The ex-premier of Queensland wore a stately grey suit with a navy tie. The ponytailed preacher – on day release from jail – wore a purple kaftan with denim jeans. He represented himself.

"I am a minister of God," said Michael, cross-examining his accuser. "Why on earth would you interpret my spiritual warning as a death threat?"

"Your disciple threatened my children," said Ahern. "He was arrested on my front lawn! You wrote a letter stating that I was about to die."

Mike Ahern detailed the expensive security precautions that followed the death threat. Michael Shelley counterattacked with a meticulous history of the corruption within the Bjelke-Petersen government that Ahern belonged to.

"This is a vexatious and malicious prosecution based upon the considerable guilt of those bringing the charge against me," said Michael.

Ahern had a change of heart. Exhausted, he directed the Department of Public Prosecutions to drop the charges. Next, Michael faced the Queensland Supreme Court on charges of menacing Anna Bligh. He pleaded guilty and was released from prison on a five-year good behaviour bond.

Michael turned his attention to a new dispute. He represented Mary at the Mental Health Tribunal. He denied that his wife was schizophrenic, or that she required any kind of mood stabilisers.

"For over three years, Mary has been trying without success to organise one five-minute phone call with her daughter," he said. "Why is that so difficult?"

Surprisingly, Michael and Mary found an ally. Mary had spent months being analysed by Diana Lange, Queensland's most senior public psychiatrist. She had perused all the unredacted files about the Shelleys.

The Stolen Generations loomed large over a new generation of government officials. Lange critiqued the original basis for permanently removing Elijah, Saul, Joshua and Hannah from their mother's custody. Some of the Shelleys' eccentric beliefs about diet had since become mainstream.

"Many of the paediatric reports about a failure to thrive do not have findings that are persuasive, with the exception of one child where there is clear evidence of a problem, but the causation is less evident," wrote Lange.

Diana Lange disagreed with Mary's diagnosis of schizophrenia. She asserted that bipolar remained her most likely mental illness. According to the psychiatrist, Mary's was bereaved and occasionally manic, but not totally psychotic. Her sense of persecution was partly grounded in reality.

"I have not become aware of any evidence providing adequate reasons for the total removal of the children and refusal of access," wrote Lange. "There has been no physical violence or sexual assault, the parents are not substance abusers, and far sicker people than Mary have had access to their children."

At long last: vindication! Michael disagreed that Mary was suffering from *any* mental illness. But a well-credentialled expert had verified two decades' worth of gripes against the Queensland government. Nothing happened. There was no public apology or financial compensation. Social workers didn't deliver Saul, Joshua and Hannah to the courtroom doors for a family reunion. They were still hidden, with fake names and fake parents.

"There is no middle ground here," wrote Michael. "The time for fence-sitting is over. Our case divides the corrupt from the caring; the cowardly from the courageous; the dastardly from the decent; the horrendous from the humane."

++

The Shelleys went back to where it all began: Sydney. Michael's mother, Marie, had died of old age. Her house on the Lower North Shore was now worth a seven-figure sum. But Marie explicitly disinherited Michael, due to his harassment of her. His younger brother, Tom – a happy-go-lucky postman – was living in the house.

Tom accommodated Michael and Mary. At night, while Tom was asleep, Michael rifled through Marie's files. He found extensive correspondence between Marie Shelley and Susan King, dating back to the early 1980s.

"My son, Michael, was an intelligent young man with the world at his feet," wrote Marie. "But he ruined his mind with alcohol and drugs. Now, he is a dangerous narcissist. I feel sorry for his wife and my grandchildren."

The duplicity! Michael wished that she could die twice. But he stumbled upon a silver lining to the betrayal: the identities of his children.

There were regular letters between Marie and a foster carer named Lenore Blaine. They arranged phone calls and visits to Sydney for Michael's children, escorted by a man named Tom. He was presumably Lenore's husband. And he was presumably the obese redneck in photos with Michael's mother and children, eating a deep-fried dagwood dog at Darling Harbour.

Saul and Joshua had been renamed Steven and John. Hannah's name had stayed the same. Marie received hundreds of photographs as they grew up. Michael became sleepless with schemes. He was sitting on something much better than an inheritance: the return address on the most recent letter.

31 Gowrie Street, Toowoomba, Queensland, 4350.

The Parable of the Black Sheep

John Blaine was horrified by the re-emergence of Michael and Mary Shelley. They threatened to expose the biological barcode hiding below his mask. In his final year of high school, John performed a leading role in the mafia musical *Bugsy Malone*. He had an unexpectedly beautiful singing voice.

My father went to the Empire Theatre. But he couldn't fabricate the same level of rapture he channelled towards Steven's sporting exploits.

"Bravo, mate," Dad said to John on the drive home. "Bloody bravo!"

John had grown taller and slimmer, but he was still shivering in Steven's shadow. At school, he was stuck in a clique of C-list nerds. John played the euphonium in the school band. His marks stagnated in the high Cs. The more disillusioned my parents grew, the further his marks deteriorated.

"I don't want to be Steve!" yelled John. "Stop comparing me to him!"

John was afflicted by a gut-wrenching dread. Soon, it was a struggle just to open both eyelids and shuffle to the kitchen table for a bowl of cereal. Mundane tasks such as tying his shoelaces and brushing his teeth seemed unbearable. He constantly felt on the verge of bursting into tears.

"What the fuck is wrong with me?" he wondered.

At night, John suffered from involuntary visions. In his mind's eye, he watched a simulation of himself climb onto the corrugated iron roof of the garage out the back. From there, he nosedived onto the concrete driveway.

John called in sick to school with complaints of migraines.

"I'm worried about you, Johnnie," said Mum. "What's going on?"

"I just feel like shit, all the time," John said. "Nothing feels good."

My mother organised meetings with John's teachers. They provided extensions on his assignments. A GP diagnosed John with textbook depression. He was prescribed Prozac as a pick-me-up before exams. In a spring cricket game, the broad-shouldered fast bowler took five wickets for ten runs. This included an in-swinger that snapped the middle stump.

"Back to the pavilion!" John shouted at the embarrassed batter.

The Shelley Curse had lifted. John flunked his final exams but passed a driving test. He bought a green two-door Daewoo Lanos. On the first night of Schoolies Week 2001, John got blotto. He pierced his nipple and dyed his hair blue. It turned blond in the waves of Surfers Paradise. So he dyed it green.

John came home looking and acting like The Joker, with a bundle of elaborate gifts. I received a bucket hat and a shark-tooth necklace.

"Why's John in such a good mood?" I asked Dad.

Whereas Mum was always finding psychological excuses for strange behaviour, Dad suspected the erratic mood patterns had a chemical origin.

"Your brother's been smoking meth," he said.

The only university course that would accept John was early childhood education. Late on a Friday night in March 2002, he drove alone into Queens Park. The hoon ripped high-speed donuts around the cricket pitch, shredding the infield, while crooning "Come Fly with Me" by Frank Sinatra. Then he pulled the handbrake. The tyres incinerated the artificial grass.

Sirens appeared from the park's entrance. John played dead. He turned the headlights off. But as the police car neared, he hit the accelerator. The police pursued him at high speed. At a busy intersection, John indicated left. He turned right at the last minute and ran a red light. The Daewoo was five seconds from being t-boned by a Nissan Patrol.

John felt a strange acceptance of his fate. All those nights he nearly killed himself. Now he'd cheated death again. Maybe God was real. Maybe the Shelleys were right. Maybe John was divine. He surrendered outside the police station.

"You got me," said John, offering his wrists.

The copper was John's old junior cricket coach, Ian.

"Your dad will kill you," Ian said. "How much have you had to drink?"

"I'm sober!" said John, truthfully.

Ian was well aware of the fuss being caused by the Shelleys. He condensed half-a-dozen infringements into a single ticket. John kept his licence. He wouldn't have to go to court or have his face emblazoned in the newspaper.

"But you need to tell your mum and dad," said Ian. "Or I will."

On Saturday night, following a shift pushing trolleys, John handed the rap sheet to Mum. She wept for her failure as a mother. John was a menace.

"I swear I'm not on drugs," he said. "But I feel high all the time."

The next day, Mum took him to a psychiatrist. John completed a series of quizzes. The diagnosis: bipolar II. He was prescribed serious mood stabilisers.

"This isn't your fault, Johnnie," cried Mum. "I love you so much!"

John shuffled to the corner store. His nostrils filled with grease. Out the back, Dad was watching the horseracing. The TV remote rested on his rising and falling gut. They stared at each other in silence.

"What's the matter, Dizzy?" asked Dad, muting the horseracing.

"They reckon I've got bipolar," said John.

"Shit, hey," said my father. "Everyone's got something, but."

John burst into tears. Dad allowed him to whimper and snivel into his warm chest without censorship. The diagnosis went way beyond a sibling rivalry with Steven. Antidepressants had been a short-term solution to the stress of final exams. This implied something lifelong and unfixable.

"I don't want to go on the medication," said John.

Dad glared at his son with sympathy and irritation.

"It's a disease," said Dad. "Just like I've got diabetes. So cut this poor-me bullshit and take your tablets, mate. Or you'll end up in the nuthouse."

The speech wasn't politically correct, but it did the trick. John swallowed two purple mood stabilisers with a glass of tank water. In this way, bipolar diverged from being a potential death sentence to a sly quirk of John's nature.

The Ascension

Three days after John was diagnosed with bipolar, Michael and Mary Shelley drove up the Great Dividing Range in a 1978 white Chrysler Valiant. They parked the Valiant on the main strip of Toowoomba. Then they checked into a queen suite on the seventh floor of the Burke and Wills Hotel.

The Shelleys walked to the Mort Estate. Michael sported a white t-shirt with a blue cross on the front. Mary wore a purple dress that sailed above her sandals. Our house was much uglier than either of them had envisioned. Michael was facing instant prison time if caught within touching distance of Hannah. He went back to the hotel. Mary opened the wrought-iron gate.

In the sunroom, my mother sat reading. Mary rang the bell. Mum looked at the clock. 5.01 pm. Nobody who knew us entered via the front. It was too late for business visits. Mum answered the insistent knocking.

"Jeez Louise," said my mother.

Finally, Mary came face-to-face with the woman who had replaced her. Mum wore Ugg boots and tracksuit pants. A black-and-white striped t-shirt. Shapeless face and oversized reading glasses. Grey hair cut short.

"My name is Mary Shelley," Mary said, with the fading trace of an upper-class British accent. "I am here to see Saul, Joshua and Hannah. *My* children."

"G'day, Mary," said Mum, regaining her composure. "Can I just get you to wait out the back for a few minutes, while I see if any of them are free?"

"Please don't keep me waiting," said Mary.

Mary inspected the property in a state of bliss and disgust. She stood under the rusted breezeway. It was occupied by a wobbly ping-pong table. "LAST PUB 897 KM" read a yellow sign beside the dartboard.

Mum moved through the house in a fugue. Dad was at cricket training with me. He had left his mobile in the bedroom. Steven was at work. Rebecca was watching TV while Hannah showered. John was shooting people on Nintendo 64.

"John," said Mum. "Mary Shelley is here."

"You're kidding," he said.

"I kid you not," she said.

John moaned and punched his mattress.

"Tell her to get fucked," he said.

"No, I shan't be telling her to do that," said Mum. "Please don't get angry. Can you get Hannah from the bathroom? I'm going to call the police."

In no shirt and a pair of Brisbane Lions shorts, John opened the bathroom door. Hannah hid behind the shower curtain, hair frothing with shampoo. John's intrusion was weird even by his recent standards.

"John, get the hell out!" she said.

"Our mother is here," he said.

The statement made zero sense. Hannah believed innately in the state-created fiction that Lenore Blaine was her mother. It didn't occur to her for even a split second that John meant their non-fictional mother Mary Shelley.

"I know she's here, you freak," said Hannah.

"Our *real* mother," said John.

"Jeez Louise," Hannah whispered.

John waited in the laundry for Hannah to dry off and get dressed. Through the back window, he watched Mary having an argument with the bird.

"G'day, mate!" squawked Jack, the corella.

"Silence, you stupid cockatoo!" shouted Mary.

Hannah's short, wet hair was slicked back with bobby pins. She wore shorts and a tight red singlet that said *GIRLS KICK HARDER THAN BOYS*. Mum opened the back door and led them to the unplanned reunion.

"My daughter!" cried Mary. "What have they done to you?"

Hannah was a public-speaking enthusiast. But the chatterbox was tongue-tied. Mary hugged her numb body. She relished the scent of her shampooed hair. A decade without the brush of Hannah's skin or the sound of her voice. A decade of emptiness, overcome with a single touch.

"I love you so much, Hannah," said Mary. "Do you know that?"

Hannah's brain floated above the embrace like a spaceship. Her nose and throat choked on the overflowing incense. She pulled away from Mary.

"We have the same blood," said Mary. "God made you from me."

John loomed between them, chest naked like a boxer.

"Don't touch her," said John.

"Joshua Shelley, how dare you speak to me like that!" said Mary.

"My name is John," he said. "John *Blaine*. B-L-A-I-N-E."

"Blasphemy. I am your mother. After all that I've done …"

"I wouldn't piss on ya if you were on fire. It'd be a waste of piss."

Hannah's lack of affection ruined Mary's beautiful delusion that her daughter had been waiting impatiently to be saved from the Blaines. John's profanity distracted Mary from confronting the fruitlessness of her pursuit.

"I refuse to listen to you without a shirt on!" she said.

"You'll be waitin' a long fuckin' time, mate," said John.

John stalked off down the driveway. Hannah was shaking like the final leaves of autumn. Rebecca ran outside and embraced her younger sister.

"Please don't kidnap Hannah!" sobbed Rebecca.

"And what is your name?" asked Mary.

"Rebecca Blaine," she whispered.

"There is plenty of room in heaven for a sister of Hannah," said Mary.

My mother stood on the driveway with a cordless phone in one hand. She twisted an unlit cigarette in the other. Mum smiled diplomatically to hide her anxiety, while trying to maintain eye contact with Mary out of politeness.

"How are you liking Toowoomba, Mary?" asked my mother.

"Why are you smiling at me, Satan's handmaiden?" asked Mary. "You have desecrated my daughter's beautiful hair. She looks like a shemale, like you!"

Mum studied Hannah, mystified. She had made peace with her own lack of attractiveness. But how could anyone look at Hannah and not see pure beauty?

"That's the way she likes it," said Mum. "I don't make her do anything. Hannah is an independent young woman. You should be really proud of her."

At this point, Steven's Mitsubishi Magna squealed to a stop on the street. He marched up the driveway, trailed by the two dogs. Rebecca and Hannah used the decoy of his arrival to slip inside the house. Mary studied the insult of her son's name badge from Amart All-Sports: *STEVEN*.

"Saul!" cried Mary. "Your name is Saul!"

Her son awkwardly reciprocated the hug. Mary Shelley didn't measure up to the female goliath of Steven's childhood reveries. His biological mother was short. Her wrinkled face was brimming with misery.

"Steve, if you could explain to Mary that your dad and me aren't molesting Hannah, that'd be greatly appreciated," said my mother wryly, going back inside.

Mum called the police to request more urgency. She made a quick diary entry. *5.01 pm – the arrival of Mary Shelley. LIFE WILL NEVER BE THE SAME AGAIN!!!* Then she went to the girls' bedroom. Hannah wept into a pillow. Rebecca clung to her sister's body. Mum embraced both of them.

"I don't wanna go to heaven yet!" cried Rebecca.

Steven and Mary discussed the custody battle under the breezeway.

"You can't just rock up out of the blue like this," said Steven.

"Saul, what choice did I have?" said Mary. "I am your mother. Nothing can change that. I haven't seen my own children in ten years."

Steven felt a pregnant pang of anger. It dissipated into pity.

"You need to go through the department," he said.

"I tried!" she said. "I really tried! They locked me up and threw away the key. They called me a 'schizophrenic'. Why? Because I love my children *too* much."

Steven found it hard to argue. He was at risk of capitulating to a damsel in distress. So he concentrated on the sinister spectre of Michael.

"Hannah isn't responsible for any of this," he said. "She's eleven. And she's freaked out that Michael and you are going to try and kidnap her."

"Listen to yourself, Saul," said Mary. "You've been brainwashed."

"I haven't been brainwashed," he said. "You kidnapped Elijah. You threatened to kidnap Hannah. I've read the letters. What have I got wrong?"

For almost two decades, the word "kidnap" had been used to deny Mary. To her, it was a nonsensical slur. She had been kidnapped in the middle of the night by her father and taken to Australia. Elijah had been saved. Just like Hannah would be saved if they managed to do it again. A police officer's definition of kidnapping was a mother's definition of a rescue mission.

"Hannah was kidnapped from us!" she said.

Steven offered an olive branch. He agreed to meet with Michael and Mary for dinner in Brisbane. If they could demonstrate civility towards him, he would attempt to facilitate direct contact between them and Hannah.

"But you need to leave," said Steven. "Or I won't help you."

"Do you promise to come?" asked Mary.

"Of course," Steven said. "I promise."

Mary Shelley kissed her son on the cheek. Then she left without saying goodbye to Hannah. Their true reunion would come soon enough.

The Nightwatchman

After cricket training, my father and I arrived at a crime scene. On the footpath, four police officers were taking statements from Steven and Mum. Dad shuffled grumpily towards them. I watched with a lump in my throat.

"What's goin' on?" asked Dad.

"The Shelleys know where we live," said Mum.

"Fuck me dead," said my father.

In the kitchen, we were greeted by silence. John, Rebecca and Hannah sat at the table. My mother had a frozen lasagne in the oven for us and a rump steak thawing on the sink for Dad. He sizzled the meat himself. Mum's mashed potato was even lumpier than usual. She didn't touch her food. John and I halved her uneaten lasagne.

"We need to leave," said Mum.

It wouldn't be difficult for the Shelleys to establish where Hannah went to primary school. Toowoomba North was fifty metres from our house. Mum wanted to protect Hannah from Michael, and Michael from my father.

"I'm staying," said Dad. "Never give in to tax collectors or terrorists."

"Dad's right," said John. "I'll flog the fuck out of Michael Shelley."

"What would that achieve?" asked Steven. "You'd be no better than him."

"Yeah, maybe we should have a debate," said John. "That'll do the trick."

My mother sat at the head of the table, stewing over the truth.

"Steve's right," she said. "Violence isn't the answer. That's exactly what Michael wants. A big fight. The department will put Hannah into another foster home if they don't think she's safe with us. Like they did with Elijah."

It was a blunt reminder of just how much lay outside of our control, and how many fronts we were now fighting on. Years of peace had allowed us to take independence for granted. The Blaines were a fake family.

✠

It was decided: the seven of us would stay at 31 Gowrie Street for the time being. That first night was terrifying. I refused to sleep in the sunroom. Dad sat on the edge of my bed with a cricket bat.

"Sleep with your mum," he said. "I'll be the nightwatchman."

Dad was kept awake by adrenaline and Diet Coke. A white Chrysler Valiant arrived in the early morning. It idled outside the house. Mary climbed from the passenger's seat in a long, white dress. Dad opened the front door. This triggered the sensor light.

"Where's ya husband?" Dad murmured.

Mary didn't seem surprised to see him standing there.

"Thomas Blaine, you can't fight Michael with a cricket bat," she said.

At the letterbox, Mary made the sign of the cross. She slipped an envelope through the slit. Then she and the Chrysler disappeared from the silent street. Dad collected the envelope. It was addressed to him. The back leaf featured a crucifix sticker with a black X hanging above it. Back inside, he turned on the sunroom light and read the letter on the edge of my bed.

"AS GOD'S CHOSEN PROPHETESS," wrote Mary, "I GIVE YOU A FINAL WARNING FROM GOD. I NEED MY DAUGHTER HANNAH RETURNED TO MICHAEL + I TODAY WITH APPROPRIATE COMPENSATION ($100,000 WOULD BE A NICE START) OR GOD WILL SEND HIS NEVERENDING WRATH UPON YOUR HEAD."

The words "GOD", "HANNAH", "MICHAEL" and "WRATH" were inscribed with a gold-gel pen, love hearts scribbled above. The rest was written in black. It included directions to read Proverbs 10:2, and email addresses for Michael and Mary: michael_the_one@yahoo.com and mary_the_missionary@yahoo.co.uk.

Dad had never used a computer, let alone the internet. He went to the master bedroom. Mum and I were asleep. The bible in the drawer was a family heirloom. He turned on the light in the kitchen and flipped to Proverbs 10:2.

"Righteousness delivereth from death," it read.

My father cracked a grin. They were trying to extort a non-existent $100,000 from an atheist via bible verses. How did the Shelleys intend to get rid of their Judas? A crucifixion? He was certainly too heavy for a cross.

++

Mum didn't see the funny side. Neither did the police officers or the social workers. The following morning, our house was overrun by public servants. They treated the letter as a legitimate act of blackmail: return Hannah or die.

The Department of Child Safety booked us into a three-star motel across the road from the racecourse. We stayed there under a fake surname. On Friday night, the Blaine family ate takeaway pizzas. Steven and John shared a twin suite at the motel. The rest of us crammed into a family room. At 5 am, we were startled awake by the approach of an apocalyptic clattering.

"It's just the trackwork jockeys," said my father.

Nobody got back to sleep. That morning, Dad and I drove to my junior rugby league game. Mum took Rebecca and Hannah to the hockey club. Steven went to do a shift at work. John insisted on returning to Gowrie Street.

"Someone needs to feed the dogs," he said.

"Are you sure?" asked my mother.

"What are they going to do to me?" he scoffed.

Crisis required routine. John got changed into a Brisbane Lions jersey and joggers. He took great pride in being better at manual labour than Steven. He whipper-snipped first, and then collected the grass shavings with the mower.

A white Chrysler Valiant pulled up on the street. Red upholstery glowed through tinted windows. White rosary beads swayed from the rear-view mirror.

"Oh, fuck," whispered John.

Mary Shelley climbed from the passenger's seat. She slipped another envelope into the letterbox. Michael Shelley climbed from the driver's seat. A white, billowy robe ran to the tips of his skinny wrists and ankles.

"Good morning, Joshua," said Michael. "I finally get to speak to you, man to man. You need to stop running from the truth of who you are."

John preferred his fictional identity to the factual one that the Shelleys were determined to unearth and widely publicise. Michael moved closer to the fence line. John exploded into flight. He sprinted up the driveway.

"Don't be a coward, Joshua!" called Michael.

The motor of the mower kept going. John high-jumped the back fence. He bounced from the trampoline onto the grass. He bolted through the back door of a neighbouring boarding house. The pensioner pointed him to the phone on the kitchen bench. John dialled 000. But the story he told made little sense.

"My name is Joshua Shelley," said John. "I mean John Blaine! My parents just arrived at my house. Michael and Mary Shelley. 31 Gowrie Street."

"Are you in danger?" asked the operator.

"Extreme danger!" he said. "They want to kidnap my sister."

"Your sister is their daughter, I presume?"

"We're fostered. They aren't allowed to be here!"

The Shelleys waited in vain at the front gate for Joshua to return. They heard sirens in the middle distance. Mary wandered around the corner, just before the arrival of three police cars. Michael pointed towards 31 Gowrie Street and explained the situation. He was handcuffed on suspicion of stalking.

"What an enormous waste of police resources," said Michael.

"That's for us to worry about," said a cop. "Where's ya wife?"

"Mary operates under her own spiritual jurisdiction," said Michael.

Michael was taken to the watchhouse of the police station. Mary was arrested while praying at the cathedral beside the Burke and Wills Hotel.

Back at the motel, John collapsed into Mum's arms.

"I just want 'em to fuck off," he cried.

"I know, Johnnie," said Mum. "I do too."

One of the police officers handed Mum an envelope addressed to her in messy capital letters. It contained the unmistakable smell of Mary's incense.

THE YEAR OF OUR LORD 2002

To: Lenore Blaine,

How have you managed to pull the wool over Tom's eyes for so long? You are quite clearly a closeted lesbian. Hard, shut-off, asexual yet masculine. That is how women become when their fat husbands don't know how to satisfy them.

You are a LESBIAN + a PEDOPHILE, ugly, grossly ugly. How could you ever make love? There is no love in your empty heart, no love in your ugly home, no love in the lives of our children except what we send them continuously.

Your husband, Tom, is a fat pig, and all grossly overweight people are child abusers. GOD will hold YOU responsible for the rape of Hannah. She is edgy + jumpy + angry + confused. <u>THERE IS NO EXCUSE FOR CHILD ABUSE EVER</u>!

11 years – 11 years! + you have the gall to sit there + say: "It isn't my fault, it is the Department of Families". <u>LIAR</u>! You have chosen to be part of the system for years, so that you can extort money in the name of "fostering". You foster DECEIT, LIES & HALF-TRUTHS in our children's hearts.

Today, it is your choice to continue to serve the depravity of the Department, or to effect the return of Hannah. Simply + swiftly. I am a chosen prophetess of GOD + Michael is a prophet. "At that time will Michael stand up and there will be a time of trouble such as the world has never seen." Just for your information, that is my husband. Well, Lenore, the Lord of Israel is about to set you + Tom some overdue limits.

I am giving you a chance to get down on your knees and beg GOD for forgiveness. If you choose not to repent, GOD will afflict you with a terminal illness. Fear, pain + dread all the time, just like you + Tom have done to Saul, Joshua + Hannah for decades. <u>HOW JUST</u>!

You wish to tempt GOD, well go right ahead, but take another look at what GOD <u>allowed</u> to happen to New York on 9/11. When you stand before HIM – and you will – HE will say: "I never knew you! To hell for ETERNITY." When it happens, remember that <u>I warned you</u>.

Faithfully,
MARY SHELLEY – <u>HANNAH'S MOTHER</u>

P.S. You don't look like a female, dress like a female, or speak like a female. What do you have to teach Hannah about womanhood? YOU ARE A <u>TRANSVESTITE</u>!

Mum read what seemed like a blatant death threat three times in quick succession, while chain-smoking cigarettes to pacify a rising panic attack.

"What does it say, Mum?" asked John.

Her eyes were wide. She sighed out a cloud of smoke.

"Long story short?" asked Mum. "The end is nigh."

Now it was her turn to cry in his arms.

A Plague of Paranoia

Mum was right. Our lives were never the same after the second coming of the Shelleys. There was a clear dividing line. BM. AM. *Before Mary. After Mary.*

In the short term, Hannah went to stay on a farm half an hour outside of town with the family of a hockey teammate. Dad dropped her to the hideout at dusk on a Monday. He watched the rear-view for a white Chrysler Valiant.

"What are you looking for?" asked Hannah.

"Dead roos," lied my father.

Dad's cheeks were even more beetroot-streaked than usual. He parked the Toyota Camry outside the farmhouse. Dust hovered in the headlights. Hannah hugged him before he had time to remove his seatbelt or the car keys.

"What's wrong with these people?" asked Hannah, sobbing.

Hannah's terror tapped a paternal urge that my father found hard to muzzle. He tried to come up with a diplomatic way of summarising the situation.

"Ya real mum and dad just aren't the full quid," he said.

"Do you think they'll actually try to kidnap me?" she asked.

Whenever my father contemplated the possibility of a kidnapping plot, he was gripped by extremely detailed visions of grabbing Michael's ponytail with one hand and feeding him full of uppercuts with the other.

"I reckon they're all hiss and no sting," he said. "But just remember one thing, darlin': I'd jump in front of a truck before I let anyone lay a finger on you."

My father was a man prepared to die for his daughter. She trusted this.

"Dad, I love you to bits," said Hannah, smiling through the tears.

"I love ya to bits, too," he said. "We'll be right. You'll see."

☨

Hannah got the easy way out. The rest of us needed to sleep at home. Through the windows of the sunroom, I searched for the faces of two moonlit lunatics.

That week, Mary Shelley's white dress was frequently seen fluttering in the dark beneath the branches of the camphor laurel. She hung a plastic bag of dead flowers on the front gate. The mailbox was inundated with letters for Steven, John, Hannah, and also Rebecca, whom Mary promised to liberate too.

Rebecca started sleepwalking. On the way to school in the morning, we could smell Mary's lingering incense. On another frightening night, Mary left a fresh death threat for my parents. The envelope contained white powder.

"Don't touch it!" Mum cried to my father at the kitchen table.

Mum was convinced the Shelleys had launched an anthrax attack.

"If that's anthrax, I'll eat my hat," said Dad.

"Michael has a degree in chemical engineering," said Mum.

The police took away the envelope for testing. The mysterious white powder was Wizz Fizz, the sherbet children ate with small plastic spoons.

Mary was arrested again on a separate trespassing charge. She was transferred to a local psychiatric hospital. The department sought a restraining order for Hannah. The court date was set for September. It was still only April.

Hannah came home. John dropped out of university and got a job as a roofer. He moved out with some cricket teammates. I gratefully claimed John's bedroom but was beset by sleep paralysis. My mother barely slept. Her GP prescribed Normison for the insomnia and Valium for the panic attacks.

Mum doubled the numbness by upgrading from mid-strength XXXX Gold stubbies to heavy cans of Bundaberg Rum and Coke. The cocktail of benzos and liquor made her feel amazingly dazed, until it inevitably wore off.

"They're my calm-me-down pills," said Mum.

Hannah packed lunches for Rebecca, herself and me. None of us spoke about Mum's unpredictable shifts between distress and listlessness. Nor did we talk about our fear of being kidnapped. We were in survival mode.

++

Mary Shelley was released from the psychiatric hospital. We steeled ourselves for looming attack. But the Shelleys took off to New Zealand.

Peter – the social worker responsible for taking Hannah to Australia – still lived on Waiheke Island. On an autumn afternoon, he took his children to the beach. Upon their return, Peter's son came into the house, pale-faced.

"Dad," he said. "There's a strange lady in our teepee."

Peter found Mary Shelley sitting cross-legged in the backyard tent.

"Mary, what are you doing here?" he asked.

Mary regurgitated Michael's gospel, without the same eloquence. She claimed to have seen a letter from Susan King imploring New Zealand police officers to "find these people and take their daughter no matter what".

Peter sent his children to their rooms. He invited Mary inside for a tea. Dried laundry was stacked on the dining table. Mary had been in the house. She had taken socks and underwear from the clothesline and carefully folded them up.

"How can you cast judgement on *me* as a mother?" asked Mary. "Just look at the state of your son's socks! They are disgusting. You know nothing."

Peter didn't feel threatened, merely unsettled. He saw a mother craving the embrace of her daughter. Mary gate-crashed the New Zealand Parliament. She was found sleeping in the gazebo of Jenny Shipley, the former prime minister. Mary was sent to a psych ward in Point Chevalier.

"It is Mary's unchangeable view her mental illness can be managed with prayer, meditation and swimming, rather than medication," wrote the psychiatrist.

Hannah's social worker announced the Shelleys' return to New Zealand, and her biological mother's incarceration in a psychiatric ward.

"That's the best news I've ever heard," said Hannah.

Hannah was too in the thick of panic for pity. On paper, we were safe. On paper, the Shelleys were two ageing bodies, restricted by the laws of physics.

But Mum didn't stop imagining the kidnapping of Hannah. Dad didn't stop shadowboxing with the revenant of Michael inside his head. Rebecca didn't stop sleepwalking. I didn't stop dreaming. Steven and John didn't stop spotting doppelgangers for Michael and Mary. Hannah didn't stop fretting that they were around every corner.

We felt as if Michael and Mary could hear our thoughts. The Shelleys seemed almighty, more like gods than human beings. Their paranoia was contagious. We were incapable of seeing their frailties or feeling their pains.

CHAPTER EIGHT

The Wheel of Fortune

During the height of the crisis, my father decided to sell the shop and buy a pub. But the only lease in his price range was a dive on the main street named the Metropole Hotel. Affordable, because there was no lease fee, just rent and bills.

"Eureka," said Dad, when he took Steven and John for an inspection.

The pub was one hundred years old. The corrugated iron roof was red and rusted. The brick exterior was covered with camel-coloured tiles that were sliding off. The doors and windows were shuttered with timber.

"It's a bit of a fixer-upper," said Dad.

The front bar smelled of stale liquor and fresh mould. The ceilings were yellowed by cigarette smoke. Cockroaches procreated beneath the beer mats. The underground cellar was a fruiting chamber for mushrooms.

"Are you sure this is a wise idea?" asked Steven.

Steven, the commerce student, saw a money pit. John saw a money tree. Eight pokies in the back bar. Enough space for two pool tables and a jukebox.

"Sign me up," said John.

Dad didn't need convincing. He opened the double-hung front door, shining light on the mice droppings scattered across the cracked tiles.

"You can buy a brand-new pub," said Dad. "Fresh paint. Flash furniture. But the one thing money can't buy is character. This place has got it in spades."

Up a carpeted flight of stairs, there were fifteen one-star hotel rooms occupied by pensioners and junkies. They paid $120 a week, cash-in-hand, for a single bed and a sink. The bathrooms and toilets were communal.

There was no paperwork between the landlord and the tenants. It was a handshake agreement. That night, my father had a recruitment meeting with John on the back patio. He saw a younger version of himself.

"Dizzy, whaddayawant from life?" asked my father.

John wouldn't be eighteen for another four months. He had somewhat stabilised since his bipolar diagnosis. But university hadn't worked out. Labouring for a minimum wage on rooftops was a stopgap, not a vocation.

"I want to work hard," said John. "Like you. That's it."

Nothing made John feel better than the exhaustion after a ten-hour shift in the sun, pushing trolleys or ripping up corrugated iron.

"Mate, you've got all the potential in the world," said my father. "You just haven't found a way to use it yet. Cause you're street smart, not book smart."

John nodded, spine tingling with his idol's praise.

"I'll do whatever you want," said John.

"This is about you," said Dad. "I wanna offer ya a job. Number two under me at the pub. Master and apprentice. I'll show ya everything I know."

++

Steven and John moved into the dark, grimy private quarters of the Metropole Hotel. It was a downtown bachelor pad. In return for free rent, Steven agreed to do my father's bookkeeping and the occasional shift behind the front bar.

"We need a slogan," said my father.

"Meet your mates at the Met," said Steven.

"John Singleton, eat ya heart out!" said Dad.

The Metropole reopened on 1 July 2002, a Monday morning. John removed the shutters with a hammerhead. *UNDER NEW MANAGEMENT*, my father wrote crookedly on the chalkboards adorning the exterior walls. *CHEAP BEER. NO DRESS CODE. MEET YOUR MATES AT THE MET.*

John wore a yellow XXXX Gold t-shirt, cargo shorts and Dunlop Volleys, his new uniform. He put a $300 float in the front till and a $200 float in the back till. At 10 am, John drew back the blinds and unlocked the four doors. Nobody came, except an old bushie with Tourette's named Kevin. He was banned from every other establishment in town for profanity.

"Fuck a platypus," Kevin mumbled at John, after his third pot of port.

John had a meeting with my father in the sound-proof cold-room.

"Do you want me to boot him?" asked John.

"No, mate," said my father. "If he pays, he stays."

"But I can smell him from here!" said John.

My father saw the public bar as society's last great leveller.

"Kev needs some excitement in his life, too," he said. "Everyone has a yarn. We all drink from the same cup. And we all shit from the same hole."

That first week, Kevin was the only regular customer. Dad was disappointed but unflustered. It would take time to attract the old regulars back from their new haunts. None of them had mobile phones or internet. The only avenues for advertising were chalkboards and word-of-mouth.

"Don't worry," Dad told John. "Eyes on the prize."

Dad installed a dartboard in the corner of the front bar. He rented two pool tables and a jukebox for the back rooms. And he called a leadership spill at the Darts and 8-Ball Associations. My father was elected president of both. It was an incredible power move. He also became president of a local branch of the Labor Party. The CFMEU and ETU held their meetings in the back bar.

"Solidarity forever!" Dad sang with the trade unionists.

Lastly, Dad erected a "Wheel of Fortune" in the front bar. Nails divided the clock-shaped board into ten-cent increments: $2 down to $1. Every Thursday at 3.59 pm, the bartender would twirl the wheel. Whatever number it landed on would be the price of a pot of beer for the next hour.

"This will get 'em interested," Dad told John.

Word spread. The Wheel of Fortune offered customers a democratic oasis of exhilaration. By Thursday afternoon of the third week, the bar was packed with an odd assortment of tradies and drifters. Men and women. Old and young. To the uninitiated, it sounded as if they were speaking in tongues.

On the jukebox, "Copperhead Road" segued into "Rivers of Babylon". John entered a flow state. He poured schooners and collected empties. He swapped trays of clean glasses for dirties. He changed the kegs when the taps shot froth.

The clock ticked towards 4 pm. In the bar, breath was bated. Dad let John do the honours. He spun the wheel, fast and hard. The drinkers stared at the spinner like stockbrokers on Wall Street. It hovered on the $1 segment. The bar roared. But then the spinner clipped over to $2. Happy Hour as usual.

The Hand of God intervened. My father tipped the spinner back to $1. The forsaken hailed their saviour. Fists lifted. Faces blazing with amazement. John wanted to be a great man, too. He committed the barflies' names and drink choices to memory. He recycled Dad's one-liners to widespread mirth.

"You've got 'em eating out the palm of your hand," muttered Dad.

The distribution of sin produced an incredible togetherness. The father and the son. The son and the father. It was the oldest story in the book.

Goanna

Hannah flew to Townsville for the under-twelves state hockey titles. She was captain of Darling Downs. But on the flight north, her dream of making the Queensland team was derailed by a deep fever and throbbing tonsils.

Upon arrival, Hannah was diagnosed with the flu. She was placed in isolation at the team hotel. Throat aching from the coughing fits. Brain drained by the antibiotics. On the second day, Hannah woke up to a knock on the door. It was my father. He wasn't meant to be coming. She hugged him.

"What are you doing here?" she coughed.

"I booked the first flight up," he said. "I'm next door to you."

Dad fetched Butter Menthols for Hannah's throat and Vicks for her chest. He delivered fresh orange juice, banana smoothies and chicken soup. He refrigerated cold towels for her hot sweats and poured warm baths for her aches. Hannah missed the whole week of games. By Friday, she had gotten through the worst of the flu. But she was still too weak to play in the semi-finals.

"It's too late," said Hannah.

There was no way the selectors would pick her for Queensland without participating in a single game at the tournament. My grinning father poured another glass of saltwater for Hannah to gargle.

"A little birdy told me that if you're right by Sunday, the selectors will pick ya for the Possibles–Probables game," he said. "Because you're that bloody good."

"Are you for real?" asked Hannah.

"Dead set," he said. "But if you're too sick, you're too sick."

By Saturday night, Hannah had revitalised. She went for a jog around the block without feeling nauseous. Dad waited at the front door. They high-fived.

"Lazarus!" he yelled.

Sunday afternoon was humid. Hannah put on her shinpads and slapped her hockey stick against them for good luck. She played as a central defender for the Possibles. Thanks to her impregnable defence, the underdogs won.

"Hannah Blaine," proclaimed the loudspeaker, the final name.

☨

The national hockey titles were in Adelaide, late August. The Shelleys' court case was a few weeks later in Toowoomba. Hannah distracted herself by doing push-ups, sit-ups and shuttle runs in the back paddock. I joined the sprints.

"One more set," yelled Hannah.

"I'm done," I said, collapsing on the trampoline.

Mum remained on Valium-induced autopilot. Hannah cooked dinner: grilled chicken and fish with vegetables. She got stronger. I grew slimmer.

"You think Mum will always be like this?" I asked during a fitness session.

"Like what?" asked Hannah.

"I dunno," I said. "So afraid."

Hannah dropped into a set of squats.

"She'll be right," Hannah panted. "When we get a restraining order."

We had become strangely acquainted with the legal jargon.

"But what if they just vi-arr-late the restraining order?" I asked.

"Don't be a worryguts," she said, with my father's calmness.

Hannah went to a training camp in Brisbane before the carnival. She was a born leader. Friendly but not sycophantic. Confident but not arrogant. The last-minute selection was unanimously voted captain of the Queensland team.

"Here's a good-luck charm, skipper," said my father at the airport.

It was a Nokia 3316 with thirty dollars' credit.

"Thanks, Dad!" said Hannah. "You're a dead-set legend!"

On Thursday, Queensland qualified for the grand final. It was on Saturday afternoon in Adelaide against New South Wales, perennial favourites. My father couldn't really afford a holiday, but he bought flights for him and me to Adelaide and back. Hannah had no idea that the two of us were coming. We caught a cab from the Adelaide airport to the arena.

In matching Queensland Maroons jerseys, my father and I slipped into the grandstand on the sideline with two meat pies and a carton of hot chips. He was noticeably more obese than the lean, well-spoken hockey dads. We crystallised our uncouthness by booing the New South Wales team.

"The Queensland side," said the announcer, "led out by Hannah Blaine."

Hannah sprinted onto the artificial turf, strangling the stick and staring heroically into nowhere. She wore a maroon headband with a white Nike tick.

"Goanna!" yelled my father. "Goanna!"

Hannah smiled at us, dumbstruck and vulnerable, but only for a moment. This was no time to be overwhelmed by sentiment. She withdrew the mouthguard lodged between her shin pads and socks. Queensland lost the toss. It was nil–all at halftime. Hannah flashed her crooked teeth at us.

"What are you two ratbags doing here?" she asked.

"I wouldn't have missed this for a million bucks!" said Dad.

The second half was a nail-biter. Hannah was everywhere in defence and counterattack. She tackled the stars from Sydney without deference. My father took a socially unacceptable level of satisfaction from the brutal collisions.

"Give it to 'em, Goanna!" he barked, to the shock of the hockey mums.

From a corner, one of Hannah's teammates trapped the flying white ball. With minimal backswing, Hannah smashed it into the net. She didn't let the moment go to her head. A few high-fives, and then eyes down on the way back.

"Let's go, girls," she yelled. "Ten more minutes."

Queensland won 1–0. Hannah, the captain, was declared player of the match. She made a magnanimous victory speech, thanking New South Wales for a fair game and her teammates for their never-say-die attitude.

"I just wanna thank my dad and brother for coming down this far south," she said in closing. "It's been a tough few months. But I love you heaps, Dad."

My father coughed with his mouth shut, tears in his eyes.

"Gee whiz," he whispered to me. "She's a good egg."

Like my father, Hannah worshipped at the altar of winning. And like Michael Shelley, her skin didn't flinch from the flame of adrenaline.

✠

Hannah's social worker applied for a twelve-month child protection order forbidding any direct or indirect contact between the Shelleys and their daughter. Mum submitted an affidavit to the Queensland Children's Court.

> Since Mary and Michael Shelley have become aware of our address, it has disrupted the lives of our children. John has moved out of

the house due to the visits. He has since suffered from suicidal ideation. Hannah's personal life has been disrupted in the form of needing to be accompanied by an adult at all times. Another child in our care, Rebecca, has been extremely distressed, fearing Mary will abduct Hannah and herself.

At the Children's Court in Brisbane, Michael tried to have himself struck from the child protection order, given he had no recent contact with Hannah. He magnified the risk of Mary undertaking a kidnapping mission.

"I have never threatened to abduct Hannah, and I never would," he said. "I see it as inappropriate at this stage. But I fully understand how Mary feels. If Mary did accomplish this rescue, it would be far, far less of an illegal act than what the department has done on three occasions with four of our children."

The judge didn't budge from the position of the social workers. The court awarded Hannah a twelve-month child protection order.

No visits. No phone calls. No letters. No birthday cards.

Eternity Is Forever

It was only a matter of time until Michael Shelley, evangelical PI, discovered that my parents had purchased the lease of the Metropole Hotel. He called up on the Sunday morning after the court case. My father and I were in the cold-room cleaning the keg lines. I answered the cordless phone.

"Metropole Hotel," I said, brightly. "This is Lech speaking."

"How old are you, Rex?" asked a male voice. "I take it that you are just another one of Tom and Lenore Blaine's godforsaken foster children."

I dropped the phone. My father picked up the receiver.

"Tom Blaine," he muttered with bloodshot eyes.

The voice on the other end of the line was shrill and quick, like a cassette tape in rewind. The publican received a Sunday morning sermon.

"You should thank me," said my father. "I brought up ya kids, 'cause ya couldn't hold down a job, ya bludger! You've never worked a hard day in ya life."

Dad hung up. We went back to cleaning, drenched in a baptism of beer and bleach. Usually, it was a great bonding exercise. But the phone kept ringing, and ringing, and ringing. Dad answered. Michael persisted.

"The asylum just rang me," said Dad, with an irritable grin. "They've got a straitjacket with your name on it, mate. Cuckoo, you fucking lunatic!"

Then he smashed the cordless phone against the concrete floor.

A few days later, Dad received an epistle from Michael. The protection order didn't extend to my parents or to their business. The fifty-cent stamp had a picture of a puppy. The back of the envelope was littered with stickers of bones.

To: Thomas Blaine

Because you haven't the guts to talk to me on the phone & keep hanging up, I needed to write down what I was trying to say for your edification.

You, Thomas Blaine, are an obese, ugly brute. An emotional infant. A real parasite. A foul-mouthed, cowardly thug. An abuser of women & children. You have not "brought up" my children, you freeloading leech. You have thieved off their spirits, ruined their childhoods, tried to make them clones of you – even my beautiful daughter! You have destroyed everything that was special about her.

You are a bully & misuse your size & strength to intimidate

& assault people around you into cowed silence. That is also why you are so IGNORANT, STUPID, ARROGANT & INTOLERANT of difference. Look at yourself in the mirror – not a pretty picture!

It is hard to believe that anyone who is such a FAT UGLY GLUTTON & ALCOHOLIC OAF could open their piggish mouth to express an opinion. Let alone have the gall, presumption & temerity to impertinently insult one of GOD's ministers. In truth, you have deprived, neglected, abused, assaulted & violated my children. It is no exaggeration to call you a depraved deviate & perverted paedophile.

When I consider why GOD would deliver my daughter into the wandering hands of someone like you – a trivial, irrelevant piece of human garbage – I realise how special she must be to survive such privation. You don't work. You just indulge other unweaned infants like you with continuous schooners of beer, and help fill their lives with distractions, such as sport & gambling. You are the BLUDGER, not me.

You couldn't keep a real woman if you wanted to. Your wife wears her hair like a boy. What's wrong, Tom? Why did you marry a woman who looks like a man? Perhaps because she looks like your mother – A FAT, FEMALE EUNUCH!

Dad kept his composure relatively well, until Michael called his dead mother a eunuch. He punched a hole in the wall. The letter finished with a threat:

I have asked GOD, whom Mary & I serve, to expunge your unwanted presence from the planet. And I encourage you to broadcast your derision & contempt for this warning. That way, when GOD clearly executes His judgement upon you – SOON – my ungrateful children might learn to fear HIM & return to their rightful place. So, Thomas Blaine, as you keep saying to me: "CYA LATER!" What a blessing!

Yours faithfully,
Michael

It took a couple of hours for my father to identify the pain in his chest as more than anger. An ambulance came. The publican was taken for CAT scans.

"Do you want the good news or the bad news first?" asked the doctor.

"The good news would be good," said my father.

"The good news is the heart attack was small, by your standards," he said. "But your arteries are very clogged. I think you're heading for a heart bypass."

"What's the *bad* news?" asked Dad. "I've got cock cancer?"

"The scans picked up a bunch of cysts on your kidney," said the doctor. "Unlikely to kill you. But you'll need an operation to remove them. Pronto."

Dad refused to be seduced by the idea of divine intervention. According to the doctor, the cysts were likely caused by the discharge of adrenaline from glands on the kidneys. The fight-or-flight factory. Michael was trying to kill his nemesis with repressed stress. It was a war of attrition.

++

Michael's next epistle to my father arrived on 3 January 2003. Marked *CONFIDENTIAL*, the threat had been sent from Dubbo on New Year's Day. Dad read the letter in the back bar, ringed by the jingling pokies. There were goosebumps on his bruised knuckles.

"We therefore need to give you a <u>final warning</u>, Thomas Blaine, on behalf of GOD," wrote Michael. "TO SAY THAT YOU ARE OUT

OF YOUR DEPTH IS A CONSIDERABLE UNDERSTATEMENT. YOU NEED TO REALISE LENORE + YOU ARE ENDANGERING YOUR LIVES IN THIS WORLD + IN THE NEXT. ETERNITY IS FOREVER!"

Dad fell into a rotten mood. Mum double-dropped Valiums. On a Thursday night, we ate dinner at the pub. Dad stayed behind to finish the late shift. Rebecca, Hannah and I climbed into the Toyota Camry with Mum.

"There they are!" shrieked Hannah.

A XXXX Gold sign hung above the front door. Michael and Mary were apparitions lit up underneath it. Neon preachers. I hadn't seen Michael in the flesh before. He was petrifying. I felt like I might die just by laying eyes on him. Suddenly, Michael and Mary were looking directly at us.

"Drive, Mum!" cried Rebecca.

Mum rose to the occasion. The Camry pulled away from the curb. We drove five blocks to the police station. At the counter, Rebecca, Hannah and I huddled around Mum. Shaking, she explained the violated restraining order.

"Their names are Michael and Mary Shelley," said Mum. "They sent a letter last week warning that mine and my husband's lives are in danger."

"I know who you're talking about," said the desk sergeant.

Two pairs of cops stormed from the station to their cars. They departed in a blaze of sirens. This didn't make me feel safer. Worst case, the Shelleys had shot, stabbed or blown up Dad. I listened for an explosion.

"We better go to the motel," said my mother.

Mum drove to the same old three-star motel near the racecourse. Our car flashed past the grimly familiar landmarks. In the backseat, Rebecca, Hannah and I held hands while hyperventilating. How was this our life now?

"Your dad will be fine," said my mother. "He's tough."

The motel owner let Mum call my father from the front desk. Mary had been arrested. Michael hadn't entered the pub. He was on the loose. We curled up with Mum in the queen bed of the family suite. Dad was alive. Our tears dried up. But there was a pressure in everyone's heads and chests.

"Will I need to go somewhere else to live?" asked Hannah.

Just getting Hannah to ponder this possibility was revolutionary. Like King Solomon, the Shelleys were setting my mother a test. How much do you really love our daughter? Enough to suffer this much dread on a daily basis?

"Over my dead body," said Mum.

It was a stalemate. Short of killing her, no amount of domestic terrorism could make Mum willingly surrender custody. The rival mothers had something in common. They loved Hannah too much for their own sanity.

Supply and Demand

To the naked eye, the life of Steven Blaine seemed perfect. He received straight distinctions at university. He also made the Australian University Rugby League team. But there was something missing. Steven had no desire to finish a degree, get a high-paying job and invest the proceeds in the property market. He read books about economic inequality and imperialism.

"Don't let ya brains go to ya head, mate," warned Dad.

On a Friday afternoon, while John poured schooners for a flock of barflies, Steven went to a lecture at the University of Southern Queensland. A long-haired man burst through the entrance to the lecture hall. He was carrying a bouquet of sunflowers. Steven whiplashed against his seat. The stalker had talked a receptionist into giving him Steven's lecture schedule.

"This is very important," said Michael Shelley.

Michael's deep, lucid voice astounded Steven. He didn't sound deranged. If Steven closed his eyes, and ignored the purple poncho worn over a tie-dyed t-shirt, it might have been the vice-chancellor speaking.

"Aloha, dude," said the lecturer to Michael. The commerce students were now wide awake and laughing loudly at the bizarre scenario.

"My fingernail has a higher IQ than you!" said Michael.

"Nice to meet you, too," said the lecturer. "How can I help you?"

"I need to speak to Steven Blaine," said Michael.

The lecturer looked blankly into the hall. A few people who knew Steven turned towards the back row. In a daze, Steven walked to the front of the lecture hall. He wore black Converse sneakers. Michael handed Steven the bouquet of sunflowers. They walked wordlessly towards a gazebo outside.

Michael delivered a lecture. It started with more autobiography than theology. Steven folded his arms and listened with interest. The fable was erudite and insightful. It turned out they shared similar reservations about capitalism. Michael tried to stay calm. But moving into the present-day battle for custody, his breathless voice became suffused with megalomania.

"The department could not have done a worse job of finding you decent foster carers," he said. "So why did they do something that they knew would distress and infuriate us? In answering this question, you will uncover the deceit and treachery that has been a feature of your entire childhood."

Students from the lecture streamed past the gazebo. The musk of autumn wafted upon the breeze. Dusk was coming in. Steven tried to contain his indignation.

"Michael, you don't know Lenore and Tom from a bar of soap," he said. "They are unbelievably kind. You're judging a book by its cover. It's pure snobbery."

"My children needed guardians who were educated, artistic, cultured and physically active," said Michael. "Not obese, illiterate, liquor-swilling hillbillies!"

"Mum is one of the smartest people I've ever met," said Steven. "The only reason she doesn't have a degree and a PhD is because her family was too poor. And she dedicated her life to looking after us. Unlike you."

Michael's face twisted. He was overwhelmed by outrage.

"Where do you think you get your looks from, Saul? Where does your intelligence come from? Me! The Blaines have never set foot in a university."

Steven stared at his biological father. There was nothing he wished to recognise or perpetuate. He stood up and left the sunflowers on the bench.

"There's no reason we couldn't have a relationship right now," said Steven. "But you can't swallow your pride. You can't bite your tongue. You would rather believe we were raised by paedophiles than two people who love us."

The son was done. He walked off. Birds circled above, chirping in short bursts. Steven heard a wail of anger. But he couldn't make out the words.

The Other Cheek

Mick Bishop's abandonment of Latoya and Jason was a fait accompli. He packed up his belongings. Jason was three, the same age as Mick when he was kidnapped. Back when his name was Elijah Shelley. Now, Jason studied his father's exodus through the big windows. Little fingerprints smudged the glass. He cried for him to stay.

"Can you take him away?" Mick begged Latoya.

"No," she said. "He's allowed to watch you leave."

Cyclone Michael swept Latoya off her feet as a teenager. She had felt calmer in the eye of the storm. When it had seemed like she was wind, too, and not just debris. Now he shacked up with a series of short-term flings.

Latoya's parents helped raise Jason, without child support from Mick. One afternoon, Latoya heard a knock on the front door. It wasn't Mick. It was one of his degenerate buddies, Clint, a drifter who rode around Beef City on a two-speed pushbike. Clint had gotten wind that Latoya was single.

Clint moved in. Pretty quickly, he started hitting Latoya, even more remorselessly than Mick. One afternoon, he demanded the keys to Latoya's car. She refused. Clint threatened to flog Jason if she didn't hand them over. She still refused. He hit the toddler, leaving a welt on Jason's body.

Latoya reached her limit. She was fair game. Jason was untouchable. Drawing on an emergency reserve of strength, she called the police and reported the domestic violence. She took out an AVO against Clint. He left.

Latoya decided to be a single mum for good. To relinquish the opportunity for love in return for the safety of her son Jason. Loneliness was better than risking another slapped cheek, another split lip, another Mick.

++

In Rockhampton, word circulated that Mick Bishop was ripping off customers by cutting his product too thin. He caught a bus north to Cairns, near his birthplace. Mick was arrested for theft and drug possession. He was spared an immediate prison sentence by an episode of drug-induced psychosis. Police admitted him against his will to a Cairns psychiatric ward. He had no one to call but Michael Shelley. He dialled Michael's mobile number.

"Dad, I need your help," said Mick.

"Hallelujah!" said Michael.

Michael and Mary flew straight to Cairns. Their estranged child had been released from the psych ward and was awaiting a court date. They found him in a seedy hotel room above a pub. Mick was in bed with a teenage girl. The benches were covered with needles, spoons and heroin.

"Heathens!" screeched Mary. Michael disposed of the drugs.

The Shelleys dragged their son to a cheap caravan park. Mary nursed Mick through the hot and cold sweats of drug withdrawal. In the cabin, she wiped the vomit from his chin, while Michael Shelley recited scriptures.

Finally, the Shelleys had one of their children to nurture. Finally, Mick had some unconditional love. He submitted to their sermons in return for tenderness and a full stomach. At night, the three of them sang together.

"You have the voice of an angel!" Mary told Mick.

Michael taught Mick to play the acoustic guitar. His tar-stained fingers memorised the chords. It was hard not to be seduced by Michael's approval.

"You're a natural, Elijah," said Michael. "You have a gift!"

Michael bought a disposable camera. He took a photo of Mick sheepishly smoking a cigarette beside a beaming Mary on the front steps of the caravan. Mary took a photo of Michael handing his 23-year-old son a teddy bear. His father, triumphant, got the family photos developed at Big W. He sent the snapshots to "Saul" and "Joshua" at the Metropole Hotel.

"Elijah is back with the only parents who ever loved him," wrote Michael. "He has learned more about faith in two weeks than the past twenty years. We are going to do the same for the both of you. GOD needs us to be together!"

Michael dictated letters for Elijah to write to his younger brothers and sister. They received a stream of epistles from their born-again

Christian brother. He regurgitated the heinous accusations against Lenore and Tom. This cut the final tie of kinship between Mick and his biological siblings.

⁌

Michael Shelley wanted to turn a minor criminal trial into an airing of grievances about the Department of Child Safety. He offered to train his son to represent himself. Mick wanted to plead guilty to the theft and drug possession charges. He deserved them. And he had committed worse sins.

"The only thing you are guilty of is cowardice, Elijah!" said Michael.

As Mick grew cleaner, the sermons sounded less agreeable and more unhinged. His mother was mentally ill and under Michael's thumb. Michael demanded that his eldest son join their crusade for the custody of Hannah.

"I need some peace in my life," said Mick.

"The path to peace is paved with sacrifice!" cried Michael.

Worse, "Michael Bishop" refused to change his name by deed poll to Elijah Shelley. Shelley wasn't the surname on his son's birth certificate. Mick still yearned to be Jason's father. Michael insisted he get a paternity test for Jason. He accused Latoya – whom he'd never met – of being a black Jezebel.

"Dad, Jason is my son," said Mick. "He looks like me."

"You don't want to see the truth!" said Michael.

Mick had no fight left in him. In the middle of the night, he filled a backpack with his few belongings. He slept in a park near the courthouse. The next morning, he pleaded guilty. He was sentenced to six months in prison. Mick refused visits from Michael Shelley and ignored the hectoring letters.

"You have learned to be a manipulator from your foster parents," wrote Michael Shelley. "It is CRUNCH TIME. As my eldest son &

heir, you have a responsibility to save your sister from the Blaines. If you had done what I told you to do, you might not be such a disobedient burden on us now."

Mick resisted this mission. He pulled free from Michael's charisma, insistent as a rip in the ocean. But he was now permanently adrift from Steven, John and Hannah. They were afraid of him. He was no one's brother and no one's son.

Those Who Trespass Against Us

By the spring of 2003, my mother had a false sense of security. One lunchtime, she and Rebecca went grocery shopping. They left Hannah and me alone at home. Hannah was thirteen. I was eleven. Hannah sat in the lounge room watching *The Simpsons*. I checked the back door was locked every few minutes, while playing on the computer in the kitchen.

There was a shadow in the tinted windows. Mary Shelley rushed up the driveway. She looked inside. I could see her, but she couldn't see me. My body convulsed. I grabbed the cordless phone and sprinted into the lounge room.

"What's wrong, Peck-sta?" asked Hannah.

I put an index finger to my lips.

"Mary is here," I whispered.

Hannah muted the TV. We slid under the metal frame of our parents' queen bed, met by the smell of dust and rust. Hannah dialled triple zero.

"My name is Hannah Blaine," she whispered. "I have a restraining order against my biological mother, Mary Shelley. She just arrived at our house."

Mum didn't have a mobile phone. Hannah called Dad at the pub. Then we waited. Hannah's skin was the temperature of porcelain. My father drove straight through the front gate. Hannah and I ran to the back door. Through the windows, we watched Dad search the garage. But Mary had vanished.

"Let me in," said Dad.

I opened the door, hesitantly, as if it might be a trick. Dad came inside. I locked the door again. Hannah and I hugged him, weeping deliriously.

"Are you dead certain she was here?" asked my father.

"She was here," I cried.

The police arrived, followed by Mum and Rebecca. Mary was nowhere to be found. The cops left to search the surrounding streets. They had no luck locating the Shelleys. Dad went back to the pub, believing the Shelleys were heading downtown.

"I'm just a phone call away," he said.

Hannah had recently moved into Steven's old granny flat. In the late afternoon, she returned to her bedroom. Nobody had thought to check there.

Mary lay on Hannah's bed. White dress ablaze with sunlight. Eyes shut. Fingers clinging to her daughter's clothing. A framed photo of Hannah on her chest. Mary's wrinkled face was so at peace, her breathing so discreet, that Hannah thought she had stumbled upon a successful suicide.

Mary's eyes slid open. Hannah screamed. She saw a monster.

"I just wanted to be near you," said Mary, apologetically.

Hannah ran back to the house and locked the doors. Mum called the police again. She called my father. She called Steven. He arrived first. Mary refused to vacate the granny flat. Steven's deep reserves of diplomacy ran out.

"Get up!" yelled Steven. "I'm sick of this."

Mary sat on the edge of the bed.

"You're sick of this?" asked Mary. "Saul, why can't you walk a mile in my shoes?"

The argument continued on the back patio, mother and son

screaming, eyes opened but blinkered. He was blind with hate. She was blind with love.

"You hate me for loving you too much!" said Mary.

Rebecca, Hannah and I listened from the kitchen table. I had never heard Steven so impatient, so uncontained, so willing to cause another person pain.

"You don't love *us*," he yelled. "You hate everything about us! You love the idea of your own love. You're in love with a delusion."

"Oh, Saul," cried Mary. "You are such a cruel, naïve young man. You have never made love to a soulmate. You have never created a life from that love. You have never given birth. You have never had a baby taken from you!"

"Put yourself in Hannah's shoes," he said. "She was happy before. That's what hurts, isn't it? That's why you're so determined to fuck up her life."

Four police officers had arrived. They stood to the side of the breezeway, letting the old woman and young man finish their argument.

"I will never stop loving Hannah," said Mary. "I will never stop loving Elijah, Joshua and you. I can't stop trying. I would rather die! One day, when you have your own children, you might understand just how much I love you."

The police ushered Mary up the driveway. Hannah and I watched through the blinds of Hannah's bedroom window. There were no rainbows lately, just red and blue cones spinning underneath the thick tree. The bark was brown. The leaves were dark green.

The Covenant

Mary was charged with unlawful stalking. Social workers applied to extend the restraining order. Hannah moved back into the main house. A few days after finding Mary in the granny flat, she composed a letter to the Shelleys on the computer.

hi,

Well I read your recent letters. Do you want to know the truth??? I'm not being brainwashed or abused!!! I'm not stupid. I only believe what I want to believe. My foster parents are FANTASTIC! They do anything for me no matter what. The things you say about them are SO disgusting.

I love my life. It was perfect. But now I'm really disturbed. The way you act frightens me! You don't act exactly normal. It scares me to death. How would you like being told that you are going to be kidnapped??? It's not exactly the best thing to read.

Coming to my house was scary and going on my bed made me SUPER uncomfortable. Now I won't sleep up there or go outside alone. It was an invasion of privacy. Stealing my pictures was really wrong. They were VERY special to me. You say that you love me. Well, you stole from your own daughter. If you'd asked, maybe.

When you came to my house for the first time, you said that I was angry and confused. But I was just shocked and scared. I didn't know what to think! But I've grown up since then. I know what I'm doing with my life. I appreciate why you want to make contact. But I really think you're going the wrong way about it. I'm asking you to please stop coming to my house and writing threatening letters to my parents. Maybe some good things might happen :) I just want to live a normal life and not fear that I'm going to get kidnapped every corner I turn.

Anyway, I've got to go. Cya Later

hannah

Hannah sent her first letter to the Shelleys. Mary was released on bail. A few days later, my mother heard a quiet rattling on the front door. It was a quarter past four on a Wednesday afternoon. Mum opened up. Mary stood on the porch. She had been separated from Michael for more than a week, due to her imprisonment.

"Hello, Lenore," said Mary. "I know I shouldn't be here. Please don't call the police. You don't need to open the security screen. I just want to talk."

"Okay, Mary," said my mother. "What do you want to talk about?"

"Do you know what it's like to lose a child?" asked Mary.

"Yes, I do," said my mother. "The grief never goes away."

The two women had more in common than either of them knew. They had both married fearless, egotistical men and suffered six miscarriages each.

"All I ever wanted was to see Hannah," said Mary.

"Mary, I never would've tried to stop you from seeing or speaking to Hannah," said Mum. "I never pretended to be her biological mother. She always knew that a woman named Mary gave birth to her. And that you loved her."

For the first time, the two women regarded each other as mothers, not monsters. An uncommon bond between them. They loved the same children.

"I guess I get carried away sometimes," said Mary. "When I first met you, I thought: 'Terrorist!' But there's much more to you than that, isn't there? I can see that Hannah really loves you. It makes me jealous, Lenore."

Hannah sat cross-legged on the lounge room floor, listening to the conversation. Her fear of Mary softened. She stood in the hallway. Mum saw her. Hannah pointed at herself; then towards the door; then mimed a talking mouth; then gave Mum a thumbs up. Translation: I want to speak to Mary.

"Mary, would you like to talk to Hannah?" asked my mother. "I can't open the security screen. Don't take it personally. She is still quite scared."

"Oh, Lenore," said Mary. "It would mean the world to me!"

Hannah walked to the front door. She was trembling. The thirteen-year-old girl summoned all of her courage to smile.

"Hi, Mary," said Hannah.

"Oh, Hannah," said Mary. "My daughter. You're beautiful. I'm so sorry for scaring you. I don't want you to live in fear. I don't want you to hate me."

"I don't want to hate you," said Hannah.

They spoke through the flyscreen for half an hour.

"What do you want me to do, Hannah?" asked Mary. "Would you like to be adopted by Lenore? Would that create the possibility of regular contact?"

Adoption had never occurred to Hannah as a possibility.

"I would love that," said Hannah. "You've got no idea how grateful I would be! And we could go from there. I don't want to not know you."

"I will need to talk to Michael," said Mary. "Your father is stubborn."

Dusk settled upon the front porch. The dogs barked for their dinner.

"That might be enough for today, Mary," said Mum.

Her sad face flashed with a pang of hope.

"Can I have a hug?" asked Mary. "Just one?"

Hannah nodded. Mum opened the door. Hannah stood on the porch. Mary embraced her. The hug went for a few minutes. Eventually, Mary let go.

"I love you, Hannah," said Mary. "Please never forget that."

Hannah didn't feel love for her biological mother; just sympathy.

"Thanks, Mary," said Hannah. "See ya later."

Mary left through the front gate. There were no sirens waiting.

++

A few days later, Hannah received a letter from Michael Shelley.

Dearest Hannah,

I needed to write to you, following your recent letter, and the conversation that you had with Mary at Gowrie Street. How could you be such a TRAITOR to contemplate a formal adoption by the Blaines? As your father, I will NEVER agree to this. It would be a betrayal of Mary, & would break her heart, whether she admits to it or not.

Yes, Hannah, you have been "brainwashed". Misled and conditioned by the forces of evil arrayed against us. You are so much a part of the depraved foster care subculture that you are not aware of the real world outside, or the corruption inside your delusional bubble.

Hannah, you actually complained about Mary taking two photographs. Instead of thinking about how difficult life is for you, think about how difficult life is for us. Consider the enormous burden of grief that Mary carries every single day without resorting to violence. Why don't you think about how she felt being in your room, Hannah, that awful little shack they trap you in, trying to ease the pain in her heart.

For a change, why don't you try to understand how we feel. Four children stolen illegally from us. Our daughter neglected & molested while defenceless. Mary & I are very sensitive to the symptoms of sexual abuse. I am sure that Tom Blaine is capable of committing it. If you are lost to any "lusts of the flesh", you are lost to them all. You are only so outraged about this, Hannah, because you know it to be true.

GOD loves you, pities you for all that you have suffered, & needs us to reunite as a family. This absurd scenario has been going on quite long enough. It is time to muster all the courage

& integrity in your soul, to persevere & strive for a true reunion. You could do so much good, not only for yourself, but for other survivors of sexual abuse.

Although I have the greatest compassion for all that you have endured during your awful foster care placement – none of which is my fault – I have to say that you are making life much, much more difficult for yourself and for us: your real parents!

I notice you have all the time in the world to make complaints about us to the social workers who destroyed your childhood. But you won't expend the same energy communicating with me, your real father, despite all the enriching information I send. I need to have regular & ongoing contact with you starting now, & that is final. If you squander this God-given opportunity, you will regret it until your dying days.

We will NEVER go away, no matter how many times you ask.

Faithfully,
Your Father-in-Christ,
Michael

Michael vs Goliath

On a Thursday afternoon, Michael strode through the doors of the Metropole Hotel. The customers did a fuzzy double-take at the ponytailed man wearing a white robe and sandals. He stuck out like a kangaroo on the moon.

"Last drinks, boys," said one of the drunks. "Jesus escaped his cave!"

"I can guarantee He won't be coming back to save *you*!" said Michael.

For the first time, my father made eye contact with Michael. They stared at each other from opposite sides of the bar. The publican threw down a coaster.

"Mick, ya mad prick," said Dad. "What are you drinkin'?"

"My name is Michael!" said the prophet.

"Six of one, brother," said Dad. "Half-a-dozen of the other."

Dad lifted a tray of dripping, clinking schooners from the dishwasher. He put them back into the bar fridge. Michael's disappointment was immense.

"You're an enabler of alcoholics!" said Michael. "Look at all these animals. You think you are a businessman. No, Thomas: you are a zookeeper!"

The zoo went silent. A dozen or so gorillas directed thousand-yard stares at the gazelle. Their initial bemusement turned rapidly to indignation.

"You've got a lot of teeth for a smart cunt," said Fish, a mechanic with no front teeth from a pub fight. "Tom, want me to knock him out?"

Dad was more physically intimidated by Fish than by Michael.

"Nah," said Dad. "He's an old mate of mine." Dad gave a thumbs up to Audrey, the puzzled barmaid. "Me and me mate Mick need to have a quick yarn."

The publican nodded towards the pokies lounge. Michael followed him. The gambling den had misty windows and flashing screens. Dad cracked open a Diet Coke and poured Michael a water. He offered him a bowl of salted cashews.

"I don't want to even *touch* those disgusting peanuts!" said Michael.

"Suit yaself," said Dad, swallowing some. "What *do* ya want, mate?"

The two boomers – one skinny, the other obese – were an odd picture. Both had been blond, ambitious little boys, the apples of their mothers' eyes. Both had cheated on their first wives. And both had tried to build hospitality empires while dabbling in illicit side-hustles. They had been seduced by the promise of post-war prosperity. Dad's lust for money had lasted the distance.

"I'm indubitably not your mate, Thomas Blaine," said Michael. "I have forensically elucidated the proof of your dissoluteness."

Slowly, my father had grown impervious to Michael's verbose provocations. A) Because most of Michael's vocabulary made zero sense. B) Because he wasn't physically afraid of him. C) Because he was a devout atheist, so the forecasts of damnation didn't raise a sweat. And D) Because he believed, at a fundamental level, that Michael was mad as a cut snake.

The prophet was a pest, not a killer. Dad poured cashew crumbs into his mouth. He gulped some Diet Coke and burped into a clenched fist. In that moment, he reminded Michael Shelley more of Homer Simpson than Satan.

"Are you retarded?" asked Michael. "Is any of this getting through your thick skull? How can you be so blasé? Your existence is in limbo!"

Dad's lips flitted between a playful grin and a grimace.

"Fuck, you must have shit for brains," said Dad. "Poor bloke."

Michael realised that the fat, uneducated philistine pitied *him*, the Chosen One. Michael wanted to shock my father out of his complacency.

"Do you think that you are a good man, Thomas?" asked Michael.

My father contemplated Michael's question for a long time. This seemed like a positive development. Michael wanted proof of consciousness. A sign that the publican knew what he was doing and continued to do it.

"Nah," said my father. "Not really. Bitta good. Bitta bad."

"You have spent decades tempting men and women with evil," said Michael. "What kind of example are you setting for *my* children?"

My father sighed and smiled. He recognised Michael's eyes.

"There was a bloke I used to know," said Dad. "Mad Catholic. Hated me. Thought *I* was a bad influence on kids. All 'cause I liked a drink and a punt."

"Maybe you should have paid attention to him!" said Michael.

The smile fell south from my father's mouth.

"I found out this do-gooder was a kiddie fiddler," said Dad.

"That's why I left Ipswich. I was gonna kill him. That's why I agreed to be a foster carer."

"What does any of this rambling nonsense have to do with me, Thomas?" asked Michael. "I have spent twenty years crusading against child abuse!"

In the back bar, Dad's grey eyes weighed up two bright blue ones.

"He used to look at me just like you do, mate," said my father. "He needed a bad man to make him feel good. I reckon you've done things that would make my skin crawl. That's why ya tryin' so hard to make up for it."

Michael had lost control of the philosophical contest.

"You indecent beast!" cried Michael. "You slobbering yobbo! The paedophile was you, wasn't it? And you never stopped. *You* – you fat behemoth!"

Dad took great satisfaction from not giving him what he wanted: a left fist to the chin. Short of Michael murdering my father, it would be the only way to emancipate Hannah from his custody.

The publican placed both big elbows on the bar mat. His hairy face was adjacent to the thin minister's. Dad weighed more than two of Michael.

"I can't be that bad," said Dad. "My kids love me. They hate you, mate."

For once, Michael was tongue-tied. He was crucified by the truth. The prophet of God vanished from hell's front lobby via the fire escape.

Praying for Sheep Stations

Mary Shelley returned to Michael's authority. All bets were off. The threats kept coming. It was as if the conversation about adoption had never happened. Michael sent letters to everyone in Queensland with the surname Blaine, informing them that their relative – Thomas – was Australia's worst paedophile.

Mary gate-crashed a parliamentary inquiry into sexual abuse. On the national news, a woman with a blurred-out face and posh accent claimed her daughter was being molested by foster carers: childless Toowoomba publicans.

At night, Mum sat on her recliner with an instant coffee and a stack of parliamentary Hansards. She began cramming the *Queensland Defamation Act*.

"Defamatory matter!" she announced to the loungeroom.

My sisters and I were trying to watch *Home and Away*.

"What's that, Mum?" asked Rebecca.

"Any imputation concerning any person, by which the reputation of that person is likely to be injured, or by which that person is likely to be injured in the person's profession, or by which other persons are likely to be induced to shun or avoid or despise the person, is called defamatory," she said, quietly.

Mum couldn't work out what hurt most: being called a paedophile, or being called childless. The Shelleys still hadn't cottoned on to the fact she wasn't infertile.

"What is wrong with your own womb, Lenore?" Mary wrote in a letter to my mother. "It is so withered and useless you stole three children from me!"

Mum kept these slurs from us. But we got the gist. The Shelleys were trying to sully her greatest source of pride: motherhood. I put my ear to the door of the master bedroom and eavesdropped on my parents.

"How can we keep going on like this?" asked Mum. "They're trying to give you a heart attack and drive me mad. And they're not far off, to be honest."

"Giving me a heart attack is no great achievement," said Dad.

"I'm over it, Thomas," she said. "I feel like I'm being suffocated. If we were politicians, the government would give us 24-hour police protection."

"Whaddayado, love?" he asked. "They're nuttier than a packet of Nobbies. But they're going to be very old and lonely one day. We won't be."

"I suppose you're right," she sighed.

The next day, I stayed home from school with no particular sickness. Rain pitter-pattered against the corrugated iron. Occasional thunder. Otherwise, the house was quiet. My mother and I sat in the loungeroom, legs under a blanket.

"Isn't this wonderful?" she asked.

"This is living," I said, taking a sip from a hot Milo.

Mum was inhaling *True History of the Kelly Gang* by Peter Carey. I was reading her old copy of *My Brilliant Career* by Miles Franklin.

"If only the Shelley Gang knew about you, baby," she said.

Her conspiratorial grin had a hint of self-satisfaction.

"What the hell is that supposed to mean?" I asked.

"*Their* children are the athletes!" she said, exasperated. "Not mine!"

I was a beautiful counterargument to the delusion that my parents had brainwashed Steven, John and Hannah into being short-haired jocks. Their sporting success was a genetic gift from the Shelleys, not from Lenore Blaine. Mum hated all sports equally. She just didn't feel the need to piss on anyone else's passion.

"I'm good at sport!" I said, defensively.

I loved cricket and football, but I was thus far bad at them. My hair was long and curly. I was in the school choir. My wrists and fingers were thin.

"Of course you are, darling," Mum lied.

From my mother, I had inherited hazel-green eyes, flat feet and hifalutin thinking patterns. We were addicted to words and sentences, memories and premonitions. She blamed our French genes.

"It's just that Michael Shelley thinks he is exclusively responsible for the intelligence of his kin," she continued. "Little does the narcissist know."

"What's a narcissist?" I asked.

"They sniff their own farts," she said.

I began panicking. Secretly, I was partial to the aroma of my own farts. I looked up *narcissist* in the dictionary. In some ways, I was not dissimilar to a young Michael: academically gifted, with a Napoleonic self-confidence.

"Am I a narcissist, Mum?" I asked.

"You are actually miraculous," she said.

I was suddenly worried that Michael might take a liking to me, if only he knew. I listened to the Cat Stevens mixtapes that he sent to Hannah. In the bathroom mirror, I sang "Wild World" and "The First Cut Is the Deepest", with a hairbrush as microphone. I was so afraid of the Shelleys that I had begun praying to God to save us from them. They made me a believer.

"Mum, you aren't going to tell them about me?" I asked.

"No way, Jose," she said.

Mum feared that the Shelleys would try to kidnap me as blackmail for Hannah. Her membership of the childbirth club remained confidential. Outside, there was lightning in the sky. On the couch, she hugged me.

"I love you, Lech," she said, eyes wet. "I hope I'm a good mum."

I was stunned. How could she not know her own wow factor? That was a major difference between us. She'd never been showered with this much love.

"I love you too, Mum!" I said. "Dad reckons you're the only genius he's ever met besides Gough Whitlam. You're dead-set the best mum ever!"

Mum smiled at me shyly, as if I might be lying to her face. It was a pity the Shelleys frightened me so much. I wanted to kill them, or at least wash their filthy mouths out with soap until they apologised to my mother.

"I'll write a book about the Shelley Gang one day," she said.

"Cool," I said, half-heartedly. "That'll be an absolute hoot."

I couldn't imagine anything worse than reading a book about the Shelleys. That night, in the privacy of my bedroom, I flicked off the light switch and knelt down. I made the sign of the cross and put my hands together.

"G'day, God," I prayed. "Can you please get Michael and Mary to rack off? Life was going great guns before they showed up. You can't seriously believe that they're real Christians. It gives me the shits! Pardon my French. I'm just worried about Mum. She seems a bit sad all the time."

Then I counted sheep – thousands of them – until I fell asleep.

Salt of the Earth

There was one sport I was actually better at than Hannah: eight-ball. My ambition at the age of eleven was to make the under-twelves Queensland team for eight-ball, like John had done. Each afternoon, I strutted downtown to the pub in my school uniform. I played pool against the customers until dinner time. No butterflies in my stomach. The Shelleys were irrelevant.

"Ya son's a pool shark, Tom," said one of the drunks.

"Pity about the mugs he's up against," said my father.

John was one of the best senior eight-ball players in the state. I became his protégé, just like he was my father's protégé. I played with my left hand, the same as them, even though I wrote and bowled with my right hand.

"Don't hit the white ball so hard, Lech," said John. "You're about as subtle as a kookaburra. Count the numbers. Soft touch. Nice and fuckin' soft!"

I studied John for hours. Then we played against each other. He refused to let me win. But he taught me how to see seven shots ahead. When I was snookered, I learned how to spin the white ball in ungodly directions off the cush of the pool table by hitting it with precision at the top or bottom.

"I reckon he's ready," John told Dad one Sunday arvo.

My father unveiled an aluminium case from behind the back bar. Inside was a mystical object: John's first pool cue. The shaft was made of maple wood. It had a nylon ferrule with a felt tip. The handle was signed by Eddie Charlton, Australia's greatest snooker player. Years ago, Dad had paid for Charlton to give John a masterclass at the Country Club Hotel.

"Now we're talking!" said Dad.

There was a surprising final item in the case. A piece of sheepskin from Otago in New Zealand. Michael Shelley had sent the keepsake when John was in primary school. John used the wool to wipe the oil from his cue after every few shots.

"Smooth," I said.

Dad decided it was time for me to sink or swim. I filled in for a C-grade team. The eight-ball crowd was a motley crew of blue-collar workers and small-time criminals. My captain was a lesbian CFMEU member named Maggie. She wore a flannelette shirt with denim jeans. I wore an oversized XXXX Bitter polo shirt.

"Little Lechy Blaine," said Maggie. "All grown up."

It was a school night in October. Maggie drank schooners of Victoria Bitter. I drank tequila sunrises, without tequila. We played at a white fibreglass table in the back room. Dad had an A-grade game in the front bar. He kept popping out to watch me. I won my first three games.

"Tommy," said Maggie. "Your boy has actually got some balls!"

"I've got more balls than you!" I protested.

"We both know that's bullshit," she said.

Maggie and I joined up for doubles. It was half past nine. My curfew was 10 pm. We edged towards victory. The winning shot was mine. I wiped the cue with the sheepskin and lined up the black ball.

Then Mary Shelley appeared. She whirled around the pool room, shouting scriptures.

"Hang on," said Maggie. "We're on the eight-ball, mate!"

A haze of blue chalk and cigarette smoke hung above the green mat of the table. Mary sized up Maggie's mullet with undisguised revulsion.

"Are you a man or a woman?" asked Mary.

Maggie's laugh sounded like the blast of a car motor.

"I piss like a chick and root like a dude," said Maggie.

Everyone in the pool room cracked up, except for me. Mary clicked her tongue with disgust. Her horrified eyes met mine.

"Is this your godforsaken child?" Mary shrieked, pointing at me.

"No, you dumb fuck," said Maggie. "That's Tommy Blaine's son."

"Thomas Blaine's foster son?" asked Mary.

Maggie used to babysit Rebecca, Hannah and me when we were little kids. She knew about our different DNA. I pouted at Maggie, silently pleading for her to shut up. But I couldn't get words out quickly enough to explain the situation.

"Nah, his real son," said Maggie. "Tommy's one good nut. Unless Lenore was doing the dirty on him when she got knocked up."

Mary deciphered me. She was perplexed, then incensed. Her trump card had vanished. She held my shaking hands. I was silent and terrified.

"This boy is possessed by the devil!" Mary cried.

Dad arrived during my exorcism. He lurched towards us. Mary let go of me. Dad chased her around the pool table.

"Get out!" yelled my father. "Get the fuck out of my pub!"

Mary reached into her purple fabric handbag. I expected a gun or a knife. Instead, she produced a salt shaker flogged from a table in the dining room. She twisted off its silver lid and chucked the salt into my father's face.

"Paedophile!" shouted Mary. "This man is a paedophile!"

Dad removed his glasses. He wiped the salt from the lenses and licked the salt from his thick, white moustache. Maggie came to the rescue. She grabbed Mary by the arm and dragged her away. Dad called the police.

"This is assault!" Mary wailed. "Defiled by a transvestite!"

Such random outbursts of absurdity weren't irregular at the pub. After a brief intermission, the pool game continued. I missed the black ball. We lost.

"Who was that crazy mofo?" Maggie asked me.

"Nobody," I said.

Mary located my father's ute. The red personalised number plates were a dead giveaway: 80-TOM. From inside the pub, we heard a loud shattering. She had smashed a big glass ashtray through the windscreen.

Mary was arrested for theft and vandalism. Dad made a statement to the police. Two cops searched the block for Michael Shelley's white Chrysler. My curfew fell by the wayside. I wanted to be here, close to my father, not bunkered down with Mum. He locked the doors and grumpily counted the tills.

"You could not make this shit up," he muttered.

I sat at the side of the bar watching the big-screen TV. There was a stop sign right outside the window. A cop car pulled up. Michael Shelley sat in the back seat. I stared at him. He stared at me. Was there a new plot in his wide eyes, or just plain old rage? It was hard to judge. Then he was gone.

Bloody Mary

The Shelleys refused to swallow their pride. In Warwick, they were arrested for disturbing a church service and assaulting a pastor's wife. Then Mary was arrested for breaking into the house of Peter Beattie, the Queensland premier. Beattie's wife, Heather, took out a restraining order.

Hannah reiterated to her social worker that she wanted no contact with either of the Shelleys. A prosecutor applied to extend Hannah's restraining order to protect my parents, and for it to cover their place of business.

Michael and Mary appeared at the Toowoomba Magistrates Court. They were charged with the unlawful stalking of Hannah and the unlawful stalking of my parents. They were also charged with a litany of bail breaches and failures to appear at court. Michael attempted to excuse himself from the stalking charges.

"I'm not my wife's keeper," he told the judge. "If my wife makes decisions that she believes are important, I need to abide by them. If that means I get caught between a rock and a hard place, well, I try to sort this out."

Michael was his wife's keeper only with psychiatrists. To the naked eye, he seemed to be the sane spouse, dragged into the rip of his wife's madness. Yet it was Mary who occasionally showed flashes of pragmatism.

"Your Worship, my contact with Hannah has been minimal to say the least," said Michael. He was technically correct. Mary had acted as his messenger, his prophetess, his scapegoat. And she bore far more of the brunt.

Michael was convicted and sentenced to three months' imprisonment. The Shelleys were ordered not to make any contact with Hannah or my parents for two years. Mary wept. The attention of the courtroom turned to her.

"Your Worship, my client feels – rightly or wrongly – that Hannah was wrongly removed as a breastfeeding baby," said Mary's solicitor.

"If you'd stand up then, please, Mrs Shelley," said the judge.

Mary stood up. In the past five years, she had spent ninety-nine nights in police watchhouses for the crime of loving her daughter too much.

"Here I am, close to Hannah, and you want me not to see her for another year, and another year, and another year," said Mary. "Don't you think I deserve some peace in my life? Some joy? Like I could see my daughter smile at me for an hour? I can't speak to my own daughter. I can't send her a birthday present."

"Well, maybe if you—" said the judge. Mary interrupted him.

"She's my daughter. She looks just like me. She looks like Michael, too. Why does no-one want me to have her? I don't understand. It is inhumane."

"Hang on," said the judge, over Mary's protestations. "Hang on for just a second, please. You understand that there are legal provisions in place?"

"What provisions?" asked Mary.

"Well, the Children's Services Act for a start," said the judge.

"It states that they need to reconcile families!" said Mary.

"Don't worry about what's written, okay?" said the judge. "Orders are made. When Hannah turns eighteen, she'll be able to make her own decisions."

"Oh, yes," said Mary. "Just like Elijah, Saul and Joshua. My own sons loathe me. I'm alone twenty-four hours a day, seven days a week, trying to find out what I am supposed to do. This is too much pain for one life."

"Mrs Shelley, are you going to listen to me?" asked the judge. "Or do you want to go back into the watchhouse cell until you are ready to listen?"

"Not particularly, no," said Mary. "The cell is beyond depressing."

"Righto," said the judge. "I'm not surprised to hear that."

For the charges of failing to appear, Mary was convicted and sentenced to twelve months' imprisonment, suspended for a period of two years. For the charges of unlawful stalking, Mary was convicted and sentenced to twelve months' imprisonment, also suspended for two years.

"Stalking is a serious matter," said the judge. "It needs to be deterred. These people have a right to live their life without being pursued and harassed."

The judge showed some mercy, owing to the bullying that Mary faced in prison. She was released on a strict good behaviour bond. But if she made any contact with the Blaines, she would be sent to prison for at least two years.

"Do you understand?" asked the judge.

"Yes," said Mary.

"That tidies it all up, I think," said the judge.

Mary left the courtroom. Her wrists were uncuffed, but her heart was muzzled. All that suffering for nothing. So much love lost. No love gained.

The Promised Land

My parents didn't trust the sanctity of the new restraining order. Mary Shelley had ignored the paperwork before. Hannah no longer felt safe sleeping at 31 Gowrie Street. Mum had wanted to stay there at all costs. But she gave up.

The bank pre-approved my parents for a $250,000 home loan. We went to property inspections in Glenvale, a western suburb. This part of town was brown from drought. But the street names evoked the Garden of Eden.

Liquidambar Street. Honeysuckle Drive. Silky Oak Crescent.

1 Evergreen Court was the jewel in the crown of a cul-de-sac. A four-bedroom house with a two-bedroom granny flat attached. Cork floors in the kitchen. A dishwasher. Built-in wardrobes. Exhaust fans in the bathroom.

"It's too much for us, surely?" asked my mother.

"Not anymore," said my father.

Gowrie Street was sold. We moved just before Christmas. Dad bought an 8-Ball table for the new house. He covered the walls of the pool room with Allan Langer memorabilia, along with three framed portraits of Steven, John and Hannah in their maroon Queensland outfits. Lastly, my parents acquired a jacuzzi for the back patio as a collective Christmas present.

At 7 am on Christmas Day, Mum hit play on "All I Want for Christmas Is You" by Mariah Carey. Dad put on his socks and joggers.

"Get up, ya bludgers!" my father bellowed.

Rebecca, Hannah and I went on our annual Christmas pilgrimage. We walked through the sprawling suburb. For a fat behemoth, Dad was fleet-footed. Shoulders arched inwards, thick forearms swinging. A plastic bag for Mazda's dog shit flapped from his pocket. Hannah held the red leash of the Dalmatian.

In neat front yards, blue flags hung from white poles. *LOVE IT OR LEAVE IT* read the bumper sticker on a brand-new 4WD ute. There was a Southern Cross on the back windscreen, five astronomical exclamation marks.

"All the cars are so clean," said Hannah.

We talked the same, but second-hand cars and clothing were a thing of the past. The Blaines were metamorphosing into a middle-class family. By stalking us, the Shelleys had delivered Hannah deeper into the belly of the beast that Michael had failed to slay: the Australian Dream.

"G'day, maaate!" squawked Jack upon our arrival home.

We toasted ham sandwiches for breakfast. Mum, Rebecca and Hannah added slices of fresh tomato. Dad and I opted for tomato sauce. Mum presented a cardboard tray of ripe mangoes. Our mouths watered. Dad slit the skin from five heart-shaped pieces of fruit. The juice dripped down our chins.

"I could eat a hundred of them!" said Hannah.

Afterwards, Rebecca and Hannah changed into new bikinis. Dad and I slipped into footy shorts, shirtless. Mum stayed fully clothed. The rest of us hopped into the hot tub on the back patio. Dad took his glasses off. The crest of his huge stomach nudged above the water. Rebecca, Hannah and I splashed bubbles at each other.

Mum sat to the side with a cup of instant coffee.

"No flatulence in the spa, Thomas," said my mother.

Steven and John arrived with Trent, a surprise visitor. He was back from working on the mines out west. Their noses and lips were white with zinc. Steven carried a cricket bat and metal wickets. John carried a carton of beers. Mum hugged and kissed her grown-up sons.

"Merry Christmas, Mum," the three of them chimed at the same time.

"What did I do right in a past life to deserve this?" she asked.

No mention of the Shelleys was permitted on Christmas Day. That morning, my parents beamed with glee. Mum felt safe. Dad felt rich. The war had been won. We hadn't fallen apart.

Act Three

CHAPTER NINE

This Is Australia

As a reward for being stalked by the Shelleys, my father decided to take Hannah and me on a summer pilgrimage to the Sydney Cricket Ground. Mum and Rebecca stayed home. They were both afraid of flying and indifferent to cricket.

"I wish I could come," Mum lied as we said goodbye.

Mum never stopped waiting for the Shelleys to arrive. She still flinched when the phone or doorbell rang. Hannah and I were relieved to get a breather from her nervousness. Dad was tugged between being a bodyguard to his wife and encouraging his kids to be young and free.

"Are you worried about Mum?" I asked on the way to the airport.

"What do you mean?" asked Dad.

"Nothing," I said, cheeks flushed.

My father stared at the vanishing point. I felt like a traitor.

"She'll be apples," he said. "Your Mum's tougher than me. I could spin you some yarns one day. Poor thing's just a bit high-strung at the moment."

This made her sound like a horse. We weren't familiar with PTSD. And my mother wasn't keen to put a label on her malaise, for fear social workers might grow suspicious. She was meant to be the sane and stable anchor.

Persecution had the opposite effect on Dad. It made him thirsty for more of the same, enlarging the personality traits that Michael hated most.

"What's your new year's resolution, Dad?" asked Hannah.

"Eat more meat," he said. "I'm wasting away!"

Hannah was thirteen turning fourteen. I was eleven turning twelve. She didn't tower over me so much anymore. I was getting taller and less chubby. We were two chatty high achievers. She was aiming to make the Hockeyroos squad for the 2008 Beijing Olympics. I was aiming to be prime minister or a famous writer.

"Hannibal and Lecter," said Dad. "Youse can be anything."

"Not necessarily *anything*," I said.

"This is Australia, mate!" said Dad.

My father's delusions of grandeur were contagious. It was a different kind of blind faith from Michael Shelley's. We were the stars of his visions, not him.

++

The three of us flew into Sydney on New Year's Day. The harbour glinted through the plane windows. In the arrival lounge, Hannah shadow-batted against my invisible leg spinners. Trains took us from the airport to Kings Cross.

"The Cross is the best place to get the train," Dad always explained, with wise eyes, as if the red-light district contained the only train station in Sydney.

A gust of hot, dank air hustled us onto Darlinghurst Road. It stank of grease and liquor, sweat and piss. Yet Hannah and I felt much safer in Kings Cross than on the sedate streets of Toowoomba. The Shelleys weren't lurking.

"Sin City," said Dad. "How good is it?"

"It'd be even better if we got kebabs for dinner," I said.

"If you stop pervin' on the pretty girls, Mervyn," he said.

We checked into a three-star hotel with an all-you-can-eat breakfast. Dad left enough space in his travel bag to fill it with toilet paper, soap and condiments from the kitchenette. His wallet was brimming with $50 notes, but he still felt poorer than an orphan. We ate $5 kebabs as the sun set.

"Could you live here, Dad?" asked Hannah.

"I could live anywhere," he said. "Except Paris. That place stank."

Dad bought me two disposable cameras from the chemist. He took a photo of Hannah and me grinning in front of the El Alamein Fountain. It was across the road from the building that had once contained the Chelsea Restaurant, owned by Sidney Newgrosh, Hannah's biological grandfather.

"Can we go to the movies?" asked Hannah.

"Bloody oath," said Dad.

We caught a bus into the well-lit city. My father purchased three large popcorns, three frozen Cokes, a packet of Maltesers and three tickets to *Love Actually.* The tough publican was a sucker for an English romcom. In the dark cinema, laughter howled from our mouths, our spit saltier than the Dead Sea.

Dad passed around the Maltesers. Hannah and I were less numb in his bare-knuckled company. The frozen Coke tasted sweeter. The future shined brighter. Every joke was doubly funny, and any threat half as petrifying.

✣

The next day, we marched towards the SCG. Hannah wore her New Zealand one-day cricket shirt. I wore a yellow Australian one-day shirt. Our faces were shaded by matching Greg Chappell hats with broad brims.

"Aussie, Aussie, Aussie!" barked my father outside the ground.

Dad sported a XXXXL Australian Wallabies jersey and a Brisbane Broncos cap. He carried a brown leather case containing vintage black binoculars.

"Oi, oi, oi!" Hannah and I chanted.

Stewards handed out red handkerchiefs emblazoned with Steve Waugh's name. It was the captain's last test match. He was my father's favourite batsman since Doug Walters. They were both brilliant, but with an egalitarian streak.

Today, the opponent was Sachin Tendulkar's India. We sat next to an Indian family in the Bill O'Reilly Stand. The crowd clapped the approach of the opening ball from Brett Lee. Hannah and I shivered with excitement.

For morning tea, Dad fetched Hannah and me meat pies and Solos from the canteen. Prime Minister John Howard appeared on the big screen. Dad booed him vigorously. After lunch, sweat leaked through the sunscreen on our cheeks. The Indian father passed us a spray bottle filled with water to cool down.

"Legend," said my father.

Dad bought them some hot chips to repay the favour. Then, from a hip flask in his pocket, he tipped scotch into a 600 ml bottle of Diet Coke. I took turns squeezing a tennis ball in each hand. This was an exercise to improve my leg spin and help my wrists and fingers grow as thick as Dad's.

Waugh's final test match went awry. Tendulkar arrived at the crease and didn't budge, en route to a double century. At an ear-splitting pitch, my father sneezed repeatedly into the souvenir handkerchief. Hannah and I grew pink and dehydrated. I pulled out my diary and blue biro to catalogue the day's events.

"Look up and smell the roses," said Dad.

Dad watched Tendulkar through his 1950s binoculars. They were a kaleidoscope. The present swirled together with the past. Occasionally, he lowered them and let slip a memory from a day just like this one.

"Dougie Walters against the Poms," he said. "1965. The Gabba. Tonne on debut. You would not read about it! Jeez we had some fun on the hill."

"Who'd you go with?" asked Hannah.

There was a sting in his eyes. I thought it might be the sunscreen.

"Your pop," he said. "His last test match, now that I think of it."

Dad was two years younger than his mother had been when she died in 1963. He was giving us what his father had given him: a happy distraction. Sport was more than win and loss, bat and ball. It was history. It was kinship. It helped ordinary people to believe in the possibility of persistence.

"You wouldn't be dead for quids," said Dad.

Mum fought mortality by writing everything down. Dad fought mortality by telling stories at the cricket.

Parable of the Tall Poppy

Steven accepted a graduate job at Toowoomba's biggest accounting firm. On a Friday night, he sat with my father at the bar of the Metropole Hotel. Steven drank bourbon. Dad drank scotch. They ate 300-gram steaks. Business was booming. John regaled the barflies with far-fetched yarns about fighting.

"Your brother was born with the gift of the gab," Dad said to Steven, nodding towards John. "You count a few beans this week, or what?"

Steven envied the bare-knuckled intimacy between John and my father. They were both stubborn, short-tempered and unfiltered during disagreements. This produced explosive blow-ups between the master and the apprentice, but also a hard-won camaraderie. Whereas Dad applauded Steven's academic achievements with a slightly baffled admiration.

"Accounting isn't all it's cracked up to be," said Steven. "I'm bored."

"Come and work for me!" said Dad.

"*Here?*" asked Steven.

"Nah, mate," said my father. "This is just the start."

Dad wanted to create a succession plan. Luckily, he had two hyper-competitive sons. My father offered to buy the lease of another hotel — something bigger and better than the Metropole — and get Steven to run it.

"I'm in!" said Steven.

Neither of them questioned whether Steven was suited to running a country pub. Dad organised a surprise business meeting with Steven and John. Steven suggested to John that his accounting degree could take the Blaine Family Trust from the outhouse to the penthouse of the hotel industry.

"What's wrong with the Metropole?" asked John.

"You've done a great job," said Steven. "But it's not making a fortune."

John was apocalyptically pissed off. For the first time, he had found an existential connection that bonded him to my father, the same way rugby league bonded my father to Steven, or biology bonded my father to me. Of course Steven wanted in. He couldn't stomach John's newfound importance. And of course he expected the golden handshake of a swankier establishment, without serving a shit-kicking apprenticeship at the Metropole.

"He's not a publican's arsehole," John scoffed to Dad afterwards.

"Your brother is one smart cookie," said Dad.

And I'm not? thought John.

"People don't come here to eat spreadsheets," said John.

My father dismissed John's objections. Dad and Steven searched for a suitable venture. They drove thirty minutes west from Toowoomba to Oakey. On the surface, it was a sunny and dusty country town. Behind the tranquillity of the faces on the main street was a profound allergy to outsiders.

The Bernborough Tavern was named after a famous dead racehorse. There was a statue of Bernborough out front and a creek bed out back. The shiny one-storey pub was newly built to profit from the mining boom.

Thus, it contained all the mod cons the Metropole Hotel lacked. A drive-through bottle-o with a forklift. A games room with PlayStations for the kids, away from a private pokies den for their parents. Air-conditioning in the front bar. No scent of stale beer or the fading trace of cigarette smoke.

"Bullseye," said my father.

His small business career was leading towards this moment. Dad borrowed $250,000 to buy the lease, using his property portfolio as collateral, against the objections of my mother. They had no superannuation or shares. He was betting their retirement plan on Steven's success as a publican.

On the first day of operations, Steven wore a button-up white shirt. Long sleeves. Striped tie. Black pants with a black belt and black shoes. Cheeks clean-shaven and dimpled. Hair brushed into a quiff. He was fit and tanned and grinning indiscriminately, like an actor on the red carpet.

"Who the fuck do *you* think you are?" asked a barfly named Brad.

Brad was a fat, balding meatworker with skin that looked like a leg of ham left in the sun. He was the chief shit-stirrer in a group of afternoon dribblers. They had patriotic tattoos on their arms and fillings on their teeth.

"G'day, fellas," said Steven. "My name is Steven Blaine."

Big Bad Brad saw a young man physically impressive enough to trigger his inferiority complex, yet way too sophisticated to lay a fist on his chin. He squinted at the supple skin of Steven's extended hand with disgust.

"I didn't ask for a fuckin' handjob," he said. "Get me a XXXX Gold."

The target demographic of the bar was men who had dropped out of school at the end of grade ten to get a job at the local abattoir. Steven hoped that his objective toughness as a rugby league player might win them over. It didn't. After he regaled them with the exploits of his career, there was a hostile silence. They stared at him with crossed arms and flushed cheeks.

"If you're so fucking good at football," asked Brad's sidekick Pat, "why are you pouring schooners for us and not playing in the NRL?"

The fact that Steven had played representative rugby league actually made him more unlikeable. When battlers looked over the bar, they wanted to see a mirror, not a magnifying glass for their own flaws.

"Cause his dad bought the uppity fucker a pub," muttered Brad.

There it was: the rumour that spread through Oakey like the flu. The perception was that Steven had been born with a silver spoon in his mouth. Pubs were where simple men went to feel like kings. Steven reminded them that they were peasants. So they were going to knock him down a few pegs. He spent most of that first week getting heckled by menacing strangers.

John the Baptist

After a few months, Steven was tiptoeing along the tightrope of a nervous breakdown. The Blaine Family Trust was on the precipice of bankruptcy. My father, Steven and John had an emergency honesty session in the front bar of the Bernborough Tavern after closing time. It was 10 pm on a Sunday night.

"We're going broke," said Steven, bursting into tears. "I've fucked it up. The pub is going down the gurgler. You'll lose the houses."

All of Steven's business plans had failed to win over the locals. Dad sat on a bar stool with folded arms. He took a sip from a stiff scotch.

"It can't be that bad," said John, secretly vindicated.

"You don't understand," said Steven. "It's not like the Metropole. There are loan repayments. We're not making enough money to meet them."

"Oh, is that how loans work?" asked John. "There ya go."

My father's growing empire was ablaze. He sized up Steven and John like they were fire extinguishers. He could only pick one of them. The choice would be gravely humiliating for one, and an opportunity for the other.

"John, you're gonna run this place for a week," said Dad. "Steve, you'll take over at the Metropole for a week. Ya need to look after yaself."

Steven's face was grief-stricken. His coronation as the perfect son had turned into a public defrocking. He finished his beer and departed. John poured himself another drink. His face was filled with an *I told you so* glow.

"Wipe that grin off ya lips," said Dad. "This isn't a job promotion. Don't cut off your dick for a kiss on the cheek."

John sat back down on the bar stool. His chastened face opened back up for the forthcoming motivational speech. My father laid out a game plan.

"This pub isn't about you, or your brother, or me," he said. "It belongs to the people of Oakey. We're just running it for 'em. Show some humility. But don't let anyone treat ya like a mug. Or the others will smell blood in the water."

On Monday morning, John drove to Oakey in a battered two-door hatchback. He wore a t-shirt, cargo shorts and a pair of Dunlop Volleys. Thanks to a daily intake of steak sandwiches, he had packed on weight since high school. The bartender was 186 centimetres and 105 kilograms.

"Are you the ugly brother?" asked Brad at the start of Happy Hour.

John had the hint of a double chin and a mouthful of haphazard teeth. He smiled like a crocodile at Brad and his buzz of blue-collar barflies.

"I'm the brother who loves punching people," said John.

The meatworkers winced. And then they burst into laughter. Truth be told, they were a little bit intimidated by him. But they liked it! John listened to their stories about pig hunting in rapture. His amusement was uproarious and authentic, because deep down he found the men funny, not disgusting. He reciprocated with his own tales of barroom brawls and getting arrested.

"You're a breath of fresh air, mate," said Brad, clapping his hands.

In the space of a single rounded vowel, they could tell that Steven Blaine wasn't one of them. Yet they forgave John for going to a Catholic school, living in Toowoomba and running his father's pub. Why? Because he was a politically incorrect strongman, not a white-collar arse-kisser.

Word circulated around town that the tavern had a new operator, a proper knockabout. On Friday night, the front bar was packed for karaoke. In less than a week, John had resurrected the cashflow of the Bernborough.

"In half an hour, call me up to sing a song," John whispered to Brenda, the karaoke master. "I'll say no way. But don't take no for an answer. Right?"

"Rightio," she said with confusion.

The plan went off without a hitch. On the microphone, Brenda invited John to the stage. He shook his head with a fabricated embarrassment. The bar started egging him on to sing a song, just like he suspected they would.

"Ah, fuck," he said, shrugging his shoulders. "One song, I guess."

John shuffled onto the stage. He directed Brenda to play "Khe Sanh" by Cold Chisel. Those unmistakable opening notes of piano lilted from the speakers. The singer filled his lungs. Ocker poetry flowed from his throat. His voice was beautiful. Those present swore it was better than Jimmy Barnes': deeper and more soulful. A new nickname was bestowed. *Jukebox Johnnie.*

At the end of the song, someone handed John a jug of beer, not realising that he was born without a gag reflex. The beer disappeared like a bucket of water down a storm drain. People were speechless. What had they just seen? Who would believe them? In five minutes flat, the black sheep of the Blaine family had converted sixty witnesses into fanatical disciples.

Feeding the Multitude

My father had seen the light. He sold the lease of the Metropole Hotel. John was put in charge of the front bar of the Bernborough Tavern. Steven was put in charge of the restaurant and business operations. Dad ran the bottle-o.

The Blaines assimilated. Dad played lawn bowls in Oakey twice a week, targeting the over-sixty demographic. The Bernborough became the major sponsor of the Oakey Bears, the local rugby league team. Steven became captain and star player of the A-grade team. John played B-grade.

Trent moved back from out west to work as Dad's right-hand man in the bottle-o. Then he moonlighted as a glassie and security guard. Rebecca and Hannah worked as waitresses in the restaurant. I was given responsibility for the dishwasher in the kitchen on Friday and Saturday nights.

The head cook, Will, was a goateed introvert who blasted country music in the kitchen. He taught Hannah how to judge the doneness of a steak with her thumb and finger. Hannah, fifteen, decided she wanted to be a chef.

Unbeknownst to Mary Shelley, Hannah had grown curves and long, thick hair. The gangly tomboy was becoming a woman. She got braces for her teeth, paid for by the Department of Child Safety. Her first serious boyfriend was a footballer from St Mary's. She wasn't ashamed of sex.

On a Friday night in winter, Mum drove Rebecca, Hannah and me from the suburbs of Toowoomba to Oakey. The three of us wore matching black pants and white polo shirts. The car passed half-lit, drought-stricken farm paddocks. The sun was setting above our destination in the west. We arrived at the tavern.

"It's a clusterfuck," Steven announced in the kitchen.

The cook had called in sick. So had the main waitress. None of the substitutes were available. Hannah would be head chef and Steven her sous chef. Rebecca and I were waiters. We were prone to panic. Hannah wasn't.

"Let's do this," she said.

By 6 pm, the bistro was at capacity. By 7 pm, the bar was full with the overflow from the bistro. It was so busy that people were eating dinner in the pokies room. Steven looked like a man evading flames that no one else could see. Oakey had given us another chance. Now it could all go up in smoke.

Hannah stood at the grill in a black apron and white chef's hat. The hot plate was covered with sixteen seemingly indistinguishable cuts of rumps and rib fillets, to be succeeded by sixteen more, and then sixteen more. Some needed to be covered with prawns and garlic sauce for the surf and turf.

The steaks ranged from rare, to medium rare, to medium, to medium well, to well done. Customers would detect too much or not enough blood. Steven manned the deep fryer. He laid out the plates of vegetables and salad for Hannah. She distributed the steaks and added ladles of gravy.

"Order up," said Hannah.

Rebecca and I carried three meals at a time to the impatient tables, then collected the finished ones and rushed the plates back to the dishwasher.

"Scuse me, mate," a meatworker said to me.

His face was solemn. The rest of the table went quiet.

"Yep?" I asked.

"That was the best fuckin' steak I've had in ten years," he said, cracking his knuckles over a protruding gut. "Tell the chef he's a genius."

"It's a she!" I said.

"Well, she needs a pay rise."

A fifteen-year-old girl had cooked 150 dinners without a single complaint. Customers left twenty-dollar tips. The tavern had an atmosphere of affection and respect. My father watched John and Trent serving the drunks, Hannah and Steven feeding the hungry, and Rebecca and me cleaning up the scraps. The best thing of all: we didn't need him to save us.

✣

Pretty soon, the Bernborough Tavern was turning over $60,000 a week. John claimed personal responsibility for the dramatic turnaround.

"Running a pub is money for jam, mate," he told Steven.

From Steven's perspective, John deserved no more credit for the high turnover than my father or he did. The front bar actually provided less revenue than the other three sectors: the pokies, the restaurant and the bottle-o.

"John, you do realise that charging people two dollars a pot during happy hour is losing the business money?" asked Steven. "It's not 1995."

"But the smiling faces are priceless, mate," said John.

The truth was somewhere in the middle. John's popularity filtered into the pokies, the restaurant and the bottle-o. His congregation of blue-collar barflies brought their families to the restaurant rather than to the RSL and bought cartons from the bottle-o rather than more cheaply in Toowoomba.

Steven's liberation from the bar had allowed him to relax. He formed close friendships with public servants, business owners and farmers. Many of them found John lewd. The two brothers' personalities appealed to different people. And their strengths counterbalanced each other's weaknesses.

But Steven had tunnel vision for the people who disliked him. John had tunnel vision for the people who loved him. Each day, Steven was confronted by the sight of John being worshipped by the meatworkers and coalminers. He listened to John mimicking their bloodthirsty lingo.

"When did you become an expert on pig hunting?" Steven asked.

"I take an interest in other people's interests, mate," said John. "Not all of us flog our cocks to economics textbooks and history documentaries."

"At least I'm not a chameleon," said Steven. "I am who I am."

John was the one who'd changed. Like a snake shedding its skin, he'd shaken off his identity as a high school drama kid, reinventing himself as a larrikin.

"You're about as real as a fake tan, mate," said John.

Not that long ago, John had wanted to be Steven. Now, Steven was tortured by his failure to be John.

There was rarely a handover between shifts that didn't devolve into a slanging match. Politics added another layer to their sibling rivalry. They had both deviated from my parents' tribal loyalty to the Labor Party. Steven voted for the Greens. John voted for the Liberal Party. In the bottle-o, John overheard Steven proselytising to me about climate change.

"That sounds like a pipedream, mate," scoffed John.

"It's science," said Steven. "Something you don't know much about."

"People used to think that the world was flat, too," said John.

"That's the exact opposite of this scenario!" said Steven.

"Righto, mate," said John. "Let's see what comes out in the wash."

One brother went to university. The other brother didn't. Steven saw higher education as a virtue. He worshipped at the altar of reason.

John saw Steven as an elitist. He trusted his gut. For Steven, his success in life was a testament to the basic morality of the welfare state. For John, his survival proved that the only obstacle to a battler raising themselves up by the bootstraps was laziness.

This Baby Business

John had been dating a young woman from Toowoomba named Merkilla. She was thin and pretty with blonde hair. One Saturday night, John's girlfriend arrived at the front bar of the tavern. He was surprised but pleased to see her.

"Hey, babe," said John. "What do you want to drink?"

"Just a Coke," she said, forebodingly.

Merkilla chewed on her straw and tore apart a paper coaster. John finished his shift with a terrible presentiment of rejection. He called last drinks earlier than usual. Then he sat on a stool next to her.

"What's wrong?" he asked.

Merkilla crossed her shaking arms, like she was naked in a cold lake.

"I'm pregnant," she said, grinning in a disturbed way.

Merkilla was nineteen. John was twenty. They had been seeing each other for less than six months. It hadn't been uncomplicated. He put his arm around her.

"Your thoughts?" asked Merkilla, before bursting into tears.

All John could think about was his mother and father: Lenore and Tom, not Michael and Mary. Just the vision of his parents nipped the possibility of self-pity in the bud. Nothing could be tougher than what they'd done.

"I won't let you down," said John.

John still needed to officially meet Merkilla's parents. On Monday, he went around to their house in the suburban sprawl south of Toowoomba. They all sat at the living-room table. The face of Merkilla's mother was a beacon of warmth. Merkilla had inherited her mother's prettiness and her father's no-bullshit glare. He was a big, tough truck mechanic.

The conversation was mostly between John and Merkilla's mum. He gave them a condensed rendition of his childhood. Her father ignored John's witty one-liners and interjected with the reason for the meeting.

"This baby business, mate," he said.

"Oh, mate," said John. "It goes without saying."

Merkilla's father studied John with a skin-tingling animosity.

"No," he said. "It don't go without saying. That's why I'm saying it."

John took a deep breath. He stared into the other man's eyes.

"I'm in love with your daughter," said John. "I wasn't planning to be a father this quick. But I'm sure as shit gonna throw the kitchen sink at it."

John and Merk moved into a two-bedroom house next to the airport. The fibro slats were yellow. The timber stairs to the door were green. They bought second-hand furniture and linen, cutlery and crockery from Kmart. Her parents donated a fridge. His parents donated a washing machine. In winter, Merkilla went for her first ultrasound while John was at work.

"Boy or girl?" asked John when she phoned him.

"Girl," said Merkilla.

"Ripper," said John. "Let's hope she looks like you."

There was a long hesitation from the other end of the line.

"Another thing," said Merkilla.

"What's that?" asked John.

"There's two of them," she said.

++

Merkilla was scheduled for an elective caesarean first thing in the morning. Maternity nurses prepped the expectant mother and father.

The epidural took a long time to work. John, twenty-one, wore a cap, gloves and teal scrubs.

"Love, are you sure you want to be here for this?" one of the nurses asked John. "You can sit behind the curtains. It's a lot for you to watch."

John was hellbent on seeing the birth.

"I'll be right," he said.

Blood and guts flooded from Merkilla's body. John felt like he was holding his breath under water, brain weightless. He squeezed Merkilla's hand so hard it cut the circulation. The first baby came at 10.38 am. The second baby came at 10.41 am. They were both screaming at the top of their lungs.

John's heart stopped. He had never experienced such fear and euphoria. Everything that had happened to him divided into before and after. He was no longer Joshua Shelley, bipolar foster boy. He was John Blaine, partner and father.

"Are you okay?" groaned Merkilla, eyes glazed and face pale.

"I love you," said John, weeping through his fingers.

They named the first girl Sophie and the second girl Amelia. Sophie *Blaine*. Amelia *Blaine*. This was John's offering to my parents for all their unspoken sacrifice. A two-for-one birth, their first grandchildren.

"Twin girls," said my mother. "This is just the best."

On Tuesday afternoon, I went to the hospital with my chuffed parents. Mum was fifty-two. Dad was fifty-seven. There had never been any hint of disapproval on their behalf. They didn't care that John was unmarried, or that he would rather spend his wages on the rent than on an engagement ring.

"John will be a good dad," said Dad. "He's got a big heart."

It was sweet and sad to see my parents nurse the twins for the first time. Mum's love of children was satisfied without the paralysing fear that she couldn't protect them. Dad beamed into their little faces without needing to offer a model of strength. They were grandparents.

The Engagement

At high school, Rebecca struggled academically. She fought with teachers. Seeing the cruelty of schoolgirls made Hannah feel guilty about her past nastiness. She helped Rebecca with her homework and tried to shield her from persecution. It was no use. Eventually, Mum organised for Rebecca to switch from St Saviour's to a school for teenagers with learning difficulties.

"I'll never make it to uni," Rebecca cried to Mum. "I'm too dumb!"

"You don't need to go to university," my mother told her. "Look at me. I didn't go to university. I didn't even finish high school! Want to know the stupidest thing in the world? Thinking a piece of paper makes you a good person."

At the end of grade ten, Rebecca left school. She worked as a cleaner and trainee barmaid at the Bernborough Tavern. Each week, she helped Mum do the grocery shopping. They always stopped at the two-dollar shop. One day, the check-out boy was named Jamie. He was a skinny, tattooed teenager with blond tips and an eyebrow piercing. Rebecca fell in love at first sight.

"Oh, Mum," said Rebecca on the way home from the shopping centre. "I've got butterflies in my guts! Is this what you felt when you first met Dad?"

"Something like that," said Mum. "Why don't you ask for his number?"

"He won't like me," she said.

"Rebecca, you're beautiful!" said Mum.

Their pilgrimages to the two-dollar shop became more frequent. Rebecca grew silent in front of Jamie. He was painfully shy.

"My daughter wants to ask you on a date," said Mum at the checkout. "I'm going to take this stuff out to the car. I'll leave you two lovebirds alone."

Rebecca got Jamie's phone number and email address. They spoke every day on MSN. Jamie was a high-school dropout, too. Rebecca invited him on a date to the movies. My mother dropped her to the cinemas and picked her up.

"He doesn't say much," said Rebecca.

"Beware men who love the sound of their own voice," said Mum.

Rebecca and Jamie began spending every spare moment together. She told him about being a foster girl and her alcoholic biological mother. He told her about his father, who had been a cleaner at the meatworks. He died when Jamie was twelve.

"I love you, Jamie," she said.

"I love you, too," he said.

Rebecca and Jamie lost their virginities to each other. Jamie got a job installing roof insulation. They moved in together. Rebecca missed her period. She was eighteen. The pregnancy test from the chemist was positive. She was terrified by my mother's potential response.

"Mum, I'm pregnant!" said Rebecca.

Rebecca confessed to her fear that people would judge her for being too young, or for not having been with Jamie for long enough. But she didn't want to get an abortion. Her destiny seemed crystal clear: to be a mother.

"What should I do?" asked Rebecca.

My mother offered unconditional tenderness. It wasn't her womb. She was equally prepared to support either possibility. Rebecca wanted to keep the baby, or she didn't.

"It's totally up to you," said Mum.

For the first time, my mother told another human being about her own long-ago abortion. It seemed like yesterday. The fear of disapproval. Then the guilt from an irreversible decision that permanently damaged her fertility.

"You'd be a wonderful mum, Rebecca," said Mum. "But it isn't easy. You'll need to make some sacrifices. I'll be here for you whatever you decide."

Rebecca's shame evaporated. She gave up drinking, not just for the pregnancy, but for good. She didn't like the way alcohol made her feel. And she wanted to nip the cycle of addiction in the bud, once and for all.

Rebecca and Jamie had an engagement party over a Sunday roast at the tavern. The lunch doubled as a baby shower. Rebecca asked Hannah to be her bridesmaid. Now the old adversaries spoke on the phone every day.

"Welcome to the madhouse, mate," Dad said to Jamie, winking.

Rebecca gave birth to a healthy baby boy. *Henry.* He was followed by a daughter, Isabella; a son, Thomas, named for my father; and twin daughters, Isla and Ivy. Rebecca's children would never question, for a single second, that her affection was forever. Mum had taught her how to love them.

Hannah's Choice

At the age of sixteen, Hannah went home. She was selected in the under-seventeens Queensland hockey team for a tour of New Zealand. Getting a passport proved to be a nightmare. Hannah was a New Zealand citizen, not an Australian one. According to the birth certificate, her name was Hannah Shelley.

On the two-week tour, it occurred to Hannah that she was no longer head-and-shoulders above the other players. She was fit but not thin. Gritty but not quick. Dominance didn't come as effortlessly as it had when she was a kid. She gave up on her dream to be an Olympic athlete.

"Do whatever makes you happy," my father told her.

Back in Queensland, Hannah attended a school leadership camp. Teachers encouraged her to run for school captain. My mother proofread Hannah's leadership speech with tears in her eyes.

"It's beautiful," said Mum.

"Do you really think I could do it?" asked Hannah.

"You'll shit it in, baby," said Mum.

In front of the grade elevens, Hannah made a confession.

"Not many of you know this," she said. "But I was born in the bathtub of a motel room in New Zealand. I went into foster care when I was one. My foster mum, Lenore, taught me to never run away from someone who needs help."

Hannah knew exactly who she was. She was sick of hiding. Her speech dropped a bomb of moral seriousness into a hollow popularity contest. Hannah easily won the leadership ballot. She was the next school captain.

☩

Michael and Mary continued to lobby politicians across the country for custody of Hannah. Mum received a constant stream of emails from them.

From: Mary Shelley <seamissionary@yahoo.com.au>
Subject: HANNAH'S CHOICE

Lenore, I was thinking about Hannah on Friday, because I passed a shop with her name on it. Hannah will be eighteen soon. Where have all the years gone!!! Michael and I are her parents. Always have been, always will be. I wanted to ask whether she might want to see me when she turns eighteen. Otherwise, there's not much point in us remaining in Australia.

But only Hannah can make this decision. It's her life. It's her choice.

Mary Shelley

....

From: Lenore Blaine <lenoreblaine@hotmail.com>

Greetings Mary,

Time flies. As you say, Hannah will be eighteen soon. On this matter, I can only speak for myself. But maybe the time will come to ease up the restrictions of the past.

Of course, it will be Hannah's decision. We do not prevent her from emailing you. Michael and you will always be their birth parents. Nothing will ever change that fact. I cannot imagine how painful it must have been not to be able to parent your own children.

I can only say that we have tried our best to raise them, and to date we seem to have done a satisfactory job. They are confident, secure young people who truly love each other.

Regards,
Lenore Blaine

....

From: Michael Shelley <michael.the.one@yahoo.com.au>

Lenore,

I apologise for my wife's email. She was speaking without my permission. Let me reiterate: we will never entertain a peace deal with the devil's advocates. I often wonder what you and your grossly obese, useless excuse of a husband have done to OUR beautiful children to make them so scared of the truth, and so determined to believe in obvious lies and propaganda.

The contempt that I feel for you two child abusing deviates is profound and deserved. And I rejoice in where you are both going – HELL! When you least expect it, GOD will expunge your ugly, unwanted lesbian presence from the planet. It cannot come soon enough.

Yours faithfully,
Michael Shelley

....

From: Lenore Blaine <lenoreblaine@hotmail.com>

Hi, Hannah here.

There are many things that I have been meaning to say to you for quite a while and I've decided that now is the right time. Yes, you are both my biological parents. I can understand why you would want me back. But I've made a life of my own. Nothing is perfect. My current life comes pretty close. I wouldn't change anything about it. Not even having you as my biological parents. Because you gave me Steven and John as older brothers. I'm grateful for that.

I see Lenore and Thomas Blaine as my real parents. This will never change. They have loved Steven, John and me like we were their own children. My teachers believe that I am a very polite and intelligent young woman. This is because of the lessons I learned from the Blaines, not because of you. I hate the disgusting things that you say about them. Nothing could be further from the truth. What they have done for Steven, John and I is extraordinary. They are the loveliest people that you could ever meet. I just wish that you could see this.

You are both running around the country trying to convince leaders I should be with you. When it comes down to it, I think my freedom of speech is more important than yours. You have always seemed to assume that you know how I think and what I feel. But you barely know anything about me. Anyway, I'm sixteen. I'm old enough to make my own decisions.

From Hannah

....

From: Michael Shelley <michael.the.one@yahoo.com.au>

Hannah,

I am listening to Andrea Bocelli's album "Andrea" while I write this to you. He is a blind Italian tenor who, to quote your mother Mary, "sings like an angel". Mary discovered him for us some years ago and we have owned all of his non-operatic albums at one time or another. We love all of them – "Romanza", "Sogno", & "Tuscan Skies". I am guessing the Blaines wouldn't be familiar with Andrea Bocelli. I would recommend that you listen to him.

To your email: it is a dreadfully demeaning way to refer to anyone as just a "biological parent". This ignores the primary importance of spiritual relationships between children and their natural parents. No one can replace me as your father and no one can replace Mary as your mother. We are – as the bible says – "flesh of your flesh and bone of your bone".

It is not my intention to upset you, either, but I must be honest with you. I love you ineluctably. This love gave me the strength and courage to let you go fifteen years ago when you were being tormented by some truly awful foster carers in New Zealand. It has also allowed me to cope with the subsequent separation and the everyday anguish that I witness in Mary.

I acknowledge the importance of Lenore and Thomas Blaine in your life. At the same time, I am reminded of a famous quote by

William Shakespeare: "The lady doth protest too much, methinks". In other words, whilst I admire your loyalty, it is important to be objective.

Your "freedom of speech" – I presume that you meant "freedom of choice" – is so constrained by what has shamefully been done to you that you cannot appreciate what real freedom of choice means. You have been made to feel the way you do by emotional conditioning. It is impertinent for you to question my expertise. I have been blessed with wisdom by a GOD whom I serve faithfully. I can hear your thoughts and feel your feelings. I understand – better than you – how you think and feel. You would do well to carefully read the chapter in my manifesto titled "To Women Everywhere". This sums up much of your current denialism.

We are genuinely concerned that you will prematurely and inappropriately lose your virginity without discussing this extremely important matter with Mary. She can explain to you the difference between love and infatuation, and the difference between sex and making love. We are also concerned that you will become a drug addict (like Elijah) or an alcoholic (like Saul and Joshua) as a way of escaping how you feel about the abuse that you have suffered.

Nobody on planet earth understands these issues like me. Mary and I do a lot of anger management, addiction and relationship counselling. Who will you go to, Hannah? Thomas Blaine: an alcoholic glutton totally lost to the lusts of the flesh. Or Lenore Blaine: a masculine, competitive, shorthaired, lesbian eunuch. I think not! We are your only option. You, Saul and Joshua are our children, not theirs!

Please respond to this email in detail and use it as a basis for ongoing discussion. With all my Love and God's amazing Grace.

Your Father,
Michael Shelley

Hannah had broken up with a footballer. She wanted a nice, shy cricketer. There was a batsman at St Mary's named Jay. He was tall with thick brown sideburns and a dimple in his chin. Hannah had started going to St Mary's 1st IV games. But he barely acknowledged her.

"Hey, Jay," said Hannah, after he got caught on 43. "Good knock."

"Thanks, Blainey," he said, like she was a teammate.

On a Saturday night, Hannah hosted a party at 1 Evergreen Court. She invited some girls from St Saviour's and some boys from St Mary's. Jay was the designated driver. He and his mates sat on the fold-out sofa in the granny flat watching *A Perfect Day*, the documentary about Steve Waugh's century against England at the SCG.

At quarter to eleven, Jay announced that he needed to go home.

"See ya, Blainey," he said to Hannah.

"But you haven't even seen my bedroom yet!" said Hannah.

Her bedroom wall was covered with Keith Urban posters.

"Kiss me," said Hannah.

Jay blushed and surrendered.

"You should come over to my place on Boxing Day," he said.

"I would love that!" she said.

On Boxing Day, Hannah went to Jay's place. He lived in a brick house with a swimming pool. His father was a used-car salesman. His mother was a nurse. After lunch, Shane Warne claimed his 700th test wicket and then took another five. Jay was more captivated by Shane Warne than by Hannah.

Hannah left Jay's house without a kiss. Dad picked her up. She drove his car with L-plates on. He could tell there was something troubling her.

"Do you like this bloke?" he asked.

"Yeah, Dad," she said. "I really do."

"Well, tell him to pull his finger out of his arse," he said.

At home, Hannah lay in bed pondering the riddle of Jay's chastity.

"Hey Jay," she wrote in a text message. "I really enjoyed today. I love hanging out with you. Especially when I flog you in pool :) :) :) I'm just a bit confused about our status. Do you want to be my boyfriend? It's cool if not."

"of course I want to be your boyfriend :)," he wrote back.

Hannah's life changed. She felt strange in a good way.

The Settlement

At the start of 2007, John went away on his first family holiday with Merkilla and the twin girls. Steven saw purchases on the company credit card. When John got back, Steven confronted him with the annotated bank statement.

"So," said Steven. "I'm going to need you to pay this money back."

John shrugged his shoulders.

"I work hard, mate," said John. "Merkilla has had to put up with a lot of shit so that I can make this place run properly. I think we deserve a holiday."

"I'm disappointed about this, John," said Steven, trying to reclaim the moral high ground. "You've let the family down. You've let me down."

"I don't give a fuck what *you* think, mate," said John.

"I know you think I'm a wowser," said Steven. "But this place would fall over tomorrow without me. You don't know the first thing about accounting."

John sneered at Steven. He subconsciously saw himself as the publican and Steven as the irritating bean counter in the office, an underling.

"I saved your arse," said John. "You know so much about money you almost sent Mum and Dad broke. We would be fucked if it wasn't for me."

Steven's inferiority complex collided with John's messiah complex. The distance between them crystallised. John was bigger than Steven now. Taller, broader and heavier. He had responsibilities – children – that made him feel wiser. He no longer idolised his older brother or craved his approval.

"You're a megalomaniac," said Steven.

"At least one of us believes in ourselves," said John. "That's why you never made it as a rugby league player. You broke Dad's heart, mate."

Steven stared at the unshakeable self-confidence on John's face. For the first time in his life, he clenched his fists and shaped up to another man.

"Hit me, ya weak piece of shit," said John.

Steven punched John flush on the mouth. A dull thud. The adrenaline rush anaesthetised the sting in his fist. *This is why we fight*, he thought. The bliss of virility. For a fleeting instant, Steven had regained the ascendancy.

Alas, it didn't last. John grinned at his unshackled older brother. Blood bubbling from his lips. Zero fear in his eyes. John had lured Steven onto his preferred battlefield. He punched Steven in the eye socket, twice as hard.

The cook, Will, was the only other person at the tavern.

"Holy cow," he whispered from the doorway to the kitchen.

Steven's face was swathed with agony and embarrassment. Stars twinkled in his eyes. *This is why I don't fight*, he thought. There was a limit to inflicting injury on another human being that he wasn't willing to cross.

"You should've hit me harder when you had the chance," said John, wiping the blood from his mouth with a serviette, as if it were tomato sauce.

"How can you punch someone like that?" asked Steven.

"I could've knocked you out if I wanted to," said John.

"Thanks," said Steven.

Steven wrapped some ice in a Chux cloth and applied it to his eye. He retreated to the office. For whom was he subjecting himself to these daily disgraces? The rednecks rejected him. He was becoming one of them.

+++

Hannah had set Steven up with a hockey teammate named Prue. She was a brunette with olive skin and brown eyes. They were both type-A athletes. But Prue was outgoing, without relying on alcohol to loosen up, as socially anxious Steven did. He felt at risk of being seen. They broke up. Prue moved to Western Australia to play hockey. As soon as she left, Steven was regretful.

"I really miss you," he told her on the phone.

"Well, maybe you should move to Perth," said Prue.

"I can't just move to Perth."

"Why not?"

It was a great question. The feud with John had morphed into a cold war. The brothers ignored each other unless necessary. Steven knew that moving to Perth would leave Dad and John to run a pub together without him.

My father was sick of playing peacekeeper between them. The tavern was at its most profitable, but they were all exhausted by the long hours.

"I think it's time to pull the pin," said Dad at a business meeting.

Steven and John were both relieved, though they tried not to show it, in case my father was testing their loyalty. He took the decision out of their hands. The lease of the tavern was sold for $500,000, double what they had paid for it three years earlier. Settlement was scheduled for 1 July 2007.

Steven and John performed a stocktake. On a Friday afternoon, they handed over the keys of the tavern to the new owner, a retired soldier.

"Fancy running a pub with your brother," he said, pouring himself an afternoon bourbon. "It's a miracle yas don't want to kill each other!"

Dad honoured the momentous occasion by playing a game of lawn bowls in Toowoomba. Steven and John went to watch him. Steven wore a beret and a pair of brown aviators. John wore a trucker's cap and Oakleys.

Afterwards, they did a pub crawl through Toowoomba, ending up at the Metropole Hotel. The Blaines entered a game of poker. Steven made the quarterfinals. John and Dad drank in the front bar. Steven lost patience with the poker game. Unlike the other two, he had no interest in gambling.

"I'm sick of it," he told them. "I'm going to forfeit."

"Don't be dumb," said John.

In the toilets of the Metropole, Steven and John swapped clothes. John took Steven's place at the card table in the beret and aviators. Maybe the brothers were less distinguishable than they thought. None of the other players detected the false identity. John made the final, moving towards the jackpot.

Steven sat with my father in the same corner of the bar where they had hatched ambitions for a hospitality empire four long, lost years ago.

"I'm moving to Perth," said Steven.

"I thought ya might," said Dad.

"You don't mind?"

"Me? I'm not going to make you happy, mate. Prue will."

The father and the son discussed the mystery of love.

"How do you know?" asked Steven.

"You just do," said Dad. "It ain't all smooth sailing, believe you me. But love keeps ya honest. I wasn't a very good bloke before I met your mum."

Steven realised how little he knew about my father's heart. He wanted to map it like a cartographer. But there was a ruckus from the poker tables.

"Hang on," shouted a card player. "That's an imposter!"

John appeared in the doorway to the front bar. He was followed by a mob of angry gamblers. They had called his bluff.

"Let's make like a tree and leave," said John, finishing his schooner.

The Blaine Family Trust went to a new pub. Steven and John swapped back into their original outfits. They enjoyed each other's company for once.

"I'm proud of you two blokes," said my father.

Steven moved to Perth. He and Prue rented a unit in Fremantle. Steven became a craft-beer salesman. He persuaded pubs to sell pale ales to white-collar hipsters like him. He also took up marathons and triathlons. His feet blistered. His thighs chafed. His nipples bled. His toenails fell off. But Steven felt free.

++

John got what he had always wanted: an undivided alliance with my father. They purchased the lease of a working-class pub on the southwestern outskirts of Toowoomba: the Drayton Tavern. John had another daughter, named Caley.

"Caley *Blaine*," said my mother with a triumphant smile.

It was her fourth grandchild, and far from the last. She babysat John's twins to give Merkilla a rest. This part of Mum's life was a pleasant revelation. Three times a week, she volunteered at Lifeline, an op-shop in an industrial estate. The twin toddlers paid her visits. They were blonde, olive-skinned and identical.

"You little beauties," Mum called them.

Despite her eyesight going, my mother could instantly tell them apart. She was a student of childhood moods. Amelia was bossy. Sophie was a worrier. But they both thought that their grandma had the coolest job in the world.

"Grandma, can we get something?" asked Amelia.

"If you say the magic word," said Mum.

"Please, Grandma," said Sophie.

"Come with me," said Mum.

My mother led them by the hand around the toy and clothing sections of the musty op-shop. She was the pied piper of Lifeline.

"Thanks, Grandma!" they chimed.

"No worries, lovelies," said Mum.

The twins regarded her only as their grandma, not a foster grandma. She didn't need to worry about social workers, or custody battles, or vindictive Christian fanatics. The Shelleys had taken a lot, but not this.

CHAPTER TEN

Tasmanian Devils

In 2004, Michael and Mary Shelley went to the only state in Australia where they hadn't yet raised hell: Tasmania. They stayed at a hostel on the Derwent River in Hobart. St George's Anglican Church was built in 1836. It had a tall porch and sandstone pillars. The belltower had once served as a lighthouse.

On a Sunday morning, Michael and Mary sat down on the cedar pews. They were surrounded by white-collar Christians in expensive shoes and scarves. Michael took the floor. He harangued the congregation for ten minutes.

"You Tasmanian devils drive here in BMWs seeking fake salvation," he shouted. "But you ignore the crisis of homelessness right under your noses!"

The police arrived. Michael and Mary were arrested for disturbing a religious service. They faced the magistrate separately. Mary was bailed and placed under a mental health order. She was transferred to the psychiatric ward at the Royal Hobart Hospital. Michael was bailed only after Mary had been committed and tranquillised. He went straight to the hospital.

"There is no medical basis for this gross breach of human rights!" he cried. "Mary is even more distressed than before. What a miracle cure!"

Mary was released from the psychiatric ward. She reunited with Michael. They decided to bypass the greedy churches and go directly to those who needed them most: homeless people on the streets of Hobart.

Heather was a 54-year-old woman who chose to live in a park. She ate from rubbish bins and pissed into plastic bags. For three weeks, Michael and Mary came to Heather bearing food, cups of tea and ponchos. Yet when it rained, she merely hunched over and let the downpour drown her.

"Heather, you are a very mentally ill woman," said Michael.

The Shelleys staged an intervention. On a rainy Tasmanian morning, Michael borrowed plastic gloves from a local bakery. While Heather slept through the downpour, the Shelleys went through her belongings and put what they perceived as rubbish in the bin.

Heather reported the theft to the police. She decided not to press charges against her self-appointed guardian angels.

++

From Hobart, Michael and Mary hitchhiked north along the Derwent River, through a steep forested valley, deep into the heart of the Tasmanian wilderness. They arrived at Ellendale, a rural hamlet, population two hundred.

The main attraction was a 198-acre property called Kingsholme. Once Kingsholme had been a hop farm, supplying the first stage in the creation of beer. Now Kingsholme was a Christian retreat. The property was dotted with white crosses. At the centre of the compound sat a three-storey timber kiln with rusted turrets. It was called "The Centre for Healing".

Michael and Mary were offered cheap accommodation in the kiln. It was orbited by five cottages. The Shelleys went walking through nearby orchards and vineyards. Michael flyfished wild trout from the Tyenna River.

A couple named Alison and Simon were also staying at Kingsholme. They had a six-month-old named Sarah. Alison and Simon left Sarah in her room with a baby monitor while attending to spiritual pursuits not far from their cottage.

Mary Shelley became fixated with the baby girl. According to her, she heard Sarah crying. In broad daylight, Mary entered the cottage. She changed Sarah's saturated nappy and comforted the baby.

Sarah's father, Simon, saw Mary pacing away from the cottage with his daughter. He snatched Sarah back. Sarah's mother, Alison, was hysterically upset. The couple called the police to report an attempted kidnapping.

Before the police arrived, Michael and Mary hailed a car on the highway. They hitchhiked to Ouse, fifteen kilometres away. Michael called Children's Services to make a complaint about Sarah's parents.

The next day, Mary was arrested at an internet café while checking her emails. She was driven at high speed to the police station in Hobart and charged with child abduction. Bail was refused. Michael accused the available lawyers of colluding with the prosecution. He represented Mary in court.

"My wife has been taken hostage and held for ransom by Tasmanian terrorists!" said Michael. "An inbred, subhuman species!"

His defence went down badly with the Tasmanian judge.

"It is dangerous to be so zealously faithful to God in this day and age," said the grey, ageing magistrate, denying Michael's request for bail.

☨

Mary Shelley was taken to Risdon Women's Prison, north of Hobart. Corrugated iron walls on the ground level and naked Besser blocks on top. The warden ordered Mary to change into tracksuit pants and a t-shirt.

"Tracksuits are against my religious beliefs!" she said.

Two guards handcuffed Mary and dragged her into a van. She was taken to the Risdon Prison Hospital and held in a locked cell for twenty-three hours a day. It had a concrete plinth bed. No table or chairs.

The prison hospital was unisex. Mary shared a bathroom with men. The shower had two security cameras. On her way back from the bathroom, Mary recognised the pale, blond man in the cell opposite hers. It was Martin Bryant. In 1996, he executed thirty-five people with a semi-automatic rifle.

Mary was appalled by the guards mocking Martin Bryant. They had concocted a legal form of torture for Australia's worst mass murderer: a week of religious sermons from perhaps the only person in the country who believed he deserved redemption.

"Open your heart to God, Martin!" cried Mary.

"Please leave me alone," moaned Martin.

Mary was sent back to the women's prison. In the yard beside her room, she lectured four female inmates about the need to give up smoking. The warden warned Mary to keep quiet. He cut her recreational time in half. Mary objected. The warden responded by putting Mary into the cell next to the staff quarters. He sent the other female inmates back to their rooms.

In the early evening, Mary berated the other women from her cell. This caused an outpouring of anger from the prisoners. They bayed for Mary's blood as the guards dragged her away to solitary confinement.

Michael Shelley had stopped his wife from taking mood stabilisers. He incited her to violence, then failed to get her adequate legal representation. But he took zero responsibility. Michael brought Mary a radio, floral paper, special stamps, a pink singlet, witch-hazel cream and vitamin C tablets.

"You all suffer from delusions of grandeur!" he told the guards.

The Big Book

After his release from jail, Mick Bishop hitchhiked from Brisbane to Kings Cross in Sydney. He found a place to sleep near the El Alamein Fountain. Mick showered and ate at the Wayside Chapel. He waited for the fortnightly dole payment to hit his bank account and lived like a king for twenty-four hours. Then he busked for more drug money on Darlinghurst Road.

Sydney spat Mick out, like phlegm on the footpath. He hitchhiked from Kings Cross to St Kilda. Mick wore a beanie, a hoodie and loose jeans. On weekends, he busked underneath the deranged gaze of the Luna Park gates. On weekdays, he busked on a ramp below Flinders Street Station.

Mick unloaded to a fellow traveller at a soup kitchen. They implored him to go see a doctor who was a saviour to Melbourne's junkie underclass. There was no trace of judgement or disgust on the doctor's face. He organised for Mick to enter a rehab program in Caulfield named Oxford House.

"I knew I'd end up getting into Oxford," said Mick.

Mick lived with six male drug addicts. A support worker taught them basic life admin. Rehab had the soothing institutionalism of prison without the physical punishment and sexual assault. Mick had clean feet, a warm bed and a full stomach.

Oxford had two strict rules: total abstinence, and daily attendance at a Narcotics Anonymous meeting. The Wednesday lunchtime meeting was at St Kevin's in Hawthorn. Mick walked to a hall beside a red gravel tennis court. He smelled tennis balls, urine cakes in the toilets and sweat on the skin of his neck.

Mick sat in the back row. There were doctors and lawyers among the criminals and prostitutes. A judge who'd been straight for twenty years sat beside a homeless junkie quivering from withdrawals. Mick listened to matching tales of pain, heartbreak, craving, failure and self-hatred.

"We have a spiritual disease," said the chair.

NA members joked about the twelve-step program being a cult. But the cult was bottom-up, not top-down. The most divine members of a meeting were the vulnerable newcomers, not the pious veterans. Mick had never been so awake to the possibility of redemption. He walked to the front of the hall.

"My name is Mick Bishop," he said, trembling.

"Hey, Mick," said the group.

"I'm addicted to everything under the sun," said Mick. "It made me feel love for myself. Until I hated myself even more than before. I've lost everything."

A veteran in sneakers and jeans glanced at Mick with recognition. His nickname was Truck Driver Shane. He had been clean for twenty years.

"Thanks for sharing, Mick," said Shane. "One day at a time, brother."

After the meeting, Mick asked Truck Driver Shane to be his NA sponsor. He anticipated rejection, but Shane happily agreed to do it. He gave Mick his phone number, a timetable of NA meetings and a list of the twelve steps for homework.

1. We admitted that we were powerless over our addiction, that our lives had become unmanageable.
2. We came to believe that a Power greater than ourselves could restore us to sanity.
3. We decided to turn our will and our lives over to the care of God as we understood Him.
4. We made a searching and fearless inventory of ourselves.
5. We admitted to God, to ourselves, and to another human being the exact nature of our wrongs.
6. We were entirely ready to have God remove all these defects of character.

7. We humbly asked Him to remove our shortcomings.
8. We made a list of all the persons we had harmed and became willing to make amends to them all.
9. We made direct amends to such people wherever possible, except when to do so would injure them or others.
10. We continued to take personal inventory and when we were wrong promptly admitted it.
11. We sought through prayer and meditation to improve our conscious contact with God as we understood him, praying only for knowledge of His will for us and the power to carry that out.
12. Having had a spiritual awakening as a result of these steps, we tried to carry this message to addicts, and to practise these principles in our affairs.

Shane was a stickler for The Big Book, the bible of Alcoholics Anonymous. Mick read it in a weekend. He attended 180 NA meetings in 180 days. It was the longest that he had been clean since high school.

※

Mick was released from Oxford House. He got a job as a carer in a nursing home. At lunchtime, he serenaded the clapping and cheering geriatrics with an acoustic guitar. On the weekends, he played Aussie Rules for the Salvo Hawks at Peanut Farm Reserve. Mick had a job, a flat, a hobby and mates. He fell in love with a belly-dancer named Kylie. They moved into a flat together in Caulfield.

"We can only keep what we have by giving it away," he recited at NA.

Cameron was a 32-year-old houso with grey hair. He met the mother of his newborn son in a homeless shelter. A short romance followed.

"I'm a heroin addict," Cameron told the NA meeting at St Kevin's. "My dad was a bad alcoholic. All I wanted was to break that cycle. Now I'm the same."

Mick sat with his legs crossed in the front row, eyes shut and hand on his chest. Cameron thought the handsome young man might be having a heart attack. When he finished speaking, Mick stood up and hugged him.

"Wow, that was a power share, man," said Mick. "I really, really related to what you just said. The pain. Your dad. Your son. I'm Mick. You're safe here."

After the meeting, Mick provided Cameron with a timetable for NA meetings, some basic literature, and his mobile number. Cameron asked Mick to be his first sponsor. He said yes. They went over the twelve steps at Mick's flat in Caulfield. Mick lit some sticks of incense. He listened to Cameron's confessions. Then he placed a hand over the newcomer's heart.

"Do you want to know our problem?" asked Mick. "Our fathers weren't emotionally available. So now we don't know how to love our own sons."

Cameron had never felt so seen by another human being.

"Yes, Mick!" he cried. "You've hit the nail on the head!"

"Bro, we can't be a slave to the past," said Mick. "You need to break the cycle."

Cameron wrote the sermon down in a notebook. He began regularly visiting his baby boy. He kissed him. He said: "I love you." A weight lifted.

Mick – the parenthood guru – remained estranged from his own son and father. But at least he had stopped focusing so much on his own thoughts. More than bliss or obliteration, Mick wanted to be a shepherd for other lost souls.

Dean had a flash house, a BMW and a $3000 a week heroin habit. He deliberately tried to overdose but woke up forty-eight hours later. Dean went to a Narcotics Anonymous meeting in Hawthorn. The newcomer was in denial that he was just like the other addicts. In denial that one more hit might kill him. After half an hour, he made a beeline for the exit. Mick Bishop followed him outside.

"Hey, bro," said Mick. "What's going on?"

"This is fucked up," said Dean.

Mick gazed into Dean's ironic eyes with infinite sincerity.

"Bro, it's supposed to be fucked up," said Mick. "It's pretty good, though. You don't think it's working. And then, wham: you're finally clean."

Mick helped to convert Dean, who kept coming back. The fellowship anointed him with a nickname: Metha-Dean. Dean converted others. NA was like a Tupperware club for the strung-out and vulnerable.

Great White Saviour

Michael and Mary Shelley were done with the land down under. They purchased one-way tickets to South Africa. In Cape Town, the Shelleys visited Khayelitsha, one of the largest slums in the world. They preached to black South Africans from Cape Town to Durban, to Soweto on the outskirts of Johannesburg.

At the Johannesburg airport, Michael spotted a rival gang of Christian missionaries. They were Americans with hopeful slogans on their mass-produced t-shirts.

"God is not impressed, you spiritual invaders!" roared Michael. "Why don't you go home and look after your own children? You aren't here to help. No, you are here to impose on the locals what *you* want, not what they need!"

For three months, Michael researched a meticulous manifesto on fixing the poverty epidemic. His vision: to provide shelter for fifteen million people in ten years. The unemployed would be supervised by qualified tradespeople to assemble "simple" dwellings on government land.

"After one year, the house would be inspected to ensure that it was clean and landscaped," wrote Michael. "Then ownership would be legally transferred under strict conditions that the house could not be sold for a period of ten years."

To Michael's dismay, the African National Conference ignored his ingenious pipedream. He launched a public crusade against the ANC, accusing them of being even more corrupt than the apartheid regime they had toppled.

In Durban, Mary was mugged and beaten up. She came across a dead body on the street, triggering a nervous breakdown. She sought asylum at the British consulate and was taken to a South African psychiatric hospital.

Michael stayed at a hostel in Hermanus. From the balcony, he fed fruit to rock rabbits and watched whales do backflips in the Atlantic Ocean. White saviours were endangered. If only he were black, thought Michael, those dumb South Africans would see him as the second coming of Nelson Mandela.

Michael found a new nemesis: Desmond Tutu. In 1984, the Anglican Bishop and anti-apartheid warrior succeeded Lech Walesa as the Nobel Peace Prize winner. He became the first black Archbishop of Cape Town.

Now Tutu was a gay rights activist. Michael paid the sodomy apologist a visit at Cape Town's Anglican cathedral. He spotted Tutu climbing into a luxury car. Michael was horrified by his "eunuch-like" voice.

"Heathen!" cried Michael. "You are a grossly obese glutton! Look at your despicable double chin, while the slums starve!"

Michael handed Desmond Tutu a handwritten admonition. It blamed Tutu's normalisation of gay relationships for the AIDS epidemic. To Michael, it was a spiritual warning. To anyone else, it read a bit like a death threat.

☩

Michael Shelley was arrested and sent to Pollsmoor, a maximum-security prison famous for once housing Nelson Mandela. It was rife with AIDS and hepatitis. In their anuses, new inmates smuggled glad-wrapped drugs past the carefree security screenings. The jail was informally operated by gangs: the 26s, who profited from gambling; the 27s, who acted as muscle; and the 28s, who procured and distributed sexual partners for themselves and their allies.

Michael was placed in a packed dormitory run by a rival pastor, a Zulu Rastafarian. He chanted Satanic sermons twice a day while flashing yellow, orange and red cards at cynics such as Michael. Guards laughed at the sick and screaming inmates. A man who died of tuberculosis was left until the morning.

Michael learned rudimentary Zulu, Portuguese and Spanish. He received half an hour of sunlight per day in the central jail yard. The white, blue-eyed messiah performed church services for hundreds of black prisoners.

"Jesus Christ wasn't white!" cried Michael.

"Jesus was black?" asked a South African.

"Not quite," said Michael. "He was a dark-skinned Arab! That is a fact!"

Just as he was fostering a flock of followers, Michael was transferred to Westville, a high-security prison near Durban with 40,000 inmates. Many of them slept on the floor, a sheet between their bodies and the concrete. Michael traded spare clothes for a single bed. Lice dined out on his scalp and bed bugs on his skin.

The guards stole food rations and sold them back to the starving prisoners. They were forced to eat while standing up. No hot showers.

No toilet paper. No free bibles. Michael tried and failed to obtain an acoustic guitar to entertain the inmates. He encouraged the Zulu men to sing and dance and grin.

"Show no shame in being poor!" he cried. "It is easier for a camel to fit through the eye of a needle than for a rich man to enter the Kingdom of God!"

At 2 am, Michael was crammed into an eight-seater van with ten others. Guards provided a 600-ml bottle of Coke and a packet of Eet-Sum-Mor biscuits to share between eleven. There were no toilet stops. Michael emptied his bladder into a plastic bottle. They were heading to Lindela Repatriation Centre, a refugee camp near Johannesburg, six hours northwest.

The guards at the camp were armed with guns and dogs. Michael was placed in Section B with a thousand refugees from countries such as Sierra Leone, Senegal, Ethiopia, Somalia and the Ivory Coast. Seven hundred inmates were in the yard at one time. Michael did an interview with SABC News about the living conditions and the failed immigration policies of the ANC.

"A hard border – like Australia – is expensive and inhumane," said Michael. "The only solution is free movement for those from Swaziland and Lesotho, and six-month visas for those from Zimbabwe, Mozambique and Malawi. The current system is a recipe for corruption and human suffering!"

Michael preferred the refugee camp to Australia. But the South African government was determined to send him home, as it had already done with Mary. Michael received a deportation notice. In the yard of Lindela, Michael tearfully bid farewell to hundreds of refugees.

"I'm in love with Africa! God willing, I shall come back one day!"

Six months after arriving in South Africa, Michael was picked up from Lindela by two private sky marshals. They escorted him on a flight to Sydney.

Spiritual Mick

Mick's girlfriend, Kylie, left him for a woman. After over a year of sobriety, Mick surrendered to his addiction. Speaking at an NA meeting after a relapse was far worse than the first appearance. He went with Cameron – his best friend in NA – to play basketball at Albert Park. The sweat from shooting hoops lifted the veil of shame.

Afterwards, the shame came down again. Mick and Cameron caught a train to an NA meeting. Cameron had been clean for nearly six months. There was no compassion on Mick's face. His eyes flashed green with envy.

"How do you do it, Cam?" asked Mick.

"How do I do what, Mick?" asked Cameron.

"How do you smile? How do you laugh? How do you love?"

Cameron had reunited with his baby son, and then with his estranged father. He had forgiven his dad for abandoning him as a teenager. His dad had become a doting grandfather. The family reunion was all thanks to Mick.

"You showed me all this shit, bro!" said Cameron.

"It isn't working for me anymore," said Mick. "I'm fucked."

"One day at a time," said Cameron. "Go to meetings. Do the work. Follow the steps. Do the next right thing. I love you, dude. But you need to love yourself."

Mick realised that he'd been pulling the wool over everyone's eyes. He could present as a charismatic, happy young man. But he had skipped through the twelve steps too quickly, greedy for acceptance and admiration.

Mick needed to do the work. To pinpoint his deepest pains. To make amends with the people he'd hurt. He swapped Truck Driver Shane for a NA veteran nicknamed Hippy Rick. Once upon a time, Hippy Rick had been a wealthy alpha male.

Now, Hippy Rick had long dreadlocks. They were strewn with flowers and bird feathers. The soles of his bare feet were black. Mick sat in the courtyard of Rick's council flat. They drank homemade chai around a bonfire.

"You need to deflate your ego," said Hippy Rick. "Like sticking a pin into a balloon. Pop. You can't give a fuck about what other people think."

The foster boy couldn't help but try to flatter his new father figure with imitation. Mick metamorphosised into a younger version of Hippy Rick. He ditched the basketball sneakers for bare feet and the jeans for fisherman pants. Mick's face was covered with a six o'clock shadow. His hair grew long and knotty. He studied Buddhism and Hinduism and undertook a lomilomi massage course.

At NA meetings, Mick sat in the lotus position at the front, eyes shut and hands on his guts. The other members nicknamed him "Spiritual Mick".

++

Spiritual Mick got back onto the straight and narrow. Next minute, the aged care worker was pinballing between ATM machines and drug dealers. This relapse was worse than the first. He wanted to kill himself.

The Alfred Hospital in Prahran was a big, grey building across the river from the Melbourne Cricket Ground. Mick was admitted to the psych ward. He was diagnosed with borderline personality disorder. Finally, a name for the condition afflicting him since adolescence. He read over the familiar symptoms.

1. Frantic efforts to avoid real or imagined abandonment.
2. A pattern of unstable interpersonal relationships characterised by alternating between extremes of idealisation and devaluation.
3. Identity disturbance: persistently unstable sense of self.

4. Impulsivity in at least two areas that are potentially damaging (e.g. spending, sex, substance abuse, reckless driving).
5. Recurrent suicidal behaviour, gestures, threats, or self-mutilation.
6. Affective instability due to marked reactivity of mood (e.g. intense episodic dysphoria, irritability or anxiety).
7. Chronic feelings of emptiness.
8. Inappropriate, intense anger or difficulty controlling anger (e.g. frequent displays of temper, recurrent physical fights).
9. Transient, stress-related paranoia or severe disassociation.

Nine from nine. There was a certain sense of accomplishment. Mick was prescribed a daily dose of mirtazapine, 30 milligrams, an antidepressant. He walked free from hospital five days later. Three days after that, he came back after swallowing twenty-eight mirtazapines in one go.

Mick was released again after a five-night stint. The psych ward provided a phone number for a crisis team, a referral to a psychologist and a fresh prescription of mirtazapine. Mick lost his job as an aged care worker. He went on the disability support pension and became homeless again.

"I. Don't. Know. Why. I. Want. To. Die," he told an NA meeting, crying.

A few people sighed. They had grown desensitised to the prolific self-pity of Spiritual Mick. He had the weight of the world on his face. Pain oozed from his pores and changed the mood of the room. Ironically, the less charming he became, the more some of them thought that he was full of shit.

"Want to know your problem, Spiritual Mick?" asked Drummer Dan. Later his nickname was changed to "Drug Dealer Dan", when NA members realised he was slinging heroin to lapsed addicts. "You've got no idea who you are."

Mick decided he needed to go deeper. He confided to Hippy Rick an edited rendition of his sordid life story and the name on his birth certificate.

"Elijah Shelley," said Rick. "It's a beautiful name. I think that you need to make peace with your parents. And be true to who you really are."

"They kidnapped me when I was three," said Mick. "They're crazy."

"So are we," said Rick.

Mick left Hippy Rick's place feeling light-headed. He was twenty-six years old, yet he still didn't really have a clear idea *why* he was placed into foster care before the kidnapping, apart from a fable about a hungry toddler. He made a Freedom of Information request to the Queensland government.

Michael Bishop was a figment of a bureaucrat's imagination. He hated the alias. No more shame. Mick changed his name by deed poll to Elijah Michael Shelley. He made peace with his identity and revealed it to the universe.

"My real name is Elijah Shelley," he announced to an NA meeting. "My mother's name is Mary. My father's name is Michael."

Pilgrimage

Michael and Mary Shelley hitchhiked from Sydney to Darwin. The air was thick with humidity. A pastor paid for their passage by boat to West Timor, en route to Bali, the Indonesian island popular with Australian tourists. For three weeks, the Shelleys praised the long, flowing hair and dresses of the Balinese women and berated the drunken Australian men on the island.

"I was greatly outraged by the behaviour of my fellow Australians," wrote Michael. "They strut around with full wallets, fat bellies, and empty hearts."

Mary flew to London. The British citizen drifted through Wales, England and Scotland. Michael flew to Jakarta. He boarded a ship with a thousand Muslims. They sailed through coral reefs towards volcanic ranges. Michael got along famously with the Muslims. But he was sceptical about the Quran.

"Truthfully, Muhammad spent far too much time with an overbearing mother," wrote Michael. "Muhammad's vision of Gabriel was a total delusion, fabricated based upon major unresolved emotional issues."

Michael arrived at Bataan, a peninsula in the Philippines. It was littered with shipwrecks. He sailed from Bataan to Singapore and stayed there two weeks. He rode north on an ancient bus into southern Thailand. Then he caught a cheap sleeper train along the limestone coast to the sin of Bangkok.

In Indonesia, Mary had accidentally burnt her husband's passport with a candle. A new passport was issued by the Australian consulate in Bangkok. Michael flew from Thailand to the moral sinkhole of Western civilisation: Rome. He was evicted from the Vatican for heckling the Catholics and pestering the Swiss guards for a meeting with the Pope.

Mary travelled to Rome via Chamonix-Mont-Blanc, a ski commune in southeastern France. She was admitted to a psych ward overlooking the snow-covered Alps. The psychiatrists didn't try to fry her scalp with electroshock therapy. Dinner was prepared by a chef and served with red wine.

Michael arrived. Mary was discharged. The Shelleys travelled by bus to Les Combes di Introd. It was a mountain village in the Italian Alps. Pope Benedict spent his summer there in a stone and wood holiday home. He provided Sunday mass at a small church in the Aosta Valley.

Michael and Mary were allowed into the Pope's Sunday sermon. The altar displayed Saint Paul walking to Damascus. Michael wasn't overawed by the presence of religious royalty. He gave Joseph Aloisius Ratzinger both barrels at full blast.

"Your numbers man, George Pell, is a wicked enabler and perpetrator of child abuse," said Michael. "Game over, Joseph! I know! And God knows!"

"Hallelujah!" cried Mary.

The Pope showed no emotion or remorse. The Shelleys were expelled from the church. Michael and Mary strode heroically past the vineyards underneath the low, lacklustre sun, 1600 metres above sea level. Through the fir trees, they could see the 4800-metre peak of Mont Blanc.

The Shelleys caught a train to Venice. They stayed at a B&B built within a thousand-year-old Tuscan wall. Michael celebrated his sixtieth birthday wandering along a maze of canals. At night, Venice swarmed with visitors. The Shelleys smiled at them. Life was rife with woe. But life was rife with beauty, too. Occasionally, you needed to slow down and pay attention to the finer details, or the betrayal would swallow you whole.

Via the Greek island of Corfu, the Shelleys caught a ship to Igoumenitsa. Onwards to Crete. Then they flew to Vienna, the capital of Mary's ancestral homeland. Germany and Switzerland followed. They were evicted from the UN's Palais des Nations in Geneva and the Australian consulate in Brussels.

In France, Michael and Mary found their spiritual home. Michael's A in French at Knox Grammar finally came in handy. Unlike Tom Blaine, he loved the French language, the French architecture, the French appreciation of beauty. For six months, the Shelleys re-enacted the Gospel of Matthew.

"We travelled freely through France, never knowing where we would be at night, in faith without money," wrote Michael. "GOD never let us down!"

The Crucifixion

In the spirit of kinship and forgiveness, Elijah extended a digital olive branch to his father Michael Shelley via email from an internet café in St Kilda.

From: Elijah Shelley <silentmonk123@yahoo.com.au>

hey dad

Hope your well. I wanted to let you know that I legally changed my name back to Elijah Shelley. I know we don't exactly have the best of relationships and we don't really talk much. But I want you to know you will always be my real dad. Thank you for the first three years of my life. They were probably the best i had growing up. I think you're a very intelligent man and I love you.

Elijah

....

From: Michael Shelley <michael_the_one@yahoo.com>
Bayonne, France on the Atlantic coast near the Spanish border

About time, Elijah!!! Did you receive all the e-mails that I sent you about our life and work over the past 12 months or so? If so, response????!!!! The longer that you are silent, the harder it will be. The people that you IMMEDIATELY need to speak the truth to are:

- your brothers Saul & Joshua
- your sister Hannah
- Thomas & Lenore Blaine
- anybody & everybody in the Department of Families in Qld,

- especially that child abusing DEVIATE Susan King
- your various foster parents

Let me know how you go with this list.

Faithfully,
Your father in CHRIST
Michael Shelley +

....

From: Elijah Shelley <silentmonk123@yahoo.com.au>

hey dad

as for my childhood stuff I am in the process of recieving my file from the dept. should fill in a lot of gaps. I still find it hard to talk about all that stuff and I still feel quite angry about it all. But I am willing to move through it now.

    I was hoping we could communicate in a more peaceful way. I'd really like to get to know your likes and dislikes. Your fears and passions.

Elijah

....

From: Michael Shelley <michael_the_one@yahoo.com>
Tarbes, near Lourdes, France

Elijah,

I have sent you several letters over the past 5 months. Have the decency to thank me for them and acknowledge receipt. Simple human courtesy and respect! What about a postal address to write to and a mobile to text?

You asked me about what I like – GOD says give to those that ask of you. I like UNITY and co-operation. I like playing guitar and singing WITH people, especially my family. I like BBQs, talking, laughing and eating together with my family, thanking GOD for all that HE has blessed us with, especially one another.

I like sailing, away from land. I like PEACE, around GOD's works. I like standing under huge specimens of trees and in forests of large trees: TRUE Cathedrals! I like making things with my hands out of timber, stone, brick, leather, metal, caring for useful animals, growing vegetables, fruit, cereals, trees. I love spending time with children and putting babies to sleep in my arms.

Why have you really contacted us, Elijah? Guilt, loneliness, nothing better to do, the usual foster parent reared child picking up and then dumping people because they haven't the decency and courage to REALLY grow up, face their real feelings and get their priorities straight.

If you LOVED us as we LOVE you, you could not fail to be expressing your fully justified OUTRAGE at what has been done to you, to your own parents and to your own brothers and sisters.

Faithfully,
Michael +

....

From: Elijah Shelley <silentmonk123@yahoo.com.au>

hey dad

excluding the negativity it was good to hear from you. I really liked hearing about your likes. I like a lot of those things too.

Why did I contact you? Because you are my father and although i do not like a lot of the things you say and do, I am willing to learn to love you and if I were you i would thank God for that blessing and cease to be abusive in your e-mails.

And also forget any ideas about trying to control this because you can't. You will not be getting any other contact details for me until you learn to respect my boundaries and that's final Dad. I have tried other forms of communication in the past and this is pretty much my final attempt. So treasure it and don't abuse it or me.

Why did i contact you? Because I made a conscious decision in my heart to open the lines of communication for the benefit of my mother.

I am well, thanks for asking. Sorry that was sarcastic but have you ever noticed that all you do is talk about yourself?

Alright that is probably enough from me. I felt angry and got a little carried away. Anyway. Genuinely hope you are safe and hope too that you are well looked after.

God bless
Elijah

....

From: Michael Shelley <michael_the_one@yahoo.com>

Firstly let me be quite clear – I do NOT tell you what to do, I tell you what I know that you NEED. And my credentials for knowing this FOR YOU are impeccable. GOD has given me a gift and blessed me with more real wisdom than any man alive today – who will listen?

I have been blessed with incredible, gifted, talented children, all of whom have an importance and worth to GOD which is unique in the history of the planet, something that you are running away from.

I thought about what you wrote in the middle of the night last night. Your attitude is impertinent, stupid and nothing to do with me! Go and tell your useless, violent foster parents how you feel about THEM otherwise we have NO POSSIBILITY of a proper relationship.

I also don't appreciate and nor does Mary sending 2 very different e-mails to us. You won't play games with us, Elijah, nor divide us!

Yours is the kind of communication that I sent you for over 20 years with no reply. You are unbelievably ungrateful for all that we send. You are indulged, childish and cowardly because you don't want to face the truth about what has been done to Mary and to me.

The nice, little charming boy act will not work!!! Time to grow up and behave like a man for a change! But as you stupidly tried to put onto me: "Anyway I know YOU'RE not going to change anytime soon."

GOD's will shall prevail!!!

Faithfully,
Your father in CHRIST
Michael Shelley +

✢

Elijah received his Freedom of Information file. The bureaucratic parables that contained the clues to his existence were heavily redacted. That's how his life felt: blacked out. Elijah bought some heroin from a dealer in Chinatown. He aimed a disposable syringe at a thin blue vein. The prick, and the blood, and then the rush of love.

Elijah OD'd. He was saved by doctors at the Alfred Hospital. Then they sent him back to the psych ward that made his skin crawl.

Holier Than Thou

The French eventually betrayed the Shelleys. Mary was arrested in Lyon. She was sent to Le Vinatier psychiatric hospital. Michael went back to Paris. Notre Dame Cathedral rose from an island in the Seine. Inside, a sculpture showed the Archangel Michael having a face-off with Satan during the Last Judgement. Michael Shelley was arrested for interrupting a church service.

After being released, Michael went to the Australian consulate. The foyer was filled with Taittinger champagne for the party of a photographer who shot prepubescent children. The DFAT officer refused to give Michael money.

"You would rather waste taxpayers' money on child porn!" said Michael.

Michael bailed Mary out of the Le Vinatier hospital. They fled to London. The Shelleys were arrested for disturbing a church service at Westminster Cathedral. After release, they sought asylum at the Australian consulate. But the diplomats in London were just as unwelcoming as the ones in Paris. A DFAT officer accused the Shelleys of threatening her children.

"Any child brought up by you would be a willing recruit to a terrorist death squad," Michael told her. "You have risen above your level of competence."

The Shelleys demanded to speak to her superior, Richard Alston, the Australian High Commissioner. The DFAT officer refused. A security guard suggested that Michael was trying to scam airfares. Michael accused him of assaulting Mary. He counter-accused the Shelleys of threatening to kill him.

"I WARNED him that if he ever put his hands on my wife again that GOD would put his violence back onto him, perhaps by flying through the windscreen of a car," wrote Michael. "That would teach him a lesson. I said nothing about him dying, but I would not be disturbed if that was GOD's will."

The consulate called the police. Scotland Yard coppers arrived. The Shelleys were evicted. They sought shelter from the pouring rain at St Paul's Cathedral. There, Mary begged GOD to provide directions to the home address of the High Commissioner.

"After praying for a miracle, Mary came providentially upon the High Commissioner's residence, by complete surprise!" wrote Michael.

Richard Alston had been a minister in the Howard government. He had a regal face with blue eyes. His wife Margaret had expensive jewellery and dyed dark hair. In London, they found a drenched, vengeful Mary Shelley on their doorstep. She was arrested for stalking and abusing them.

"Mary abused no one," wrote Michael, "but she was horrified by the very ordinary quality of woman that was the wife of a High Commissioner."

The Shelleys fled to the west coast of Ireland. They sailed from Galway to Canada on a container ship. Then they caught a train from Quebec to New York City. They gate-crashed the United Nations headquarters, seeking to elevate their child custody case to the highest office on the planet.

The Shelleys caught an Amtrak train to Washington DC. Outside the White House, Michael sermonised about the Oedipus complex of George W. Bush. They caught a Greyhound bus to New Orleans, then Houston, and eventually Los Angeles. Michael tried and failed to track down Oprah Winfrey.

"Oprah Winfrey is the Queen of feckless females all over the world, distracting them with dangerous fantasies," he wrote. "She is a fat, ugly slob and pseudo-Christian hypocrite. Oprah has no hope whatsoever of going to Heaven!"

The Shelleys stayed in the USA for three months. They grew sick of the patriotism and poverty; sick of the false prophets on billboards and late-night TV shows; sick of the disgusting deep-fried food. Their daughter, Hannah, was about to turn eighteen. They bought one-way plane tickets home.

++

Pope Benedict arrived in Sydney Harbour on a yacht. Sin City had been flooded by 100,000 international pilgrims for World Youth Day. Michael and Mary heckled the Catholics and heckled the protestors who threw condoms at the Catholics. At St Mary's Cathedral, the Shelleys were arrested for trespassing.

After their release from lockup, the Shelleys had a fight. The global crusade for custody of Hannah had come to nothing. Mary blamed Michael for decades of unwavering pain; for using her womb and losing her children; for hijacking attempts to have contact with Hannah. This sparked the longest separation of their relationship. Michael hitchhiked to Victoria. He embarked on a road trip along the Great Ocean Road.

Mary flew to Alice Springs. She sent an email to Hannah.

Hi Hannah

I am in Alice Springs. It is a deeply spiritual place surrounded by mountains. The light changes all day. The colours are phenomenal. I first came here with my first husband, Lionel Long. I was nineteen. I never realised how courageous I was to put up with his violence.

The Aboriginals are the rightful owners of this land. They cared for it a long long time, always leaving it better than they found it. I feel like laughing and weeping at the exceptional beauty of

Aboriginal children. I love them and they love me. They are cast aside and lied to by foolish white men, who know nothing about life.

So tonight I'm sharing a room with a girl from England named Hannah. Her birthday is the 16th of April. How about that. She's nineteen. Her mother died of cancer. She is travelling all over the world, and so will you one day. I sailed to England on the *Fairstar* with Lionel when I was twenty. I fell pregnant at sea. I wasn't ready to be a wife or mother, Hannah. I hope that one day you will fall in love with a gentle man.

Hannah, life is so precious. Sometimes I miss you so much it is hard to keep going. I have a feeling that you will make a real difference to the lives of Aboriginal children. I implore you to live your life to the fullest every minute of every day. Never listen to the lies of white men.

YOUR BLESSED MOTHER
MARY

From Alice Springs, Mary travelled to north Queensland. She visited Barron Falls, where Michael had baptised her; and Kuranda, where Elijah was born. In Mareeba, she was arrested for failing to appear on trespassing charges. Mary was transferred to Townsville Women's Correctional Centre.

Michael flew from Melbourne to Townsville. He organised his wife some clothes for her court appearance. A colourful African dress, a burgundy singlet and pink fisherman's pants. But the careless guards lost the outfit.

Mary rocked up to court in the ugly prison smock. She faced five charges of public nuisance. The magistrate struck two of the charges. Mary received fines of $200, $200 and $150. She was slated for release from prison on 7 November 2008, the twenty-fifth anniversary of Elijah's kidnapping.

Journey of Love and Pain

Elijah was transferred from the psych ward to Edith Pardy House in Albert Park. It was a cream, colonial-style rehab centre with tall front doors and a tiled roof. There was a free interpretive dance group in Fitzroy. Elijah caught the tram with an acoustic guitar under his arm. He loosened his tense body to the music. Afterwards, he played songs for the dancers. They were originals.

"We're all trying to make a change," he sang. "Pushing past and through the pain. Time to live: I'm half-insane. Whatever it takes to make it through the day. When is that enough? Where is there enough love? Na-na-na-na-na."

The chords were Tom Petty-esque. The vocals fell to a faint, flat whisper and then ascended to a desperate falsetto, in the style of Jeff Buckley. The songs kept coming: "Distant Memory", "Broken Child", "Home with You", "The Pain of Love", "Edge of Madness", "Smoke and Mirrors".

The dancers believed that Elijah was good enough to get a recording contract. One of them had a home recording studio. During autumn, as the trees shed their leaves, Elijah caught a tram to Collingwood every few days. He recorded twelve songs. The album was called *Journey of Love and Pain*.

There was a final destination on Elijah's mind. He called Latoya in Rockhampton. He asked for permission to visit Jason, who was now eight.

"Course you can, Mick," said Latoya, not getting her hopes up.

"How is he doing?" asked Elijah.

"He's good," said Latoya. "Smart as anything. Must've come from you."

With the money from busking, Elijah purchased a plane ticket back to Queensland. He recorded one more song for the album: "Yesterday's Promise". "I'm coming home!" he sang. "I'm coming home!"

The staff at Edith Pardy House organised a flat in Elsternwick for

Elijah and a female friend from rehab. Their unit had a Gothic Revival style, with high ceilings and stained-glass windows. Elijah took the bedroom adjoining the kitchen. He put speakers on top of the brick fireplace and a double mattress in front.

On Elijah's twenty-eighth birthday, a few members of the dance group came around to the flat. They gave Elijah a bouquet of orange, blue, white and pink balloons. One of them lit the candles on a sponge cake from Coles.

"Happy birthday to you!" they sang. "Happy birthday to you!"

They threw balloons into the air of the small bedroom. Everyone tried to stop them from hitting the timber floor. Elijah sat cross-legged on his tattered mattress, a teddy bear in his lap, childlike with delight and laughter.

☩

Elijah sent his album to every record label he could find on the internet. None of them offered him a contract. The singer's untrained voice had potential. It was beautiful enough for FM radio. But his pain was just too suffocating.

The departure date for Elijah's homecoming to Queensland loomed. He tortured himself with two equally frightening possibilities: his son's excitement to be reunited, or total indifference to his recovering addict dad.

Elijah decided not to go. He hated himself for the betrayal.

Metha-Dean had replaced Hippy Rick as Elijah's NA sponsor. Elijah went around to Dean's townhouse in Brighton. Dean insisted that Elijah needed to accept professional help. Taking antidepressants wouldn't be a relapse.

"They don't work for me," said Elijah.

"Bro, there's nothing in The Big Book saying you can't take meds," said Dean.

Elijah and Dean finished the fourth step of the NA inventory. Dean dropped him home. Elijah swallowed a mouthful of pills with red wine. A friend named David drove him back to hospital. They sat in the waiting room.

"David, let me go," said Elijah. No faith. No hope. No joke.

Elijah was seen by the registrar. He described involuntary visions of jumping in front of a train. David left his name and mobile number at the front desk. He requested to be called immediately if Elijah left the psych ward.

Doctors prescribed Elijah 50 milligrams of chlorpromazine, an anti-psychotic, to be taken four times a day. Doctors set up dialectical behaviour therapy. Elijah was released from hospital. He bought six balloons of heroin for $200. In his bedroom, Elijah hit up. Nothing happened. It was Panadol.

A support worker took Elijah back to the psych ward.

"I'm a bad man," Elijah cried. "God doesn't love me."

The dose of chlorpromazine was upped to 100 milligrams. His mood lifted. Nurses observed him participating in a music therapy group. Elijah denied feeling suicidal. He was granted unescorted leave.

Doctors told him that he would be discharged if his condition continued to improve. The staff at Edith Pardy House had applied for a case worker through the mental health system. But Elijah wasn't considered mentally ill enough to qualify.

++

Friday 6 November 2008 was classic Melbourne: cool and overcast. Tomorrow was the twenty-fifth anniversary of Elijah's kidnapping. His looks had been ravaged by hot streaks of detox and relapse. But he was in a lighter mood than usual. Eyes less glazed. Stoic smile. At a group therapy session in Prahran, he spoke about hopes of getting a job.

At lunchtime, Elijah was granted two hours of unescorted leave.

No one called David. His note had been lost. Elijah caught Route 67 to Carnegie. At the start of the tramline, concrete cropped the sky into a pallid strip. Pretty soon, the buildings shrank. The sky became a million acres of grey.

Elijah got off at McDonald's. He trudged along the Nepean Highway, past the car dealerships, and turned left onto Elm Street. His flatmate was home. She was surprised to see him. He seemed perfectly normal and lively.

"I'm only here for a quick visit," he said.

Elijah went to his bedroom and shut the door. His flatmate could hear music. Elijah sat on the floor in the corner. His LG flip phone vibrated. It was the hospital trying to call. He opened a notepad and started writing.

From his wallet, Elijah withdrew a tinfoil packet. He lit the smack on a spoon and sucked it up with a clean needle. He hit a vein. He pressed the plunger with his thumb. In the blood, the heroin transformed into total morphine. Just enough numbed the pain of feeling unloved. Too much deactivated the part of the brain responsible for sending oxygen. Elijah's dying thoughts glided through the room.

His life became a distant memory. Then it went missing.

The Afterlife

A senior constable photographed Elijah Shelley's body for the coroner. There was a white residue on the dessert spoon beside him. A black wallet. A silver LG flip phone. A clean needle and a used one. Along with two suicide notes.

To all my friends,

You know who you are. Thanks for your unconditional love + support, you gave me so much! Just know that I did this to end my suffering, not for any other reason. I would love to tell you why I suffer so much, but the truth is that I don't know.

I guess in all honesty I am leaving because I do not want to go on. Simple. Lost touch with myself, you guys and God and see no way back. Maybe it's a big mistake. Hope to let you know from the other side.

♡ Elijah

The second suicide note was addressed to his son, Jason.

A quick note before I go.

If it's possible I would like all my stuff sold and the money to go to my son Jason. Let him know I love him and that I will always be watching over him. That's about all. I could write pages and pages but the meaning wouldn't get across. Some make it in life, some give up. I gave up.

Much love,
Elijah

Eliah was taken to the morgue. Dean – Elijah's final NA sponsor – received a late-night phone call from the Caulfield police station.
"This is about Elijah Shelley," said the cop.
"He killed himself, didn't he?" asked Dean.

⁜

Michael and Mary Shelley flew from Townsville to Melbourne. Dean picked them up from Tullamarine Airport. Elijah's NA sponsor had agreed to chauffeur them around until the funeral. He braced himself for outpourings of parental grief. In the arrivals lounge, the Shelleys were beaming.

"Elijah will rise on the third day!" cried Mary.

Dean packed their luggage into the boot. On the highway, he nodded diplomatically at their predictions of the apocalypse. Dean dropped the Shelleys to the funeral parlour and gave them $200 for food and shelter.

The Shelleys spoke in tongues to their dead son. Michael trimmed his beard and embalmed his stiff body with olive oil. Mary identified the slits on his left wrist as a stigmata: the same wounds as Jesus Christ on the cross.

"And at the ninth hour, Jesus cried out: 'Eli, Eli, lema sabachthani?'" said Michael. "And some of the bystanders said: 'This man is calling Elijah'."

Michael borrowed a phone at the funeral home. He called Latoya and demanded she and Jason fly south for the funeral.

"I'll think about it," said Latoya, in a state of shock.

Latoya asked if he had any photos of Elijah. Michael sent her photos of Elijah in the coffin. She immediately deleted them from her phone. Latoya's family suggested that it might be an unwise choice to reunite her son with the Christian fanatics. She informed Michael of her decision not to come. As payback, Michael never provided the suicide note addressed to Jason.

"I was hurt but not surprised that Elijah didn't really mention Mary or myself in his suicide note," wrote Michael. "He felt very guilty. This was reflected in the sycophantic suicide note thanking everyone who had failed to help him."

✢

Elijah's funeral was held at the Christ Church in St Kilda. The vicar knew Elijah from Narcotics Anonymous meetings. Hundreds of mourners showed up. They were predominantly NA members, along with some spiritual types that Elijah had met at ashrams and bush doofs.

Cameron and Metha-Dean sat on the left of the front row with Truck Driver Shane. Michael and Mary sat in the front row on the right. The Shelleys erected their son vertically in an open casket at the front.

Michael had spent the week haranguing the vicar for brainwashing his son with mainstream religion. The vicar prevented him from speaking at the funeral. Michael reluctantly agreed to let Cameron do the eulogy instead.

"I guarantee that if you've been to an NA meeting in Melbourne, Elijah was the first person to shake your hand," said Cameron. "He saved me. He made you feel special. But he didn't let that light shine on himself."

Cameron, Dean and four other NA members carried Elijah's casket to the hearse. The wake was in the same room as the weekly NA meeting. The vicar provided cake and sandwiches. Recovering drug addicts mingled with the hippies. Michael and Mary stewed in the corner of the room. Suddenly, Michael pointed an accusatory finger into Cameron's dumbstruck face.

"Judas!" roared Michael.

"Me?" whispered Cameron.

"Yes, you!" said Michael. "Your dreadful eulogy was more about your own ego than expressing genuine love for Elijah. In fact, you were jealous of our son while he was alive. And now you are just trying to occupy his space after he died!"

Unlike Michael Shelley, Cameron had spent the previous week blaming himself for Elijah's suicide. He catalogued and scrutinised every moment he didn't push harder to know his friend's pain.

A vicious argument broke out between Michael and the hippies. The gun-shy NA members removed themselves from the confrontation.

They streamed outside into a serene St Kilda afternoon. From a sunlit hill, Elijah's disciples watched Michael and Mary Shelley get kicked out by the vicar.

At last, they could see why no light shined on their dead friend.

CHAPTER ELEVEN

Ashes to Ashes

Mary spent the summer following Elijah's suicide in a psych ward. Michael warned that Judgement Day was coming. A heatwave descended. Melbourne hit 46.4°C. Bushfires ignited throughout central Victoria. 173 people died.

"As you all caused or allowed to happen to our beautiful son, so GOD has done to Victoria – reduced it to ashes!!!" wrote Michael. "Make no mistake, this is just the beginning: after the Catastrophe comes Apocalypse!"

The Shelleys drove to Adelaide. Then they rushed across the Nullarbor. Dust in the windscreen. Huge mushroom clouds of smoke in the rear-view mirror. The ashes of Elijah sat in the boot. Michael sped to Perth.

Steven was a silent voter and unlisted in the White Pages. Michael unearthed the address of his son's apartment in Fremantle. The Shelleys monitored Steven as he left for work. They followed Steven to the brewery.

At lunchtime, Steven changed into a pair of Asics for a run along Fremantle Harbour. On the busy footpath, he was ambushed by the Shelleys.

"Saul!" cried Mary.

"My son," said Michael.

"Jesus," moaned Steven.

Fremantle Beach was lined with Norfolk Island Pines. Steven didn't want to make a scene, so he walked with Michael and Mary to a gazebo.

"What are you doing here?" asked Steven.

"We brought you Elijah's ashes," said Mary.

Steven sighed. He barely knew Elijah at the end. How to make sense of his death? If only the Shelleys hadn't kidnapped Elijah from Fran and Neil Williams. Or if only the department had placed him with the Blaines.

"Elijah died for the sins of Joshua and you," said Michael. "And yet you couldn't even show your face at the funeral, Saul! What kind of brother are you?"

"What kind of father are you, Michael?" asked Steven. "You kidnapped a three-year-old boy from the only place that ever felt like home."

"Saul, I'm trying to save you from the same fate," said Michael.

"Michael, look at my life," said Steven. "I'm not homeless. I'm not a drug addict. By most people's standards, I'm a very successful young man."

"Don't talk to me about success," said Michael. "By the same age as you, I had two degrees. I owned three businesses. I had completed the Sydney to Hobart Yacht Race three times. What have you done lately, Saul?"

Steven's lunch break was nearly over. He stood up. He felt grief for Elijah, sympathy for Mary, and unmitigated hatred for Michael Shelley.

"Please never contact me again, Michael," said Steven. "I will never love you. You think you're an angel. You're just a narcissistic arsehole."

Michael roared. Mary wailed. Steven walked off without a kiss or hug goodbye. The Shelleys didn't give up. Steven's neighbours saw them wandering around the apartment complex while he was at work.

Steven and Prue's letterbox filled with handwritten condemnations. Michael sent virtual copies to their work emails. He printed photographs of Prue, annotating her defects. In his opinion, she was too physically similar to Steven for procreation. Her brown eyes betrayed "demonic" tendencies.

"What kind of woman spends her life chasing a small white hockey ball around a field?" wrote Michael. "Your face is bland; your body is hard; your heart is empty. I pity the children who end up with a mother as dreadful as you!"

Steven called the police. He wanted to take out a restraining order. But the process was slow. The harassment existed in a legal grey area. There was no violence or direct physical threats, just a steady stream of invective.

"How did your mum live with this crap for so long?" asked Prue.

"I don't know," said Steven. "She's a saint. Just a humble one."

Mary was arrested on an unrelated public nuisance charge. She spent three months at a psychiatric hospital in the western suburbs of Perth. Michael was distracted from Steven and Prue by a crusade against Mary's doctors.

Steven and Prue didn't take any chances. The couple applied for Canadian work visas. They moved overseas to the ski fields for two years.

The Psychologist

The Shelleys sent Elijah's ashes to Hannah, via my parents. They arrived in a nondescript parcel. When Hannah opened the package, the cinders of her older brother spilled onto the kitchen table. She was horrified. So was my mother.

"This never should have happened," cried Mum. "He was a beautiful boy. He should've been with us. He should've been with Steven, John and you."

Hannah was eighteen. Her gap year was ending. She was tossing up whether to study business or psychology. This tipped her towards psychology. She needed to understand why she was fine and Elijah was afflicted.

Hannah was accepted into psychology at the Queensland University of Technology. She and Jay moved into a rundown unit in Woolloongabba. Out the front was a Moreton Bay fig with a beehive. At night, bees hit the windowpanes, attacking the assignments that shone from Hannah's laptop screen.

"Come to bed," muttered Jay.

"One more journal article," said Hannah.

The lecture halls filled Hannah with awe. The tutorials produced imposter syndrome. Her stylish classmates didn't mispronounce the big words. Hannah finished every single reading in advance and mangled her answers to the questions of the professors, pitying glances be damned.

During the week, Hannah woke up at 6.15 am to make the 7 o'clock shift at a coffee shop on campus. She tied her brown hair into a long, simple ponytail. Her crooked teeth had been straightened by braces. A bus took her past the Gabba, over the brown river, through the glass and concrete city.

One morning, Hannah was clearing the plates from a table. A barefoot woman in a white dress swooped from the footpath to the front counter.

"I am a missionary of God," she said. "Today, *He* sent me to you. I would be pleased to receive a fruit salad and some toast."

Hannah froze, carrying a stack of plates in two hands, her back to the breakfast request. The voice belonged to Mary Shelley. There was no doubt.

"I'm not leaving until I've eaten," sighed Mary.

Hannah needed to walk past the counter where Mary stood. She kept her eyes straight and the plates stable. Mary glimpsed Hannah's poker face. They were within clutching distance. But there was no recognition. Mary was searching for a gangly tomboy. Hannah was too beautiful. She looked like Carole Sue Newgrosh, the eighteen-year-old iteration of Mary Shelley.

"One fruit salad and yoghurt," said the manager.

"God bless you!" said Mary, ignoring her daughter.

Hannah laid the dirty plates into the sink without breaking them. She went to hyperventilate in the bathroom. She heard the other staff members in the kitchen laughing about the crazy homeless bitch.

Hannah washed dishes for the rest of the shift. She occasionally stole glances at Mary from the counter. Her biological mother munched gleefully on the fruit salad and fed the bread to a few pigeons on the footpath.

"Poor woman," said the manager. "Her son died not that long ago."

"Did she mention me?" asked Hannah.

"No," said the manager. "Why? Do you know her?"

Hannah left through the fire escape. She caught a bus back to the flat in Woolloongabba. That night, after dinner, she and Jay curled up on the fold-out sofa. She ate ice cream straight from the tub. Hannah sobbed with a vulnerability she rarely revealed to anyone except Jay, her gentle bodyguard.

"Why am I still afraid?" asked Hannah.

How many hours had Hannah spent anticipating a kidnapping attempt? Thousands. So many years feigning strength for my parents, social workers, teachers. The fear was still there, just hidden, like rust covered with fresh paint.

"You're safe now," said Jay, clasping her in his large, warm arms. "They aren't going to take you. They *can't* take you, even if they wanted to."

Jay was right. Hannah was incapable of being abducted. She was a strong woman, not a hidden foster kid. And Mary was a frail old lady, not an almighty angel.

The Banana Tree of Being

In 2009, Hannah secretly plotted a surprise sixtieth birthday party for my father. She organised for all the old tradies, railway workers and footballers from Ipswich to descend upon the Drayton Tavern for a night of inebriated reminiscences.

On the Saturday afternoon before the party, John stood behind the front bar. A silver neck chain. Dark hair shaved number two all over by a set of clippers. Handlebar moustache merging with sprawling sideburns.

The one person John wasn't expecting to waltz through the front door was Michael Shelley. The preacher had a spring in his step and a grin on his lips. He was fresh from an arrest for stalking a priest in Lismore.

"Joshua?" asked Michael, squinting at John's double chin.

"What the hell are you doing here?" asked John.

The Shelleys had a knack for being in the right place at the wrong time. Michael studied his son from the other side of the half-empty bar.

"Oh my God, Joshua," said Michael. "You have let yourself go! Have you been on the same diet as Thomas Blaine? I barely recognise you!"

"Okay, Jenny Craig," said John. "You haven't seen ya son in six years. And the first thing ya wanna do is hang shit on me for being fat? That'll do me."

"I'm just worried about you!" said Michael. "All that cholesterol will strangle your veins. Just look at your foster father. He isn't long for this world."

John's insatiable appetite was a direct result of the mood stabilisers for bipolar II. And perhaps some subconscious hunger from his early childhood. John didn't worry about losing weight. He liked being big. It made him feel safe.

"Maybe if you'd fed me, I wouldn't be so fucking hungry," said John.

The bartender stood in front of upside-down liquor bottles. The Drayton Tavern was a moral Bermuda Triangle. Michael's own flesh and blood was the centre of gravity, sucking heathens from the diesel-drenched street. The walls of the bar were covered with sporting memorabilia: the Brisbane Broncos, the Queensland Maroons and the Australian cricket team.

"The banality!" cried Michael. "Oh, the banality! What a shameful waste of a human fate! Joshua, do you ever contemplate the banality of your being?"

"The banana tree of my being?" asked John. "What are you on about?"

"Thomas Blaine has brainwashed you into a bogan!" said Michael.

The devil entered by a side door, face sunburnt from lawn bowls, whistling an AC/DC riff. He wore white shoes, white trousers and a white polo shirt. Plus a hat with a badge of the Australian flag.

"Fuck me," sighed my father, eyeballing Michael. "Here he is."

It was too much for Michael's long-suffering soul. The same rough tongue. The same gruff glare. The same jutting gut. The same baboon-ish facial hair. Tom Blaine and Joshua Shelley were the same person, thirty-five years apart. Nurture had permanently erased the differences between their alien natures.

"Satan incarnate!" roared Michael at my father.

John rushed from behind the bar. He collected Michael's lithe body between his bicep and forearm, saving Dad from the abuse. He marched his barking biological father to the gravel car park out the back. Beyond the metal industrial bins, placid cattle chewed hay through a barbed-wire fence.

"How dare you lay your hands on *me*!" said Michael.

"Ya would've copped a flogging, ya goose," said John.

How distant they were from the sheep farm in the Blue Mountains, where John was born Joshua Shelley, the reincarnation of an Egyptian spy. How indifferent the young man seemed to the origins of his existence; the bliss of a sober mind and a fasting stomach;

his tenuous inheritance of planet earth.

"Not given to drunkenness, not violent but gentle, not a lover of money," said Michael. "Joshua, does this sound like you? God wants to give you the world. But you are throwing away the winning lottery ticket!"

"Shut up," said John. "Ya fucked up Mary's life. Ya fucked up Elijah's life. Everything ya touch turns to shit. But ya not gonna fuck up my life, mate."

John called a taxi and waited for it to arrive, persisting through a biblical earbashing. He handed the driver $50 and ushered Michael into the back seat.

✝

My mother was oblivious to Michael's arrival in Toowoomba. John decided not to ruin her afternoon. She was busy babysitting his twin daughters. Amelia and Sophie were nearly four. Thankfully, the Shelleys still hadn't gotten wind that they existed.

"Grandma, can we please get McDonald's?" asked Amelia.

"I'd really like a Happy Meal," said Sophie. "Please, Grandma."

"With manners like that, how could I say no?" asked Mum.

She strapped Amelia and Sophie into their safety seats. The twins didn't complain about listening to the country music channel, or about their driver going fifty in a sixty zone. My mother drove slowly to McDonald's. Her burger of choice was a Filet-o-Fish. The twins ate half of their cheeseburgers and then concentrated on the fries. They got soft serves afterwards.

"Thanks, Grandma!" said the twins.

"Just don't tell your father about this," said Mum.

"We won't," they said.

Back at the house, the twins helped my mother feed the dogs. The scene was old and new, brief and huge. Eucalyptus on the spring breeze. Grins on the faces of the little girls, as they traced the black spots on the Dalmatian. Then the three of them curled up together on the couch to watch *The Lion King*.

"Why didn't you have twins, Grandma?" asked Amelia.

"It wasn't for a lack of trying," said Mum.

"Grandma, do you think twins are weird?" asked Sophie.

Mum was outraged by the suggestion.

"Twins are the best thing since sliced bread!" said my mother, embracing them in each arm. "Double the hugs. And double the love."

The movie finished. The fun continued. Unlike teenagers, the twins saw nothing wrong with spending their Saturday nights listening to bush poetry. Mum recited "Clancy of the Overflow" by Banjo Paterson as they fell asleep.

Salvation

Hannah spent her twenty-third birthday drinking espresso martinis at a bar in Carlton, an inner suburb of Melbourne. She was studying for a master's degree in clinical neuropsychology at the floodlit sandstone university.

"Shots!" chanted her classmates. "Shots! Shots! Shots!"

Hannah got home to her flat in Malvern after 3 am. Jay, asleep in bed, had left two blue Gatorades in the fridge for his high school sweetheart.

"I love you, baby," slurred Hannah.

"I love you too," said Jay. "Go to sleep."

At 7.45 am, Hannah ran to the tram, scarf flapping in the wind. Most of the eighteen members of her master's program lived at home with their parents. Hangovers were manageable. Not for Hannah. After class, she caught a tram to Elsternwick. She worked as a nanny for a wealthy couple. Their mansion was blocks away from the flat where Elijah had killed himself.

Hannah was totally oblivious to the proximity, and mostly oblivious to the forces of social mobility. For decades, my parents pedalled into headwinds so that we could ride through life with the breeze at our backs.

Hannah had finished her bachelor's degree on a grade point average of 6.9 out of 7. She did placements in the psychiatric ward at the Royal Melbourne Hospital. This optimistic young woman took neat notes about men and women with bipolar and schizophrenia. They described their inability to prosper, and the difficulty of proving their impairments to Centrelink.

"I don't want to lie," said a former foster girl, now a woman, with a daughter in foster care. "I want to die most of the time."

Why were they so financially broke and emotionally broken? Why was Hannah okay? The answers to these questions meant everything.

"We aren't miracle workers," said Hannah's supervisor. "Tick the boxes. Crunch the numbers. Always go with the least-worst option. Don't blame yourself for the system. Or you'll end up becoming one of the patients."

The seasons changed. The footpaths filled with leaves. Hannah lit a gas heater in the corner of the cramped bedroom. Michael and Mary visited her dreams. She woke up and ran to the tram below the shaking branches of the naked plane trees.

✠

Hannah dusted, swept, vacuumed and mopped a spotless six-bedroom mansion in Toorak for twenty dollars an hour, cash in hand. Her boss was the philanthropist wife of a banker. Hannah made the fatal mistake of confiding two personal details to her boss: that she was fostered, and that she loved cooking.

"I have a luncheon coming up," said the banker's wife. "You should cook for us! I'll pay you the same hourly rate. It'll save me finding a caterer."

Hannah outlined hypothetical menus. The banker's wife selected coconut crumbed chicken and beetroot risotto for the main course.

"What are you thinking for dessert?" she asked.

"I could do some chocolate mousse," said Hannah.

"That's a little bit Broadmeadows," she said. "How about a tiramisu?"

The matron gave Hannah her Mastercard to go shopping for ingredients. On the day of the lunch, Hannah arrived at 8 am. She set eight places at the marble table in the dining room and filled the crystal vases with pink tulips.

At 12 pm, seven heavily perfumed women filed into the living room. They compared share portfolio performances and itineraries for overseas holidays. Hannah served the first course, and the second, and the third. She scraped the scraps into the bin and stacked the dishwasher. Hannah overheard the host regaling her guests with the trivia of the chef's upbringing.

"Hannah, forget about the dishes for now," called the host.

The banker's wife offered Hannah a seat at the head of the table. She filled her a flute from a bottle of Dom Perignon. The women insisted Hannah drink some champagne and eat her own tiramisu.

"I was telling everyone about your amazing life story," said the host. "I hope you don't mind. We all think that you are just remarkable, darling."

Hannah, sweaty and light-headed, realised that she was the final course on the menu. The drunken socialites of the eastern suburbs were gobsmacked that a foster girl from country Queensland wasn't a junkie or an alcoholic.

"You must feel incredibly lucky," said one of them.

"Not really," said Hannah. "I had a great upbringing."

"Luck" made Hannah's fate sound like the product of divine intervention. Nothing was preordained. It was the outcome of daily sacrifices made by two human beings whose pains and failures produced compassion.

"There are so many sad stories," said the host. "Most girls in your position would have a kid by the age of eighteen! It's a credit to you."

Hannah thought about Rebecca. She thought about Elijah. She thought about the temporary foster brothers and sisters she could barely remember, entangled by trauma, like caterpillars in a spiderweb. As if any of them could have been Hannah, a butterfly, with a little more effort. It was a lie. The lucky ones provided society with an excuse not to take responsibility for the Elijahs.

HMAS *Escape*

Mary Shelley was diagnosed with dementia. Michael was fit as a fiddle. But there was no temptation to outsource Mary's maintenance to a budget nursing home. The Shelleys stopped wandering. They settled in the fishing village of Port Albert, three hours east of Melbourne, population 300. Tall palm trees lined the short main street.

Around the corner from the Port Albert Yacht Club, Michael found a three-bedroom house to rent. 11 Pier Street. White weatherboard walls. A green corrugated iron roof. The final address on a gravel road into the ocean.

The windows of the living room contained panoramic views of the Bass Strait. Michael removed the flyscreens. Mary watched ballets of swans bob across the bay alongside the yachts. Flocks of cockatoos flew overhead. Stripes of red, orange, yellow, green, blue, violet and indigo arced across the sky.

"And there was a rainbow around the throne!" announced Michael.

Michael bought 1.5-kilogram tubs of honey for $15. He sweetened Mary's tea. They praised God for tealeaves. They praised God for beehives. Years passed this way. The world went to hell in a handbasket without them.

In the local *Trading Post*, Michael discovered a satin player piano from the nineteenth century for sale. It was manufactured by Fritz

Kuhla in Berlin. There was a pneumatic stack at the back. No keys required pressing.

Michael fed a music roll into the player and stepped repetitively on the metal pedals. For hours, the Shelleys' house was filled with ragtime. To the passing sailors, it sounded as if a gambler had won an eternal jackpot on a poker machine in the lounge room.

Paul Shelley – Mary's son from her first marriage, and Michael's former disciple – was living in Katoomba. By email, Michael berated him for not moving to Port Albert to help out. Paul complained about the guilt trip.

"Years of hellish trials have left me tormented and distressed," wrote Paul. "I am permanently disabled with PTSD and on serious medication to cope."

Paul wished he had never sent that goddamn death threat to the Queensland premier. It robbed from him the possibility of a normal life.

"Paul, I am not interested in what you have done for us in the past," wrote Michael. "It is a small fraction of what I have done for you."

Paul caved in. He slept in a spare bedroom and helped care for Mary. She was much sicker than Michael had let on. Paul could only handle her dementia and Michael's anal retentiveness in small doses. He found a council flat ten minutes away.

++

Hannah accepted a job in the paediatric section of the Brisbane Children's Hospital. It was the old stomping ground of Steven and John. Hannah knew she couldn't save everyone – or anyone – through the brilliance of her own insights. Her mission was to improve lifelong conditions, not to cure them.

Michael Shelley was a late convert to social media. He created a LinkedIn profile for his new business: *Christian Discipleship Training*. Occupation: *Christian Minister, Marriage Counsellor, and writer about all aspects of the human condition.* The messiah listed his full academic record.

"I can now say – without a hint of arrogance or pride – that I know more about anxiety and depression than any man alive," he wrote.

His profile picture was a photograph of Michael and Mary in Greece. Michael wore a white kaftan. Mary wore a purple bandana and brown aviator sunglasses. Michael used the same photo as a background for his Facebook profile. He had seven friends. But there was one friend he wanted: Hannah Blaine. He browsed her photos and sent a friend request in mid-October 2015.

"Hi, I don't feel comfortable accepting your friend request as my profile contains personal details that I don't want to share," Hannah wrote via Facebook Messenger. "But I am happy to chat over private message. From Hannah."

It took Michael a year to reply to the friendship rejection.

"How is my special and precious treasure of a daughter?" he wrote. "I am only just getting into Facebook and I find most of it incredibly superficial. But in this case, I am really pleased to hear from you. Michael +"

"Hi Michael," wrote Hannah. "I'm really well thank you. I spent three months travelling the world recently. I love sailing across the ocean, so I spent six weeks travelling along the Mediterranean coastline. How are you?"

Michael saw a slim window of opportunity for a family reunion. He bartered with a deceased estate to obtain a ten-metre cruising yacht called *Escape*. It was suspended above the earth by ropes and four wooden posts. He weatherproofed the hull and replaced the lead interior with timber.

"Mary & I love sailing, too," Michael wrote to Hannah. "I have attached a photograph of our new yacht. I am hoping to sail away one day, because I find the culture of this dreadful country depletes the spirit! Love Michael +"

For the next year, Michael and Hannah traded diplomatic life updates. They found a surprising source of father and daughter bonding: a mutual hatred of Donald Trump. In November 2016, he was elected president of America.

"Donald Trump is an over-opinionated imbecile and far-right fascist, most reminiscent of Adolf Hitler," wrote Michael to his biological daughter. "He is a clinical narcissist who is operating way beyond his level of competence and expertise."

"I totally agree," Hannah wrote. "It's pretty frightening."

"Do not be afraid, Hannah!" wrote Michael. "Trump is the answer to many of my recent prayers. He will isolate the USA from the rest of the world. With a bit of luck (and GOD's good grace) America will lapse into Civil War. Hip, hip hooray!"

In 2017, Hannah sent Michael a photograph of a pelican pod nesting at Burleigh Beach. Michael responded with a photograph of kangaroos at their living room window.

"Mary sends love," wrote Michael. "I spent the morning playing her the pianola on the Sabbath Day. Wonderful exercise. Good for the heart, and good for the spirit! M +"

Without fail, the Shelleys celebrated the birthdays of their children. Hannah turned twenty-seven. Michael wore a rainbow-coloured skivvy and headband. He hung a *HAPPY BIRTHDAY* banner from the window of the living room. Mary wore a purple nightgown and bandana. Hannah was everywhere she looked. A kangaroo hopped to the window. In her pouch, a joey. The animal kingdom knew the importance of a mother's milk.

Michael cooked dinner for two. Balloons bounced around the house. Poinsettias filled vases on the kitchen table. Through the glass, across the water, the setting sun had a pink tinge. Michael baked a sponge cake with thick white icing. He lit the candles. He played "Happy Birthday to You" on the ivory keys. Mary hummed along. Michael sent his daughter a photo.

"Happy Birthday to my beautiful daughter!" wrote Michael. "I baked you a cake. Take it easy, take it slow, love is the answer, wherever you go. M & M +"

Mary's memory vanished. She saw her children in stark focus. And when she remembered what had happened to them, she promptly forgot.

✝

In the southern sunlight, Mary sat in a picnic chair, watching her husband dock *Escape* at the Port Albert Yacht Club. Michael had renovated an ark. It was a getaway vessel from the grief of Mary's impending death. Destination: the Amalfi Coast. True civilisation, not this tacky colonial backwater.

"Good morning, Hannah!" wrote Michael. "Magnificent autumn day down here in Victoria. The boat is finished. I'm planning on doing some serious international expeditions. I wondered if you might be partial to joining my voyage. I could pick you up from the Gold Coast. The ocean is our oyster! M +"

In the lunchroom of the Brisbane Children's Hospital, Hannah's iPhone vibrated. Her left hand showed remnants of fake tan. There was a silver ring on the fourth finger. Hannah had married Jay on Good Friday in Toowoomba. They had used a secular celebrant. She kept the surname Blaine.

"Fuck the church, and fuck the patriarchy," she told her husband.

Hannah was no man's handmaiden. That morning, her wedding photos arrived by email. She chose a few pictures and sent them to Michael. Hopefully, this would distract him from the insane sailing invitation.

"Hi Michael," wrote Hannah. "I thought that Mary might enjoy seeing some photographs from my wedding on Good Friday. I married the man who I have been in a relationship with for ten years. It was the most perfect day."

Michael held his peace. In the chilly living room, the wedding photos glowed from his computer screen. Michael and Mary wept with joy. There was no denying it: Hannah was the reincarnation of her mother. At dusk, Michael sent Hannah a photograph. Thirty white birds with yellow bills. They spread in a straight line across the Bass Strait.

"GOD has blessed you with the loveliest head of hair, Hannah!" wrote Michael. "Mary is delighted to see that you have the courage and integrity to keep it long. We have a colony of 300 spoonbills roosting out the front of our house. They remind us of you in your white dress. So effortlessly exquisite."

A few weeks later, Michael played the satin piano for Mary. In the evening, a shadow from the firelight flickered across the bedroom ceiling. Michael kissed his wife goodnight. He fell asleep and never woke up.

Mary lay with Michael for the next two days. Nobody answered Paul's phone calls or frantic knocks on the front door. Paramedics smashed through the window. The couple were in bed. But Michael's lips were the same colour as his open eyes: blue. Dead at seventy. His lungs had been ravaged by tuberculosis, caught in a South African prison.

"Michael!" cried Mary.

Ambos put him in a body bag. They took Michael to the morgue and Mary to the hospital. Her will to live vanished without the sound of his voice. In the nursing home, Mary's brain and body staged the Shelleys' best getaway yet. She died at the age of seventy-four.

Two lovers on the run, finally at rest.

The Canonisation of John Blaine

John moved to Bundaberg, six hours from Toowoomba. Population 80,000. Cane farms to the north, south and west, and the sea to the east. John wanted a fresh start. He applied for a job as a car salesman at a Mitsubishi dealership.

"You don't have any experience in the automotive industry," said the owner of the dealership. "What makes you so confident you can succeed?"

"Mate, I could sell ice to Eskimos," said John. "I grew up in a pub. I know what makes people tick. And my old man taught me about hard work."

John got the job. He shaved his face clean and cut his greying hair. On Sunday night, he watched *The Wolf of Wall Street* for last-minute inspiration. To get a pass mark in his first month he needed to sell six cars. Ten would be incredible.

"I'm going to sell twenty cars," John told his supervisor.

"I love your chutzpah," said his boss. "But that's impossible."

In his first month, John sold twenty-four cars. The publican's son won over cynical customers in under a minute flat. He flashed heartfelt grins at wrinkled grandmothers. He dropped laconic one-liners for tattooed tradies.

"This is a miracle," said his boss. "You're a born car salesman."

"I don't sell cars, mate," said John. "I sell dreams."

In his first year, John ran second in the national Mitsubishi leaderboard. With the bonus, John and Merkilla paid a deposit on a three-bedroom brick home in the sprawl of Bundaberg. It had a rumpus room and a swimming pool.

The most satisfying part of John's week was Sunday afternoon. In a straw Bunnings hat, John chlorinated the swimming pool. He trimmed the hedges. He mowed the back and front lawns. He saved the best for last. With a high-powered hose, he washed a brand-new Mitsubishi Pajero in the driveway.

John put roast beef and potatoes in the oven for dinner. Then he sat down on the back patio to watch the football. An ice-cold stubbie of XXXX Gold from the bar fridge like my mother. A packet of salted peanuts from the pantry like my father. It was a bliss-filled ritual, no less sacred than the eucharist.

"Pig in shit," he whispered.

Life had never been better. But occasionally, when he tried to sleep, John could feel the wheel of human history spinning inside his head. On YouTube, he watched conspiracy theory videos about 9/11 and a New World Order.

John's doctor upgraded him from two mood stabilisers per day to three. Each morning, he dutifully swallowed the three purple pills with a glass of water. They stopped optimism from erupting into a manic episode. Upon my advice, John saw a therapist every few months to lessen his pent-up stress.

"Mate, how good is therapy?" John boomed to me on the phone.

"What do you mean?" I asked.

"She's not me missus. She's not me mate. I could tell her I jerked off my dog. She wouldn't blink an eyelid! I leave feeling like a million dollars."

John's twin daughters, Amelia and Sophie, were elected school captains of their public primary school. He wept at the ceremony. Caley was in grade four. She was brown-haired like John. He dropped his daughters to school in the Pajero. John lifted an index finger from the steering wheel towards other Mitsubishis on the streets.

"I sold that car," he said. "I sold that car. And I sold that car."

John was afraid his daughters would get too comfortable and not enjoy the simple things in life. He was afraid they'd get older and stop seeing pool parties with their dad as cool. He was afraid they'd get their hearts broken by insensitive young men like he had been. He was afraid they'd inherit bipolar from him.

On Facebook, John was nominated by a friend to scull a stubbie of beer followed by a shot of tequila. The viral videos were supposed to raise public awareness of mental health. His daughters watched Merkilla film their father on her iPhone. There was no beer or tequila in John's video. He stood at the kitchen bench with three purple pills and a glass of water.

"I was diagnosed with bipolar when I was seventeen," said John, wrists shaking. "I reckon that sculling a beer is gonna do nothing for my mental health. So I'm shooting a video of me taking my mood stabilisers."

++

John worked 8 am to 6 pm Monday to Friday, 8 am to 1 pm on Saturdays, and did a few hours of paperwork on Sunday mornings. A stream of tradies, small business owners and semi-retired boomers converged upon John's dream dealership. They were seduced by the double-chinned Aussie larrikin evangelising about the moral virtues of a brand-new Mitsubishi.

"I'm going to sell thirty cars in a month," John told his supervisor.

"Bullshit," said the supervisor.

That month, John sold thirty-five cars. Mitsubishi flew him to Adelaide for the national sales competition. He represented Queensland. In the City of Churches, John was up against rivals from Melbourne and Sydney. He wore a purple dress shirt, black trousers and cheap leather shoes.

In front of the CEO, the contestants had sixty minutes to answer sixty multiple-choice questions about the minutiae of different Mitsubishis.

"I'm done," John told the quizmaster after forty minutes.

"That's impossible," said the quizmaster. "Most people don't finish it."

"Well, I did," said John. "And I'm pretty sure they're all right."

John got 58 out of 60 correct. Next, the contestants demonstrated how to perform a handover to a customer. John was the only contestant who sat down with the fake married couple at the start and asked about their fake kids.

"The National Sales Champion is John Blaine," announced the CEO.

John was statesmanlike. He shook hands with the losers. Back at the hotel, he unleashed a flurry of fist-pumps and a roar of euphoria. He was overcome with love. For his mother and father. For his children and partner.

"We did it!" wept John on the phone to Merkilla. "We did it!"

Mitsubishi sent John and Merkilla to Japan on an all-expenses-paid corporate junket. The highlight of his first overseas trip was driving a go-kart through the streets of Tokyo in a Donkey Kong costume. He couldn't fathom the range of courtesy dipping sauces for chicken nuggets at McDonald's.

"It's unreal," he told his daughters on Skype. "They have *wasabi aioli*."

John spent the second night of the trip at a Mitsubishi dinner, followed by all-you-can-drink karaoke. Jukebox Johnnie wowed the Japanese crowd with "Fast Car" by Tracy Chapman. He lifted a phone to order round after round of cocktails. The next morning, John caught a taxi to the million-square-metre Mitsubishi factory. He chundered in the garden out the front.

"Food poisoning," he told the translator for the tour.

In a white helmet and hi-vis vest, the guest of honour strutted along the production line, escorted by Japanese automobile executives. John wasn't just living the Australian dream. He *was* the Australian dream: the personification of the myth that anyone could succeed and stay humble.

"Sayonara, mate," he farewelled the Japanese CEO of Mitsubishi.

Separation Anxiety

On a beach south of Perth, Steven's right palm was raised towards the sky, hailing thirty shivering children. It was spring 2022. He was thirty-nine. His face was slightly stubbled. His hands and legs were tanned. In his fluorescent orange rashie, Steven was the new coach of the under-nines nippers.

"Nippers isn't about winning," said Steven. "Nippers is about learning how to swim and making friends! Can I get an amen?"

His eight-year-old daughter, Penelope, was a mini-Steven, olive-skinned with brown hair and eyes. A green cap and pink goggles. Steven couldn't quell the wild pride that swelled in his heart as Penelope swam breaststroke through the turquoise water, more quickly than most of the boys.

"Go, Penny Blaine!" he yelled from a paddle board. "You're killing it!"

"Calm down, Dad," she said.

Steven delivered a post-swim pep speech. The other mothers and fathers helped hose the sand from the paddle boards and carry them back to the surf club. Prue brought Xavier, five, and Harriette, three, to the club for breakfast.

"How did you go, Steve?" asked Prue, kissing him on the cheek.

"I'd give myself seven out of ten," said Steven, eating avocado on toast.

"Five," whispered Penelope.

"Where's *my* avocado, Dad?" yelled Harriette.

Harriette chowed down Steven's avocado on toast. The bossy toddler looked like a younger version of Penelope. Xavier was a genetic anomaly. The same face and body shape as Steven, but blond-haired and blue-eyed, with fair skin. Michael Shelley's DNA had slipped through to the keeper.

"How's your bacon, Xav?" asked Steven.

"Great," said Xavier, in a strangely deep and gravelly voice.

Steven took Penelope and Xavier to the basketball courts. The ambidextrous father shot three-pointers with enduring hand–eye coordination. Initially, his children failed miserably to shoot hoops. Xavier improvised. He launched the basketball underhand. It swirled around and through the basket.

"Whoa!" yelled Steven. "Go, Xavier!"

"He can't even do it properly!" yelled Penelope. "They're baby shots!"

"Shut up, Penny!" yelled Xavier. "Just because you suck!"

Penelope's overhead free throws went nowhere near the hoop. Xavier nailed three in a row, then five. Steven high-fived him. This winded Penelope. Xavier's hot streak hit ten. He fist-pumped towards his older sister. Penelope screamed. She stormed from the basketball court to a sand dune on the beach. Steven followed.

"What's wrong, Penny?" asked Steven, embracing her.

"Why do you love him more than me?" she asked, tears streaming.

"I don't love him more than you," said Steven. "I love you both exactly the same. But Xavier did something good. I was just congratulating him for it."

"Why didn't you congratulate *me*?" asked Penelope.

"Because you didn't get the ball in the hoop!" said Steven.

Steven led Penelope back to the basketball hoop. Xavier continued to accrue underhand free throws, grinning with a missing front tooth. Penelope surrendered. She switched to baby shots, too. And the basketball went through the hoop. Steven cheered and high-fived his triumphant daughter.

"Congratulations, Penny!" he said.

Xavier was rocked by the sudden loss of supremacy. He began inexplicably missing shots. Penelope nailed three in a row, then five, then ten. She giggled and fist-pumped into the furious face of her younger brother.

"I! Hate! You! Penny!" cried Xavier.

Penelope and Xavier saw love as a zero-sum game. Most human beings do. We need the attention of our parents to thrive. Siblings divide their devotion. So we start hating our brothers and sisters without knowing why.

✠

Steven and Prue owned a small three-bedroom home near the beach in Perth's southern suburban sprawl. Post-Covid, Steven quit his job as a beer salesman and ran a bookkeeping business from home. Prue went back to university to do a nursing degree. Steven packed lunches and performed pick-ups and drop-offs. Each day, he took an antidepressant. The perfectionist finally accepted he had a mental illness that couldn't be cured purely by physical exercise.

In spring, Prue went interstate to visit family. The first night was a debacle. Steven forgot to pick up ingredients for dinner. He boiled some old spaghetti from the pantry, while Penelope, Xavier and Harriette watched *The Smurfs*.

"What's for dinner, Dad?" asked Xavier.

Shitonastick, thought Steven, in the gunshot bark of my father.

"Creamy pasta," said Steven. "How does that sound?"

Steven bathed the spaghetti in tomato paste and mayonnaise. He added bacon and grated cheese. Then he swallowed a mouthful to prove its tastiness.

"This is delicious!" he said.

The three kids probed at the food with their forks.

"Dad, this is a really bad dinner," said Harriette.

"Ew!" said Penelope. "I do not like this pasta!"

"Mum wouldn't make this," whispered Xavier.

"How about some more mayonnaise?" asked Steven.

"No, Dad," said Penelope, sadly. "Mayonnaise won't make a difference."

The next day, Steven dropped Harriette to day care, Xavier to preschool and Penelope to primary school. Then he stared at spreadsheets for five hours. At 2 pm, he drove to his psychologist's office in Fremantle.

Only recently had Steven discovered the exact circumstances of his premature birth: how Michael Shelley had insisted that Mary breastfeed him to the edge of death, and the lifesaving flight from Townsville to Brisbane.

"Close your eyes," said the therapist. "What was that baby feeling?"

"Afraid," said Steven.

Steven didn't see himself in the nativity scene. He saw Xavier. And he could vividly envision his son's distress if – at the age of two-and-a-half – Xavier had been dragged away from Prue by police officers. In the therapist's office, Steven suffered a panic attack that had the intensity of an exorcism.

"I never cry like this," said Steven.

"I think you learned – at an early age – that you needed to be perfect," said the therapist. "So that you wouldn't get in trouble and be taken away again."

Steven decided that perfection wasn't worth the effort. He ordered pizza and garlic bread for dinner. The kids were ecstatic. At the kitchen table, their father spontaneously narrated the murky circumstances of his birth.

"I was born Saul Shelley," he said. "But my real parents couldn't look after me. So my name was changed to Steven. Lenore and Tom Blaine became my parents. Your grandparents! That's where our last name Blaine comes from."

"Okay, Dad," yawned Harriette. "Can I have some ice cream?"

Harriette's identity rapidly adjusted. Penelope was panicking.

"Saul Shelley is a silly name!" wept Penelope. "I don't want my last name to be Shelley! The bullies at school would call me Smelly Penelope Shelley!"

Steven empathised with how extravagantly she prophesied improbable social humiliation. Apparently, they had that character trait in common.

"Penny, I think you're missing the point here slightly," said Steven. "Nobody is going to change your name. You'll be with Mum and me forever."

Xavier seemed delighted by the revelation.

"But Dad, can I change my name?" asked Xavier.

"What do you want to change your name to?" asked Steven.

"Shark," rasped Xavier. "Shark Shelley."

"No, Xav," said Steven. "You can't change your name to Shark."

"I'll ask Mum," said Xavier, grumpily.

After dinner, Steven bathed his three children. They all got changed into matching pyjamas. Steven read a bedtime story. Harriette fell asleep in his arms. Penelope and Xavier curled up together on Prue's side of the bed.

"Goodnight, guys," Steven whispered. "I love you."

"I love you, too!" said Penelope and Xavier in unison.

His kids would never question Steven's fondness. Their bond flowed beyond the daily grind, choppy but unbroken.

Nothing New Under the Sun

Hannah travelled over the Queensland–Northern Territory border at 110 km/h. The road was flat and straight and black. Jay sat in the driver's seat. All their possessions were packed in a trailer on the back. The sun was high and huge and hot. For the first time, Hannah understood the size of the sky.

Jay swerved around a kangaroo. Hannah sat in the backseat breastfeeding her one-year-old daughter: Lennie Blaine. She had Jay's dimpled chin. Hannah named her first child Lennie after Lenore. She kept her surname as a tribute to Tom, and the fact that Hannah – not Jay – survived nine months of morning sickness and eight hours of labour.

The Outlander hit Warumungu: the intersection of the Barkly and Stuart highways. Left for Alice Springs. Right for Darwin. Jay turned left. At sunset, they passed the Tropic of Capricorn. The car arrived in Alice Springs as night started falling. A galaxy of stars glittered in the pitch-black sky.

"You are my sunshine, my only sunshine," Hannah sang to a half-asleep Lennie. "You make me happy when skies are grey. You'll never know, dear, how much I love you. So please don't take my sunshine away."

++

Alice Springs wasn't the flat desert that Hannah expected. Rocky mountain ranges lined the horizon. Flocks of cockatoos and budgerigars flapped overhead. There were wildflowers on the streets: pink and purple and yellow. Hannah and Jay rented a townhouse on the east side of the wide, dry river.

The psychologist had accepted a job at an Aboriginal community-controlled health service. She treated children with foetal alcohol spectrum disorder (FASD). Hannah educated parents, teachers and social workers about how to soothe and improve the symptoms of FASD sufferers, rather than exacerbating them with arbitrary punishments.

Hannah's great-great-great-great-great-great-grandfather, William Shelley, had helped introduce liquor to a once dry continent. But this wasn't a resurrection of Michael Shelley's white saviour complex. It was the Gospel of Lenore Blaine. My mother had been decades ahead of the university-educated psychologists and social workers. She didn't cure Rebecca's brain of ADHD. But she provided shelter from the spirals of anger and shame.

"Patience, not perfection," was Hannah's psychological motto.

Hannah signed up for West Alice Springs women's Aussie Rules team. They were nicknamed "The Bloods". Their moniker was a bloodhound dog. Their guernseys were black with a red stripe, like the Essendon Bombers.

On Friday nights, the local oval glistened under floodlights. Hannah played centre half-forward. Her heart swelled at those same smells and noises from childhood. Deep Heat, greasy food and petrol fumes. Car horns and hooters. Now, a new sound: her daughter's shrill little voice on the sideline.

"Go, Mumma!" cried Lennie, in a miniature red and black guernsey.

To have experienced joy before Lennie was born seemed like an act of disloyalty. At last, Hannah fathomed the vastness of a mother's heart; the strength of a mother's love; the lengths that Mary Shelley went to find her.

☩

Then Hannah fell pregnant again. She knelt at the toilet bowl. Bile burned her throat. She vomited the little amount of food that her stomach could keep down. Lennie rubbed her mother on the back. She pretended to spew, too.

"Dadda, you've got to come!" cried Lennie. "Mumma's dying!"

"It's just morning sickness, bubba," said Hannah.

Hannah was told by a succession of male doctors that she had nothing to worry about. Finally, her body broke. She was hospitalised with dehydration. A female doctor diagnosed her with hyperemesis gravidarum.

"Severe morning sickness," said the doctor. "But the baby is fine."

The mother suffered so that the baby would grow, and so that the toddler could keep breastfeeding. Hannah didn't think she could endure one more day. Yet it kept going and going. While her belly swelled, Hannah grew thin and grey in the face. Lennie studied her mother's growing baby bump.

"Hello, Ra-Ra," said Lennie, her preferred name for the baby.

On a Tuesday morning, Hannah took Lennie out for breakfast. Lennie ate a brownie and drank an orange juice. At the table, Hannah's waters broke. She drove home. The streets shimmered in the heat. A friend came around to babysit Lennie. It was mid-November. Alice Springs was heading for 35 degrees. Jay delivered Hannah to the Alice Springs Hospital for the birth.

There was no pain the same as this. Hannah savoured each sting.

It meant her baby was imminent. The labour – ninety minutes all up – was remarkably quick. A dented head with black hair appeared between her legs. A long torso followed. Then chubby, olive-skinned legs. A penis between them.

In an instant, the nausea and physical torment vanished. Hannah's body was flooded with pure euphoria. Her memory of the past nine months went missing. This was nature's way of tricking women into getting pregnant again.

Hannah studied the dimple in her son's chin, identical to Jay's and Lennie's. Alive and quietly crying, the baby weighed 4.6 kg. She squeezed out a fetal macrosomia with no drugs except nature's greatest painkiller: 100 per cent love.

"That's a rugby league player if I've ever seen one," said Jay.

"He's going to be a ballerina!" Hannah objected, optimistically.

Hannah and Jay named their son Freddie Ra. In German, "Freddie" vaguely translated to *peaceful leader*. They chose the name for no special reason, except it sounded nice with Lennie. "Ra" was for the ancient Egyptian god of the sun. The giver of life. The bringer of warmth. The ruler of the universe.

++

In December, Alice Springs flooded. Hannah went on maternity leave. Slowly but surely, Lennie forgave Freddie for hogging Hannah's milk supply. She gave her baby brother a combover while reciting nursery rhymes. Freddie's eyes followed his sister everywhere. Hannah studied them smiling at each other.

"Mumma, Ra-Ra farted!" cackled Lennie.

Freddie's hair was dark. Lennie's hair was long, curly, and blonde. Michael Shelley's DNA would survive a nuclear bomb. On Christmas Day, Freddie's face lit up with anticipation when he heard his sister's footsteps in the hallway. Lennie – dressed as an elf – dove into bed.

"This little piggy went to market," said Lennie, fingers pricked.

Hannah swore that she saw flashes of my parents in the faces and personality traits of her children. Was it crazy to think this way? They taught her how to be just the right mix of soft and strong. Thanks to them, she knew that there was more to love than blood and more to life than pain.

"This little piggy went wee! wee! wee! all the way home," yelled Lennie.

Lennie tickled Freddie on the chin. Hannah tickled Lennie under the armpits. All three of them were breathless with gleeful laughter. The world grew small and warm and slow. The past and future were a beautiful blur.

EPILOGUE

It took me ten years of trying to find Latoya, the mother of Jason, the only child of Elijah Shelley. I had just gotten back from visiting Hannah in Alice Springs. Something about that brush with motherhood tugged at my psyche.

Sleepless, I searched through my archive of information for clues to Latoya's identity. I knew her first name and the first name of her son. Nothing else, except that she was an Aboriginal woman from Rockhampton. That she had once loved Elijah. That there had been drugs and domestic violence in their relationship. That their son, Jason, had grown up without his father.

I didn't think that I could publish a book about the Shelleys without knowing what had happened to Latoya and Jason. One clue led to another, and then another, and then another, and then another.

Latoya had become a mental health support worker for an organisation specialising in the grief and trauma of Indigenous people. I messaged her on Facebook. We arranged a time for me to call. She was outside. Birds chirped in the background. She was stunned but also bemused by this intrusion.

"Shit happens when you're young," she said.

Latoya knew little about Elijah's upbringing or what happened to him after he left, except that he died of a heroin overdose. I told her everything I knew. The family histories of mental illness. The kidnapping. The shifting foster care placements. The desperate attempts at sobriety in Melbourne. The psychiatric admissions. The final months before his death. The contents of the suicide note for Jason that Michael Shelley had kept a secret from her.

"Oh, God," she sighed. "I wish I knew then what I know now. The cycles. Trauma upon trauma upon trauma. We could've done things so differently."

Jason grew up under threat from the Shelleys. His kindergarten and primary school were given photos of Michael and Mary. Latoya feared they might show up and try to take him. She searched their names on Google every few months, checking if they had any recent activities in Queensland.

"Interesting people, the Shelleys," said Latoya. "Very interesting."

Latoya never thought she would love again after Elijah. It was more than heartbreak. This was about survival, and the safety of Jason. Finally, the spell was broken by a tradie named Craig. He raised Jason as his own child. Latoya and Craig had a daughter named Amelia when Jason was fifteen.

Craig encouraged Latoya to become more socially outgoing and financially independent. She didn't just need to stay at home and look after the kids. Latoya went back to study an alcohol and drug recovery program. That was where she learned about the cycles of trauma and addiction.

"For ages, I just thought Elijah was an arsehole," she told me. "You get into the reasons of why people behave the way that they do. That helps ease the pain a little bit. He was doing drugs to numb all the stuff he didn't address."

Growing up, Jason went to Craig with questions about his biological father, knowing it might be agonising for Latoya. He looked more like Elijah than Latoya. He was built like Steven and John, his unknown biological uncles: broad shoulders and thick forearms.

Latoya cheered from the sidelines of Jason's rugby league games. He excelled at science and mathematics. After school, he breezed through a trade apprenticeship with a big company.

"At least Jason is out of the cycle," said Latoya. "Works hard. His only vice is buying car parts. He doesn't even really drink. He's a bit of a gym junkie."

Latoya's pride was palpable. She called Jason "the boy". He was turning twenty-three later that year. Jason had started dating the love of his life when they were fourteen. The couple had recently gotten engaged during a camping trip on Fraser Island.

"Here's hoping I get a grandkid or two soon," said Latoya.

Jason was an Anglo-Aboriginal-Jewish-Sri Lankan Australian dreamer. The Shelley messiah complex had been overcome by the love of a humble black woman. Jason was mostly oblivious to the triumph of his existence. He was an everyday miracle. A tradie and a fisherman, like Jesus Christ, but not a saviour.

"The boy is happy as Larry," said Latoya. "That's all you want for your kids. And I think Elijah would be really happy with how he turned out, too."

AUTHOR'S NOTE

This book has been gestating in my imagination since I was a teenager. In 2013, I began actively researching the material and interviewing participants. Hundreds of people have offered their recollections. They include social workers, healthcare professionals, politicians and members of the general public.

I have used pseudonyms for most of the secondary characters, especially when their involvement was of a professional nature. Generally, I don't identify the witnesses for the events depicted, or reveal the full extent of their experiences. In many cases this was due to privacy. It was also due to the need for clarity. I apologise to anyone who might feel that I have minimised their role in these events.

I relied heavily upon the diary entries, letters, emails and legal files of my mother, Lenore Blaine, and the foster care files of my siblings. Extra detail was gleaned through conversations with Steven, John, Rebecca and Hannah Blaine, along with my mother, Lenore, and my father, Tom, while they were both still alive.

Michael and Mary Shelley used various names after converting to Christianity. I have maintained their names as Michael and Mary Shelley to avoid confusion. I communicated extensively with Michael Shelley. He provided a profuse number of government submissions, legal files and unpublished accounts about his and Mary's lives.

AUTHOR'S NOTE

Given the contentious nature of the custody battle involved and the fallibility of human memory, many of the accounts were contradictory. I have tried not to treat the perspective of the Blaines – and mine as author – as the only correct one. My success at this delicate balancing act will be for others to judge.

Australian Gospel is a work of creative non-fiction, not history or journalism. It was an extremely complex story to tell. I adopted a novelistic style so that readers wouldn't get bogged down in references to the sources of information. At all times, I have sought to capture the emotional truth of what happened.

ACKNOWLEDGEMENTS

Thanks to my friends and extended family for everything nonwriting related. There are too many people to mention without offending someone.

I am eternally grateful to Charlotte Wood, Tim Minchin, Grace Tame, David Marr and Sarah Krasnostein for reading *Australian Gospel* and gracing the cover with their praise. Thanks to Sandy Cull for nailing the design. Thanks to my agent, Benython Oldfield, for always taking my frenzied phone calls.

Thanks to the Australian writing community for sustaining me. The writers. The bookshops. The readers. The media. I have been blessed with friendship, mentorship and connection with strangers via the page.

One of my first pieces of literary luck was receiving a *Griffith Review* Queensland Writing Fellowship. A huge thanks to John Tague, Julianne Schultz and the *Griffith Review* team for helping to nurture the early development of this story.

In 2017, I was interviewed about the Blaines and the Shelleys on ABC's *Conversations*. Richard Fidler, Nicola Harrison and the team at *Conversations* have been steadfast believers in my writing. The interview led to an outpouring of contact from hundreds of people. It is impossible to thank them all individually, partly due to privacy and partly due to the sheer number of people who reached out.

ACKNOWLEDGEMENTS

I am indebted to Jacki Weaver, Bruce and Sue Moir, and Beverly Fleming for trusting me with their recollections. Paul Shelley shared hours of candid insights about his life. Dean Sholl and Cameron Lee helped me understand Elijah's Melbourne years. Thanks to Walter Meurant, Gavin Meurant, Bruce Willey, Brian Hooper and Peter Topzand for letting me pick their brains about the past. Carmel Osborne has provided so much love, and memories of my mother.

In 2019, I received a Brisbane Lord Mayor's Emerging Artist Fellowship. This allowed me to undertake residencies at the Varuna Writers' House in Katoomba and the Michael King Writers Centre in Auckland. I was also extremely fortunate to receive a grant from Creative Australia. This allowed me to work on the manuscript full-time for twelve months. Thanks to Judy Harris and the Charles Perkins Centre for your life-changing support of my writing career.

I'm grateful to everyone at Black Inc. who was involved in the editing and publicity process for this book. Thanks to Denise O'Dea for connecting with the story on such a deep level, for her sensitive editing, and for her patience with my tinkering. Thanks to Aira Pimping for typesetting the book and accommodating the changes. Thanks to publicist Kate Nash for spreading the word. Thanks to Caitlin Yates and Elisabeth Young for getting the gospel into bookshops. Thanks to Sophy Williams for finding a home for the audiobook. Thanks to Morry Schwartz for maintaining the faith.

A special thanks to publisher Chris Feik for tolerating my verbose emails, but not tolerating verbose books. My life has been littered with luck. Getting a quiet titan like Chris as a mentor is right up there on the list of providential events.

So is falling in love with Laura Jones. She deserves a medal for enduring the editing process of a Quarterly Essay and a book in such quick succession. Her general optimism and unique belief in the creative process kept me going.

Australian Gospel couldn't have been written without the permission

ACKNOWLEDGEMENTS

of Steven, John, Rebecca and Hannah. They were unwaveringly supportive of the project, and intrepidly honest about sharing their experiences. None of them wanted to be painted as uncomplicated angels. Brave is an understatement. What a miracle it is to be their younger brother and an uncle to their beautiful kids.

    I am lucky to be the son of Lenore and Tom Blaine. All their strengths, flaws, quirks and thirsts made me, and then shaped the way I see the world. My voice is a marriage of her reading habits and his gift of the gab. I miss them intensely. Everything I do in life is to honour the wonder of their love.

What is it like to survive a crash that kills your best friends, and how do you move on? *Car Crash* is a stunning memoir about grief, perseverance and courage.

At seventeen, Lech Blaine walked away unharmed from a car crash that killed three of his friends and left two in comas.

On a May night in 2009, seven boys in Toowoomba, Queensland, piled into a car. They never arrived at their destination. The driver made a routine error, leading to a head-on collision.

In the aftermath, rumours about speed and drink driving erupted. There was intense scrutiny from media and police. Lech used alcohol to numb his grief and social media to show stoicism, while secretly spiralling towards depression and disgrace. This is a riveting account of family, friendship, grief and love after tragedy. In a country where class and sport dominate, and car crashes compete with floods and pandemics for headlines, our connection with others is what propels us on. Heartbreaking and darkly hilarious, *Car Crash* is a story for our times.

Praise for *Car Crash*

"A heart-soaring act of literary bravery where the ongoing cost of experience is exposed in every note-perfect sentence. This is a profound reflection on the deafening soul noise heard by a beautiful group of young friends fated to live the rest of their lives with the silence of the dead. Some books just have to be written. And some books just have to be read." —**Trent Dalton**

"Scarifying and unforgettable, *Car Crash* is a story of carnage and lifelong consequences – not just from a single, sudden catastrophe but from the long, slow cataclysm of masculine confusion. A brave and unsettling account." —**Tim Winton**

"*Car Crash* is a phenomenal book. Beautiful and dark and compelling." —**Rick Morton**

"Shines with a fierce intelligence" —**Kristina Olsson**

"One of the best writers of his generation" —**Benjamin Law**

"This book is for everyone – it truly captures something of 'modern Australia' in a tenderly told story of one young man's tumultuous coming-of-age." —**Bri Lee**

Shortlisted for the Queensland Premier's Award for a work of State Significance, the Queensland Premier's Non-Fiction Book Award and the National Biography Award

Book club notes for *Car Crash* and *Australian Gospel* are available at blackincbooks.com